THE JOYS AND CHALLENGES OF RAISING A GIFTED CHILD

Susan K. Golant, M.A.

PRENTICE
HALL
PRESS

New York   London   Toronto   Sydney   Tokyo   Singapore

Other Books by Susan K. Golant, M.A.

How to Have a Smarter Baby with Dr. Susan Ludington-Hoe

No More Hysterectomies with Vicki Hufnagel, M.D.

Disciplining Your Preschooler and Feeling Good About It with Mitch Golant, Ph.D.

Kindergarten: It Isn't What It Used to Be with Mitch Golant, Ph.D.

Finding Time for Fathering with Mitch Golant, Ph.D. (forthcoming)

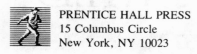 PRENTICE HALL PRESS
15 Columbus Circle
New York, NY 10023

PRENTICE HALL PRESS and colophon are registered trademarks of Simon & Schuster Inc.

Library of Congress Cataloging-in-Publication Data
Golant, Susan K.
    The joys and challenges of raising a gifted child / Susan K. Golant.
       p.   cm.
    Includes bibliographical references and index.
    ISBN 0-13-511262-1
    1. Gifted children—United States.   2. Child rearing—United States.   I. Title.
HQ773.5.G65   1991
649′.155—dc20   90-49963
                                                         CIP

Designed by Carla Weise/Levavi & Levavi

Manufactured in the United States of America

10   9   8   7   6   5   4   3   2   1

First Edition

To My Parents,
My Husband,
and
My Children

*Puis, par curieuse leçon et méditation fréquente, rompre
l'os et sucer la substantifique moelle.**

—Rabelais, *Gargantua,*
Prologue de l'auteur, 1534

* Then, by diligent reading and frequent meditation, break open the bone and suck out the
nourishing marrow.

ACKNOWLEDGMENTS

I feel grateful for having had this opportunity to study the research and explore my own feelings regarding gifted children. But authoring is no solitary effort; despite the single name on the book jacket, writing is a collaborative event fueled by the varied contributions of many.

I would like to thank my agent, Bob Tabian at International Creative Management, for his watchful efforts on my behalf and my marvelous editor, Toni Sciarra, whose wise comments and lively, inquiring spirit pushed me to examine and reexamine my subject. Without them, this book never would have come into being.

I am indebted to my many wonderful friends who contributed stories from their childhoods and their own families and challenged me with their questions and perspective. Among these, I especially acknowledge Sheila Gross, Ph.D., Dorothy Clark, Ph.D., Dorothy Dudovitz, L.C.S.W., Helana Barry, Ph.D., Barbara Becker, M.A., Janet K. Smith, Ph.D., Barbara Elias, M.A., Laura Atoian, M.A., Luba Fischer, Ph.D., Audrey Koren, M.A., Susan Perry, Beatriz Ruiz, Judy Kaplan, and Jane Zuckerman.

I am particularly grateful to Barbara Becker, gifted magnet coordinator at Wonderland Avenue School, for her taking the time to talk to me about gifted children's educational needs and allowing me to mine her volumnious files, and to psychologist Dr. Janet K. Smith for her insightful comments and suggestions regarding children's separation/individuation and parents' ego attachments. Teacher Judy Selsor at Walter Reed Junior High School provided valuable suggestions for stimulating resources as did Merrie Wartik at Wonderland Avenue School and Henriette Kleinhandler at La Merced Intermediate School. And a special thanks to Norma Kapp, L.C.S.W., the Golden(berg) family, Arla Capps, and Sheila Lane for their many profound contributions over the years.

ACKNOWLEDGMENTS

My thinking about gifted children has been deepened, broadened, and validated by the work of Dr. Robert Sternberg, psychologist at Yale University; Dr. Howard Gardner, developmental psychologist at the Harvard Graduate School of Education; Dr. Joseph Renzulli, professor of educational psychology at the University of Connecticut; Dr. Benjamin Bloom, professor of education at the University of Chicago; Dr. Barbara Clark, professor of education at California State University, Los Angeles; Dr. Linda K. Silverman of the Gifted Child Development Center at Denver University; Dr. Michael M. Piechowski, education professor at Northland College; Dr. Wendy C. Roedell, director of the Northwest Gifted Education Center in Seattle; Dr. Susan Ludington, professor of maternal-child health at UCLA's School of Nursing; and Dr. Stan Charnofsky, chairman of the educational psychology department, California State University, Northridge. I am indebted to all of these fine professionals for their years of research and their sensitive insights.

Finally, I am most grateful to my family. My mother had much to do with my being identified as a gifted child. Among other things, she spent her days recounting Greek mythology while playing "school" with me. But more importantly, she showed me with her heart what it means to be a mother. My father's generosity, sense of justice, and *menschlichkeit* helped to form my character. My sister, Henriette, has imparted to me a model of great courage and persistence in the face of seemingly insurmountable obstacles. My husband, partner, and steadfast friend, Mitch, who provides the financial and moral support essential for my writing, also contributes the vision and ever-present love that sustain my strength and growth. And last but certainly not least, my daughters, Cherie and Aimee, have enriched my life more than words can tell. In the course of our lives together, they have taught me at least as much as I have taught them.

For these gifts and all others, I am grateful.

—Susan K. Golant, M.A.

CONTENTS

PART I   INTRODUCTION   **1**

Chapter 1   Tales of the Second Grade Revisited   3

PART II   UNDERSTANDING YOUR GIFTED CHILD   **11**

Chapter 2   What Is Intelligence? Unraveling the
Tangled Skein   13

Chapter 3   What Is Giftedness?   27

Chapter 4   How Does a Child Become Gifted?   34

Chapter 5   Testing: The Good, the Bad,
the Ugly   44

**PART III   YOUR GIFTED CHILD IN THE WORLD
AND AT HOME**   **67**

Chapter 6   School Programs: Of Decisions,
Choices, . . . and Elitism   69

Chapter 7   The Complex Personality of the
Gifted Child   94

Chapter 8   The Perils of Perfectionism   108

Chapter 9   "You Gotta Have Friends . . . ":
Helping Your Gifted Child Meet Her Social Needs   121

Chapter 10   The Importance of Play   145

Chapter 11   Siblings: Giftedness Is a Tough Act to
Follow . . . or Precede   163

PART IV THE HIDDEN CHALLENGES FOR PARENTS

183

Chapter 12   Parental Responsibility: Your Secret Challenge   185

Chapter 13   Whose Life Is This Anyway? Ego and Letting Go   199

Chapter 14   Nerds, Geeks, Eggheads, and Know-It-Alls: The Changing Image of Gifted Children in Our Society   214

Appendix: Resources, Magazines, and Games   225
             Books   226

Bibliography   227

Index   239

PART I

Introduction

CHAPTER 1

Tales of the
Second Grade Revisited

---

*I wrote Bobby a letter telling him I had
started first grade and had to sit quietly at my
desk while the others learned to read. . . .*

—LYNNE SHARON SCHWARTZ, *LEAVING BROOKLYN*

WHEN I WAS SEVEN YEARS OLD, MY SECOND-GRADE TEACHER PRINTED "excessive use of lavatory" (words she knew I couldn't read) on my report card beneath the neat rows of "satisfactories" and "outstandings" for arithmetic, penmanship, and working and playing well with others. Alarmed by the possibility that I was suffering from a bladder infection, or worse yet, from some undiagnosed disorder of the kidneys, my mother rushed me to our family physician.

After taking samples of urine and performing tests that have since faded from my memory, the good doctor made his now famous (in our family) pronouncement, "This child isn't sick. In fact, there's not a thing wrong with her. She must be bored in school."

I had been found out. Indeed, I was bored. In 1955, gifted children in New York's public elementary schools were not singled out for special attention. So, after I had flashed through my reading assignments (individualized reading programs were still a thing of the future), I was required to sit quietly at my desk with hands folded while I waited for much of the rest of the class to catch up with me. Who could blame me for taking a break once in a while? What healthy, bright, seven-year-old would want to remain riveted to a hard, wooden bench for ten minutes, staring at a blank blackboard? I sure didn't.

Some fifteen years later, I was married, and soon afterward, our first child was born. By then, I had already learned the important fact that Mozart had composed music at four years of age and that Leibnitz had written philosophical essays at an equally tender age. I was very much influenced by my reading of humanistic psychologist Abraham Maslow, who had impressed upon me the fact that we humans use only

3

a tiny portion of our innate abilities; we are rooted to the ground by our own hang-ups and complexes. If only we could all live up to our potentials.

I was only twenty-one years old—hardly more than a child-bride by today's standards—optimistic, and more than a little naive. Well, I thought, here is my chance. We have this wonderful, sweet, bright-eyed baby. Why should she have to feel held back? We will raise her with love and support her at every turn. And maybe she will fulfill her human potential. Maybe she will soar.

THE JOYS

And so we innocently set about the early education of Cherie. I kept her with me most of her waking hours, pushing her around our small apartment in her stroller and talking to her about what I was doing, be it baking a cake or studying French philosophy. It didn't matter that she was only six months old. I kept up the monologue until she answered back. I read endless books to her. My husband, Mitch, engaged her in creative story telling. We did puzzles together, ad nauseum. We always purchased toys that were a few months—if not a few years—ahead of her level.

Cherie fulfilled her part by being quite remarkable. By eighteen months, she was able to recite the alphabet and could even associate the letters with their symbols. (Remember, it was in the early 1970s, long before Glen Doman introduced his Better Baby Institute flash-cards.) When Cherie started nursery school, at two years four months, her teacher asked her about her favorite color and she answered, proudly, ''magenta''!

One day, when Cherie was about two and a half years old, I read her first *Curious George* story to her. Curious George seemed like a perfect role model for Cherie precisely because that little monkey was so curious—he was always looking to discover ''what if . . .''—even if he did get himself into trouble from time to time.

Cherie found it most hilarious that George had what she called ''hands on his feet.'' Shortly after our story session, I discovered my daughter hard at play, a pair of brown leather gloves pilfered from my drawer securely pulled onto her tootsies.

''I wanted to see what it's like to be Curious George,'' Cherie declared. With a sly grin, she wiggled her new set of hands/feet. I scooped up my little monkey in my arms and together we danced around the room, uttering chimpanzee grunts and squeals.

How can a parent not delight in a child's innate inventiveness and curiosity? Cherie's game evoked more than just a laugh and a big hug. I could see that her little mind was at work and I just loved it.

Indeed, her little mind grew by leaps and bounds and craved constant stimulation. Cherie was reading those *Curious George* stories to herself at four; she read on the third-grade level by the end of nursery school. In the first grade, she scored "highly gifted" on an IQ test. In the second grade, her teacher (much to my great joy) sent her to a fifth-grade classroom every day for reading. It seems we had come full circle.

THE CHALLENGES

Of course, my husband and I were thrilled and gratified at having such an unusually bright child. But I also experienced a feeling of intensity around her achievements. Perhaps I was using our daughter's "successes" to fulfill my own ego needs. In some ways, I sought to correct the deficits in my own education by insisting that she receive the extra attention and stimulation I had wanted for myself as a child.

Only as time went on did we begin to appreciate how truly difficult it was to parent a highly gifted child appropriately. In fact, we have come to see this pursuit as a joy and a burden, a challenge and a responsibility. It is not a task lightly taken. Indeed, now that she is twenty, I have come to realize that Cherie was a youngster with *special needs*, much like a learning disabled or handicapped child. Those needs had to be addressed in order for her to make good use of her gifts.

That is why I have written *The Joys and Challenges of Raising a Gifted Child*. I think each chapter will have much to offer if you find yourself in this unique and often demanding situation. You may need help sorting through the complex feelings and situations you will be facing. There are decisions to be made and motivations to be rendered conscious. I hope you will use this book as your companion through the marvelous adventure that lies ahead of you. In it, I will share my mistakes and uncertainties as well as what my husband, clinical psychologist Dr. Mitch Golant, and I have found to be successful. I also bring you the latest research in the field of giftedness.

In browsing through the books on raising gifted children currently available in bookstores, I have found many excellent guides written by highly qualified specialists in the field. But I have not found any personal accounts written by parents who share their own experiences with their gifted children. I hope to do so, and also to share the insights I have gained from having been a gifted child myself—I know what it means to grow up gifted, which enables me to advocate on behalf of the gifted in areas where I feel we have been maligned.

By way of formal introduction, I hold a masters degree in French literature and philosophy and I have been a writer for the past ten years. With Dr. Susan Ludington, a professor of maternal-child health at UCLA, I coauthored *How to Have a Smarter Baby* (Bantam, 1987), and with Dr. Vicki Hufnagel, *No More Hysterectomies* (New American Library, 1988).

My husband and I have enjoyed combining our professional and personal relationship by collaborating on a series of books that draws on research as well as on our experiences as practiced parents. (At this point, between our two children, we have celebrated some thirty-eight birthdays!) These books include *Disciplining Your Preschooler and Feeling Good About It* (Lowell House, 1989), *Kindergarten—It Isn't What It Used to Be* (Lowell House, 1990), and the forthcoming *Finding Time for Fathering* (Ballantine, 1992).

WHAT IS IN THIS BOOK

The Joys and Challenges of Raising a Gifted Child addresses day-to-day problems that all parents of gifted children face and suggests ways to help your kids not only to become well-adjusted adults but also to feel good about their giftedness. Your challenge is to understand your individual child's needs, abilities, and areas of weakness so that together you can make decisions that will benefit him. This book provides a reasoned, well-seasoned, and pragmatic roadmap of the hurdles you and your child may face. It combines theory with my own twenty years of commonsense parenting.

Part II covers the nuts-and-bolts questions uppermost in many parents' minds. What is intelligence? What is giftedness? Can children become gifted through the proper nurturance, or are they born that way? How are gifted children identified?

As I've dug into the research, I've discovered that none of these questions have simple or singular answers. In fact, over the years psychologists and philosophers have argued a plethora of conflicting theories to explain what constitutes intelligence and giftedness. The controversy still rages today and creates a sort of domino effect. If experts can't agree on what giftedness is, how can we as parents expect them to formulate a single way to identify it and to educate appropriately? No wonder so many of us are confused about the proper way to rear and teach our children!

In chapter 2, I will help you sort through some of the many definitions of intelligence. You'll learn about the ''lumpers'' and the ''splitters'' and which point of view is in vogue with research psychologists today. In addition, we will examine the differences between right- and left-brain thinkers and how convergent thinkers may enjoy an advantage over divergent thinkers when it comes to the classroom and even IQ tests. We explore what constitutes creativity and my belief that creativity (although not accurately assessed on intelligence tests) may, in fact, be the highest form of intelligence.

In chapter 3, we'll look at some definitions of giftedness. You may be surprised to learn that giftedness is a product of one's culture—what it means to be ''gifted'' can change from generation to generation and from one society to the next. Probably one of the simplest ways to define giftedness is to observe a child's behavior. Most experts believe that parents are well aware of their children's gifts long before the kids enter school. I provide several checklists to help assess this.

In chapter 4, I courageously if not foolhardily broach the difficult question, ''How does a child become gifted?'' We'll discuss the age-old balance between nature and nurture and the latest research on how environmental stimulation can create ''smarter'' children. It's also important to remember that most people experience selective giftedness—children are not gifted in all areas—and that like all kids, gifted children mature and develop at their own rate.

In chapter 5, I share our experiences—both good and bad—with testing. We will review the most common intelligence tests and what they indicate along with a discussion about how the results should be used and why test scores are not always a valid measure of giftedness. This area is still one of heated controversy among educators and psychologists.

Part III explores how your gifted child fares at home and in the world. We'll talk about educational options, personality traits that seem common to many gifted children, the perils of perfectionism, how to help your gifted child adjust socially and get along with siblings, and finally the profound benefits of play.

Parental involvement is crucial for finding the right schools and teachers for gifted children. In chapter 6, we'll explore the many ways in which you can fulfill your child's educational needs. I share with you the choices and decisions that Mitch and I made with our two children. We'll examine the various types of gifted programs: mainstreaming, "pull-out" programs, self-contained classrooms, or acceleration; assess their pros and cons; and explain what educators mean when they refer to "differentiated learning." We'll talk about what I feel are the false accusations of *elitism*—the bugaboo of all gifted programs.

In chapter 7, we will examine how your gifted child's wonderful personality traits such as his sense of humor, his curiosity, his verbal abilities, his need for solitude, his quest for perfection, his extreme sensitivity and his own intense need to find meaning in his life can also render him difficult to live with. We will look at why some gifted children feel "different" from their peers (often because they are!) and how to validate a child's positive feelings about himself.

Perfectionism can be a problem for many gifted children and their parents, alike. In chapter 8, we will explore the origins, manifestations, and consequences of trying to be perfect. I bring together advice from many experts on how to help your child avoid falling into the perfectionism trap, and talk about the difference between striving for perfection and the attainment of a certain measure of excellence.

Sometimes it's hard to feel special. The not-so-well-hidden responsibility to *do* great things with one's life creates a heavy load of expectations. In chapter 9, we explore your child's social needs, taking into account her heightened sensitivity. Gifted children may experience conflicts and jealousy with their peers or they (especially girls) may hide their giftedness in order to fit in. Feeling different, they may be attracted to adult company rather than that of other kids. They also may become boastful. Conversely, they may suffer from name-calling and rejection such as being labeled an "egghead" or "nerd." Even their teachers may become jealous and hostile toward them. I believe that if at all possible, gifted children should find other gifted children to play with, and I suggest some ways to do this.

In chapter 10, I cover various forms of creative play, including noncompetitive games, logic puzzles, and brain teasers, as well as guidance on how to support your child's interests and curiosity using higher-level thinking skills. I also fully believe that gifted children need "downtime." We'll discuss the virtues of boredom—and the stress of the overscheduled child. I'll share with you how my daughter succeeded in creating an inner cosmology that always sustained her, and why I feel it's vital for you to encourage your gifted children to "make a mess."

Giftedness is a tough act to follow—or to precede—if you're a sibling who is not as abundantly endowed or if you are simply hiding your own gifts. In chapter 11, I share some painful stories from our own family along with interesting research in this field. I also offer strategies for coping successfully with sibling rivalry and comparisons—which your kids are bound to make, even if you don't.

In part IV, we will look at some of the hidden burdens of parenting gifted children—ones that aren't often mentioned by researchers in the field. You may experience, for instance, a monumental sense of responsibility. In chapter 12, we'll look at how some parents feel intimidated by their children's abilities or believe, as my husband and I did at times, that they had created a monster! Other parents may feel compelled to chase after every enrichment program under the sun so as not to deprive their budding genius of any opportunity—the sense of responsibility can be overwhelming. On the other hand, sometimes it's difficult for parents to accept their gifted child's areas of mediocrity as well as her everyday fears, troubles, and tantrums. It's hard to allow your future Einstein to be just a kid with kid problems. It's important to strike a sensible balance—both for you and your child.

I know that I sometimes inappropriately used my gifted children to fulfill my own achievement needs. It's easy to experience a feeling of heady elation when your kids succeed at some task, as if you had won the praise. In chapter 13, you will have the opportunity to explore the concept of your own separation from your children and your limitations as parents. In any parenting situation, especially those in which we are highly involved, we must ask ourselves the question, Whose life is this, anyway? The goal is to be a well-balanced parent of a well-balanced child.

This last task is probably the most difficult one, for as parents we all get caught up in our own unconscious needs and wishes, which we later act out on our children—to their benefit and detriment. It is possible, however, to understand our own motivations, some of which may have remained hidden to us. To facilitate your recognition of these feelings in yourself, I will share over the course of this book various stories of events in my own childhood and how they infused the approach I took in raising my children.

Finally, in chapter 14, we'll look at the uphill battle that gifted children face in our society. Many prominent researchers have pointed out how our culture devalues academic achievement and intelligence. Who knows how many children feel driven to hide their giftedness for fear of social rejection? To me, it is a tragic misuse of potential.

It is up to you, as a parent, to foster your child's confidence in his abilities and to help him understand that giftedness is a positive attribute to be used to enrich himself and others. The goal of this book, if nothing else, is to help your child feel good about his giftedness. In the words of the late psychologist Abraham Maslow, ''A person is both actuality *and* potentiality.'' Let us all be blessed with the grace to honor each child for who she is while we allow that potentiality to flower. It is our ultimate challenge.

PART II

Understanding Your Gifted Child

CHAPTER 2

What Is Intelligence?
Unraveling the Tangled Skein

The intellect is the tool to find the truth.

—SYLVIA ASHTON WARNER, *MYSELF*

This is what intelligence is: paying attention to the right thing.

—EDWARD HALL

YOU MAY REMEMBER THE INDIAN FABLE OF THE SEVEN BLIND MEN and the elephant. The first blind man grabbed hold of the elephant's tail and said, "I know what elephants are like! They are long and skinny."

The second blind man stroked the elephant's tusk and said, "Yes, and they're also smooth and hard."

The third bumped into the elephant's flank and said, "No, elephants are as wide as a house and wrinkly, too." And so on.

In truth, all of these men were right, but they were also wrong. The elephant is a composite of all of these elements, yet no one of them describes the animal fully.

Probably the same can be said for our understanding the mystery of intelligence (and by association, giftedness). There are as many theories regarding what constitutes intelligence as there are theorists. Quite a few of the theories are valid in and of themselves, but there is no one way of looking at intelligence that encompasses them all—and there is little consensus among experts in the field. Intelligence is, indeed, a tangled skein that comprises several components: Some of these, our culture affirms and supports; others, it disavows or will suppress in all but the most spirited child.

TOWARD SOLVING THE MYSTERY

It takes a heap of intelligence just to figure out what intelligence is in the first place! In general, our conception of intelligence has evolved from an earlier view that is a single, indivisible unit to current thinking that we are all endowed, to one degree or another with "multiple intelligences." Those psychologists who define intelligence as a single, overall capacity have been called the "lumpers." The more modern "splitters" believe that intelligence is made up of many different elements that operate independently of one another. In addition, there are those who theorize that intelligence is a melding of the two, somewhat like particle versus wave theory in physics.

The unraveling of the tangled skein of intelligence during the last hundred years reads much like a detective novel. The first notion—that intelligence is a quantifiable entity that actually can be studied—surfaced before the turn of the century in Britain. Francis Galton, a cousin of Charles Darwin and one of the earliest psychologists, stated in 1884 that "intellectual fitness," as he called it, was inherited. He also saw it as the product of willpower, aesthetic appreciation, moral sentiments, and capacity for abstract reasoning.

Galton developed the first "mental tests" that, surprisingly, ignored what we would consider mental abilities altogether. Rather, they focused on physical strength and how well the senses operated. Galton believed that the greater one's sensory capacity, the higher one's intelligence.

Albert Binet, the Frenchman who developed the Binet intelligence test, countered this theory. He found that the acuity of one's senses had little to do with intelligence. (He used the example of Helen Keller to refute Galton's explanation.) In 1916, Binet and his research partner, Theophile Simon, stated that intelligence is "judgment, otherwise called good sense, practical sense, initiative, the faculty of adapting one's self to circumstances. To judge well, to comprehend well, to reason well, these are the essential activities of intelligence."

Charles Spearman, a University of London professor of psychometrics, was one of Binet's disciples. Several years after Binet's pronouncements, Spearman theorized that intelligence consists of a general ability (g) and specific abilities (s) that are components of g. He argued, for example, that people who fared well or poorly on tests of intelligence would perform similarly on all other tests such as those measuring math, vocabulary, and spatial relations. This belief in a *unified, general intelligence* has been widely accepted and is the rationale for using a single criterion such as an IQ test to assess a child's ability today.

Scientists then hotly debated whether this g factor or general ability was inborn or was a product of one's environment. No one questioned the validity of the idea itself, including Dr. Lewis M. Terman, the psychology professor at Stanford University who developed the Stanford-Binet IQ test in 1916. He was the first researcher to study more than 1,500 gifted children over their lifetimes and determined that intelligence is the ability to think in abstract terms. He saw intellect as a single, global ability.

For decades thereafter, psychologists and educators relied on a single administration of an IQ test to measure what they believed were a child's intellectual abilities. Over time, however, it because increasingly clear that although IQ tests could predict school performance, a child's score on an IQ test had little to do with how successful she would be in her life. Einstein is a prime example: As a child, he was not considered an exceptionally bright student. And certainly there are scores of certifiable child prodigies and geniuses whose adult lives did not fulfill the promise of their youth.

THE SPLITTERS

And so, psychologists began to search for other answers. In 1967, for example, J. P. Guilford at the University of Southern California theorized that intelligence is no single entity but rather consists of at least 120 different types of abilities. Dr. Guilford constructed a complex three-dimensional matrix (called the *Guilford model*) to explain his ideas.

Today, the three most prominent "splitters" in the field of intelligence and giftedness are Howard Gardner, a developmental psychologist at the Harvard Graduate School of Education, Robert J. Sternberg, a research psychologist at Yale, and Joseph S. Renzulli, professor of educational psychology at the University of Connecticut and the director of the National Center on the Gifted and Talented.

In 1983, Dr. Gardner argued in his ground-breaking book, *Frames of Mind*, that intelligence is composed of seven different competencies:

- *Linguistic:* ability with meaning and order of words; facility in learning foreign languages
- *Logical-mathematical:* ability to follow a chain of reasoning and find patterns and order
- *Spatial:* ability to perceive the world with accuracy and re-create

or alter that perception; artistic or engineering skills and visual memory
- *Bodily-kinesthetic:* ability to know where one's body is in space and to move the body skillfully; athletic as well as fine motor coordination
- *Musical:* ability to recognize rhythm, pitch, meter, and tone; auditory memory
- *Interpersonal:* ability to understand and communicate with people in relationships; high social skills
- *Intrapersonal:* ability to understand one's own emotions and the emotions of others

Dr. Gardner points out that these abilities are independent of one another: One can be gifted in one or several of these areas while being average or below average in the others. By these standards of multiple intelligence, a child would be considered "gifted" if he were extraordinary in art or music (but not necessarily academics), whereas earlier theories such as those expressed by Dr. Terman limited the definition of giftedness to what can be measured by an IQ test.

Robert J. Sternberg at Yale University developed what he calls the "triarchic theory of intelligence." In 1985 he suggested that intelligence is dependent on three factors:

- The internal, mental mechanisms responsible for intelligent behavior
- The external setting that defines what will be labeled as intelligent within a given society
- The level of experience an individual has with a task or situation that is intended to measure intelligence

Dr. Sternberg believes that intelligence is made up of three factors: analytic intelligence (most valued in school and on IQ tests), synthetic intelligence (creative ability), and practical intelligence (application of intelligence to the everyday world—"street smarts").

For Dr. Sternberg and his colleague at Yale, Dr. Janet E. Davidson, it's not so much the ability to answer questions as the capacity to come up with the right problem to solve—be it artistic, mathematical, social, or scientific—that is a mark of intelligence. Other scholars seem to have made this point earlier. Social psychologist Edward Hall expressed it with elegant simplicity when he said that intelligence is "paying attention to the right things." And Albert Einstein wrote, "The *formulation* of a problem is often more essential than its solution, which may be merely a matter of mathematical or experimental skills."

Dr. Renzulli's focus is less theoretical than that of his colleagues. He conceptualizes intelligence and giftedness as composed of three interlocking circles: above-average ability (IQ of 120 or better), creativity, and task commitment.

This three-ring conception of giftedness takes into account not only children who achieve high scores on traditional intelligence tests but also those who contribute to the world by their creative production. Dr. Renzulli explains in *Conceptions of Giftedness* that "history does not remember persons who merely scored well on IQ tests or those who learned their lessons well." Yet, he also finds that many gifted programs turn their backs on most of the people that history later designates as gifted. In fact, in a recent *New York Times Magazine* interview conducted by Marie Winn, Dr. Renzulli cited Woody Allen, Charles Schulz, and Steven Spielberg as among those originally overlooked as talented students.

These newer theories of multiple intelligence have opened up our thinking about the definition, assessment, and education of gifted children, as we will see in the next several chapters. Yet I believe that we must also extract other strands from this tangled skein to get a fuller picture of the nature of human intelligence: right- and left-brain function, convergent versus divergent thinking, and as Drs. Sternberg and Renzulli suggest, the role of creativity.

RIGHT- AND LEFT-BRAIN FUNCTION

Recently, when my younger daughter Aimee and I were reading F. Scott Fitzgerald's masterpiece, *The Great Gatsby*, I was again struck by the strength of her tendency to be "right-brained." The two of us were studying the novel's symbolism and figurative language. I was using a book that my husband had used in college, while my sixteen-year-old read her own new edition.

At one point, we came to a description of a large painted sign depicting a gigantic pair of eyes—those of Dr. T. J. Eckleburg—that peered out of "enormous yellow spectacles which pass over a nonexistent nose." These eyes brooded over a road and "a solemn dumping ground'' in Queens. Rather appropriately, my husband had scribbled the word ''God'' in the margin.

"Look at what Dad wrote here,'' I said to Aimee. ''That's what this image is all about.''

Aimee peered at the handwriting in puzzlement. "Is that a truck or a boot? I can't figure it out,'' she concluded.

I was astonished by her response. "No, Aim,'' I replied. ''It's a word!''

She looked again. "Oh, I see it now,'' she answered, somewhat relieved. ''He wrote 'God.' ''

Now it was my turn to examine what my husband had written. When I shifted my gaze, I could see how my daughter had perceived the word as a series of lines and bumps. Because of her artistic abilities, Aimee is more likely to look at shapes than she is at words. She is more inclined to use the right side of her brain—the one that specializes in abstractions, spatial relations, art, music, and intuition— rather than the left side, which is more focused on logical linear thinking, language, and mathematics.

In an article in the *Training and Developmental Journal*, Ned Herrmann, former manager of Creative Educational Programs at General Electric and creator of a test that helps determine if one is right- or left-brain dominant, gives a description of how each type of thinker functions:

> Take the classic Christmas Eve "toy assembly task." In this example, we are dealing with a bicycle. The right-brain-dominant individual would look at the parts and quickly assemble them in his/her mind's eye to be a bicycle. With this wholistic view in mind, he/she would typically ignore the instruction book and proceed to assemble the parts in conformance with his/her image. Upon completion, he/she would discover seven parts left over; would cram four of them on, and place the remaining three in a bag, hang it around the handlebars and say, "good luck Jimmy." In contrast, the left-brain-dominant individual would follow the sequence in the instruction book and connect parts (a), (b), and (c) together with (d) and (e) and so on until the bicycle was assembled. The outcome in both cases is the same but the strategy, the approach and the mental process are quite different.

Clearly, a child's tendency to depend on one side of the brain can affect how he perceives and expresses information. If you are left-brain-dominant and your child is right-brain-dominant, you may have difficulty communicating with and appreciating each other. And a right-brain-dominant child, because he is less comfortable with chains of logical thought, may have more trouble in school.

STRUCTURE OF THE BRAIN

In order to better understand right- and left-brain dominance, let's take a much-simplified look at how the brain is organized. Neurologists have divided the brain into three sections. The *reptilian brain* is the simplest and oldest section. It regulates functions basic for life such as heartbeat, digestion, breathing, and the autonomic nervous system responsible for the "fight or flight" reaction. The *old mammalian brain* or *limbic system* regulates emotions, memory, attention span, and feelings of identity. Both of these constitute about one sixth of the human brain's total mass and are enveloped by the convoluted mass of tissue (the proverbial "gray matter") that we think of when imagining the brain. This tissue is called the *cerebral cortex*.

The cerebral cortex is responsible for processing information received by the sense organs, making decisions, and initiating actions. It regulates speech and language and receives, stores, and retrieves information.

If you were to look down upon the brain from above, you would notice that the cerebral cortex is split into two halves. These hemispheres are connected internally by a thick bundle of fibers known as the *corpus callosum*. It would be inaccurate to say that the left and right hemispheres function independently of one another. Actually, the corpus callosum connects the two. It is true, however, that each hemisphere has its own important areas of specialization. The left side of the brain is responsible for the right side of the body, while the right side is responsible for the left. In addition, while the whole brain is capable of performing any function, each hemisphere can assume specific duties.

There is still a great deal of brain research to be accomplished before neuroscientists truly understand how the brain's hemispheres interact with one another. Yet researchers now believe that each hemisphere responds in its own way to different types of experiences. As I alluded above, the cortex of the left hemisphere is responsible for analysis and logical thinking while the cortex of the right is responsible for metaphoric, spatial, nonverbal thought. This is true for all right-handed people and about 60 percent of the left-handed. For the remaining 40 percent of left-handers, the brain hemispheres serve the reverse function.

For some still-unexplained reason, we develop a proclivity for using one hemisphere of the brain over the other (called *hemisphere lateralization*). Depending on our dominance patterns, we structure our world accordingly. Ned Herrmann's test for assessing these patterns indicates that when we use our left-brain mode we prefer written directions, structured environments, organized tasks, checklists of items that can be crossed off when tasks are accomplished, successful results, control, and closure. When in our right-brain mode, we easily tolerate lack of closure and ambiguity, desire lots of space, see the "forest" for the "trees," appreciate artistic focus, drive cars or ski without crashing, and enjoy spontaneity and intuitive flashes.

In our family, my husband is much more right-brain-dominant than I am. He attacks the assembly of that proverbial bicycle (much to my dismay and, often, my derision) without even a glance at the instructions. He is a gifted clinical psychologist because he has tremendous intuitive abilities, yet he also was required to master certain left-brain skills in order to complete a Ph.D. in psychology.

I, who am thrilled to organize activities, cross items off a list, and neatly tie up loose ends, have learned to access my right-brain capacity in becoming a writer. Indeed, in the act of writing, I use both hemispheres in sequence: First I create—I let it all flow without stopping myself—and then I go back and reread, edit, and correct.

Ned Herrmann sees creativity as a whole-brained activity—that is, it requires both right- and left-brain input. He divides the creative act into six phases:

Interest: whole-brained

Preparation: left-brained (the rigorous task of defining a problem)

Incubation: right-brained (getting away from the problem to allow the "natural processes of the right brain to mull over [its] complexities . . . to permit the mind to come up with a new combination")

Illumination: right-brained (this is the "Aha!" when you create possible solutions)

Verification: left-brained (analysis of the new idea)

Exploitation: whole-brained (application of what you have learned)

I believe that it is important to encourage both right- and left-brain activity in children. As my co-author, Dr. Susan Ludington, put it in *How to Have a Smarter Baby*, "A universal characteristic of genius is tremendous communication and interaction between the right and left hemispheres.''

CONVERGENT VERSUS DIVERGENT THINKING

Another way to look at left- and right-brain dominance is to think of them as convergent and divergent thinking. Divergent thinking is among the 120 types of intelligence that Dr. J. P. Guilford formulated in his model of the intellect. During divergent thinking, people produce new, unique, original, and diverse ideas. They come up with many possible solutions to a particular problem.

I'm sure that you must be acquainted with at least one divergent thinker. These people can generate endless ideas. They may not be terrific at following their ideas through, but they are capable of building one notion on top of the next until an enormous but ethereal mental construct is erected. Divergent thinkers are great people to invite to a brainstorming session, where they may excitedly fire off numerous suggestions.

Divergent thinkers, such as my husband and our daughter, Aimee, rebel against multiple-choice tests. Rather than simply coming up with the right answer by a process of logical elimination, they consider why each of the choices could be plausible and often formulate reasonable explanations for why the various answers might fit. In effect, they end up questioning the questions and then answering the questions of their own creation—not necessarily those that the teacher asked!

You can see how a divergent thinker, while highly creative, may have trouble in school. Evaluation of such a student's work can be difficult for the teacher since most curriculum guidelines stress a child's ability to answer a certain number of questions correctly, and divergent thinker may challenge the questions or come up with more answers than the teacher wanted. Unfortunately, a multiplicity of answers does not fit neatly into a standardized answer key. Some teachers may feel that their authority is threatened by the divergent thinker's curiosity.

Dr. E. Paul Torrance, one of the giants in the field of the study of creativity, described in his book *Education and the Creative Potential* just such a scene that he had witnessed between a bright, divergently inclined student and a teacher during a math class:

> The boy questioned one of the rules in the book. Instead of asking him
> to prove his interpretation or trying to explain the textbook rule herself,

the teacher became quite irritated, even in the presence of the principal. Holding up the book and patting it with the other hand, she exclaimed, "So! You think you know more than this book!" The boy replied meekly. "No, I don't think I know more than the book, but I'm not satisfied about this rule." Moving to safer ground, the teacher then had the class solve problems in the text. This youngster solved the problems easily, about as rapidly as he could read them, thereby upsetting his teacher who insisted that he put down all the steps he had gone through in solving the problems. Afterwards, the teacher asked the principal to talk to her *troublesome* pupil.

As you can see, in the classroom the advantage often goes to the convergent thinker, whose way of processing information helps him to focus and therefore conform to expectations. When the teacher asks "who," "what," "where," or "when" questions, the convergent thinker's hand will shoot up with a quick "Christopher Columbus discovered America in 1492!" rather than "Do you mean the Indians or the Vikings or Columbus?" Studies have shown that teachers favor the former.

Why do I bring these issues up? Because a person who is naturally inclined toward divergent, right-brained thinking is apt to be more creative in his approach to solving problems. He is also more likely to be regarded as a maverick in the classroom. Depending on the nature of your gifted child's intelligence, therefore, his thinking style may be a factor in how bright he *feels,* and it may influence his success at school or on standardized tests. This topic is discussed further in chapters 5 and 6.

CREATIVITY AND COURAGE

What do Christopher Columbus, the French Impressionist Claude Monet, writer Henry Miller, astronomer Copernicus, and Orville and Wilbur Wright have in common? Each of these men invented a new way of envisioning reality. Each was scorned for his outlandish ideas, yet was surprisingly resilient in the face of adversity. Indeed, each was a highly original, creative individual.

Can we define creativity? According to Dr. E. Paul Torrance, creativity consists of four major elements:

- *Fluency:* the ability to think of a large number of ideas or possible solutions

- *Flexibility:* the ability to think of different approaches or strategies
- *Originality:* the ability to think of unusual possibilities, to get off the beaten track
- *Elaboration:* the ability to work out the details of an idea and implement it

All children have these abilities to a greater or lesser degree. As Dr. Torrance points out, we can't say that a child is fully functioning mentally if the abilities involved in learning and thinking creatively remain undeveloped. Creativity can be taught and enhanced but it can also be crushed (see chapter 10).

The nature of creativity is another one of those ideas that has been debated for millenia. The ancient Greeks, for example, viewed creative inspiration as descended from the gods in the form of the nine muses—daughters of Zeus. Yet even at that time, divergent, creative thinking was suspect: Socrates was put to death for his innovative notions.

In his book, *The Courage to Create*, philosopher–psychologist Rollo May insists that the creative act is an existential stance that involves risk and courage:

> If you do not express your own original ideas, if you do not listen to your own being, you will have betrayed yourself. Also, you will have betrayed our community in failing to make your contribution to the whole. . . . Whereas moral courage is the righting of wrongs, creative courage, in contrast, is the discovering of new forms, new symbols, new patterns on which a new society can be built.

Creativity is a form of thought that must be reckoned with, yet it often is studied separately from IQ. The consensus among researchers in the field points to the conclusion that above a certain threshold of intelligence, creativity is only marginally related to IQ—a high IQ does not guarantee creativity, nor does creativity guarantee a high IQ. In one of Dr. Torrance's studies, for example, there was a difference of 25 IQ points between children who were highly intelligent and those who had been previously identified as highly creative.

IQ tests aside, I believe that creative individuals can be highly intelligent. Pablo Picasso comes to mind, as does poet Robert Frost, who was thrown out of school for "daydreaming." Our civilization's most creative scientist, Albert Einstein, barely made it through high school. Perhaps creatively gifted individuals simply don't do well in the kind of structured, left-brain tests and environments our schools present.

Dr. Torrance makes the point that while highly creative children may score lower on IQ tests than their gifted peers, their achievement test scores are about the same. Perhaps the kinds of questions that IQ tests pose are inappropriate for the creative child's divergent thinking patterns. Other researchers have demonstrated that creative teachers are much more successful in helping children hone their creative skills than those who are not creative themselves.

Children are born wanting to explore their surroundings in any way they can. They become excited when generating new ideas. Creativity is a natural state for kids. For some youngsters, however, the pressure to conform to parental, educational, community, or peer standards causes them to abandon their creativity for more ''accepted'' ways of doing things.

Creativity—just like right-brain dominance and divergence—actually is not fully sanctioned in our society. Dr. Torrance conducted studies with thousands of children in which he asked the students to write imaginative fables above nonconformists such as the flying monkey, the green pig, and the duck who couldn't quack in order to gain an understanding of how children perceived nonconformity. The children's innocent stories reflect our society's views on creativity. ''In many of the stories,'' Dr. Torrance writes, ''the flying monkey is lonely, no one will play with him, no one likes him, because he can fly and they can't.''

Unfortunately, creative children can meet the same fate in the classroom. Dr. Torrance found that the most creative kids are often ridiculed by their peers (and teachers!). They have reputations for having wild and silly ideas. They are viewed as bizarre and often are shunned by their classmates.

THE UNIQUE PLEASURES OF CREATIVITY

Some youngsters manage to maintain their creativity despite the pressure to do otherwise. It takes a lot of courage and confidence. It also may attest to the fact that the act of creation is quite pleasurable— even ecstatic. A recent article in the *Los Angeles Times*, by Anne C. Roark, reports on the work of Dr. Mihaly Csikszentmihalyi, a Hungarian-born professor of psychology now at the University of

Chicago who has been exploring this joyful aspect of creativity since the 1970s.

Dr. Csikszentmihalyi discovered that people engaged in creative work seem to enter another world. They work as if in a dream state. '' 'Time is distorted, a sense of happiness and well-being overcomes them.' They have entered what he calls a state of 'flow,' 'when things seem to go just right, when you feel alive and fully attentive to what you are doing.' '' Similarly, athletes enter the ''zone'' when they make every basket or when every pitched baseball looks as big and as easy to hit as a cantaloupe.

Other scientists confirm that creative people produce brain-wave patterns dissimilar to those who are less creative. In her book *Growing Up Gifted*, Dr. Barbara Clark, a professor of gifted education at California State University, Los Angeles, explains that most people produce alpha waves (slower-than-average brain waves) while relaxing and reduce alpha production while working on a problem. Creative people, however, produce *fewer* alpha waves when relaxing and more alpha waves when working on an imaginative problem. Perhaps they experience creative work as a unique form of relaxation.

The pleasure of the creative experience can be habit-forming. In reporter Roark's words, ''Just like addicts who want drugs or athletes who seek runners' highs, truly creative people, those who are both talented *and* productive, have had an extraordinary experience, one they very much want to repeat—again and again.'' In Dr. Csikszentmihalyi's opinion, the desire to recapture this euphoria is at the root of all artistic pursuits.

As a writer, I would have to agree, since I have experienced such moments of elation in my work. Sometimes I sit down at my computer and look up ''several minutes later'' only to discover that three full hours have passed. There have been times when I've felt drawn to my work—this very book—as if it were a powerful magnet pulling me into its field.

It seems to me, then, that it makes sense to blur the distinction between creativity and IQ. Rather than viewing creativity as something separate from intelligence, some psychologists feel that it is the embodiment of intelligence—the integration of its many dimensions. Barbara Clark calls creativity ''the highest expression of giftedness'' and Rollo May says, ''The creative process must be explored . . . as representing the highest degree of emotional health, as the expression of normal people in the act of actualizing themselves.''

Despite the fact that creativity is not measured by an IQ test, and has not been factored into the traditional views of intelligence, I believe that you should take into account your gifted child's creativity and her thinking styles (as well as her academic acumen) when you try to understand her intelligence. No one has an absolute answer to the riddle of how intelligence operates. Perhaps there can be no absolute answer. It's best to look at your own child clearly to gain a better understanding of her strengths and talents. The next chapter will help you to evaluate her unique attributes.

CHAPTER 3

What Is Giftedness?

*[Queen] Elizabeth (1533–1603) . . . by the age
of 6 was proficient in both Latin and Greek,
could speak and write French fluently,
play the lute and the virginals, and was an
accomplished needlewoman. Such attainments
today would rank her as a prodigy, but then were
no more than what was expected of a royal princess. . . .*

*Einstein set down in the Australian bush a
century ago would no longer be a genius, since he would
not be very good at finding witchetty grubs and water-holes.*

—JOHN RADFORD, *CHILD PRODIGIES AND EXCEPTIONAL EARLY
ACHIEVERS*

THERE ARE AS MANY DEFINITIONS OF GIFTEDNESS AS THERE ARE
gifted people. A score on an IQ test is a start, but today all the experts
agree that IQ tests cannot measure the incalculable complexity of the
human spirit or the light that shines from within when a new idea takes
hold. Each child and adult—average or gifted—is a unique individual
who defies categorization. Besides, as I explained in the previous
chapter, many forms of intelligence such as musical ability, interpersonal and intrapersonal skills, athleticism, and creativity simply aren't
measured on standardized IQ tests.

Before we even begin to define giftedness as we currently know it,
let us keep in mind that our designation is relative. It is based on our
own culture and values. Richard Bothmer makes this point in an article
published in *Gifted Children Today*. He explains that giftedness is
simply a state of mind—a reflection of one's culture at any given
moment in time:

Suppose you were in the Australian outback with a bunch of Aborigi-
nes. . . . How much weight do you think vocabulary and verbal ability
carry? Very little, of course; they are heavily into performance. Prized,

27

here, is the ability to seek out fat lizards that can be wrung dry of juices for refreshment and then roasted. The person who has the talent to do this best is clearly in the highly superior category in that time and place.

Bothmer's point is well taken. What *we* call giftedness may be an absolutely useless concept among other peoples. "The title of 'gifted,' " he concludes, "is always a political decision. It is based on the local society's view of what is a rare and valuable ability. And this is subject to change as the society evolves."

Giftedness is also dependent on timing and perhaps more than a little luck. It has been pointed out by other psychologists that Einstein (he seems to be everyone's favorite example) might not have fared as well, had he been born fifty years earlier: The world might not have been ready for what he had to offer. Michelangelo, Leonardo da Vinci, and Rembrandt might have struggled for recognition had they lived in Manhattan during the 1960s. As Abraham J. Tannenbaum explains in a chapter of the book, *Conceptions of Giftedness*, a person's talents must match society's readiness to appreciate them; otherwise they are "stillborn"—either passé or too avant-garde.

At the moment, we're all part of late-twentieth-century Western civilization. What does our society value as being a rare ability? Clearly it's not a simple score on an IQ test. Again, we are faced with many conflicting views about the nature of giftedness. In their excellent book, *Conceptions of Giftedness*, Drs. Robert Sternberg and Janet Davidson of Yale University have amassed some *seventeen* interrelated yet distinct viewpoints on giftedness from as many experts!

This variance does not make your job any easier, but understanding giftedness is not impossible, either. I believe that children are gifted when they show a love of learning, a burning curiosity about the world and how it works, a sense of excitement over a new discovery, and a remarkable ability to integrate information and create a new reality. Throughout this chapter I will share with you how others view giftedness, as well.

But let's begin with you. As parents, perhaps one of the easiest ways to identify giftedness is to observe a child's behavior. Your child's activities are the gentle footprints of his hidden thought processes.

IT'S THE LITTLE THINGS

Many experts point to a child's advanced sense of humor as indicative of giftedness. In fact, one of the early signs of a child's giftedness is his ability to find incongruities humorous.

We derived great enjoyment from Cherie's sense of humor while she was still a baby. When Cherie was less than ten months old, she giggled if we pretended to suck on her pacifier or bottle. She thought it hilarious when we wore her training pants or her little jeans on our heads, and she absolutely cracked up when we tried to clothe her in the same absurd manner.

Indeed, funny dress-up became one of Cherie's most enjoyable games. We have pictures of her as a toddler decked out in my sister's wooden clogs, my vintage 1969 knee-length boots (the kind that went with miniskirts), and knit caps, berets, straw hats, scarves, shower caps, sailor hats, Sherlock Holmes caps, even plastic tupperware containers on her head. The best outfit included cone-shaped party hats over her ears, one pointing east, the other west. Gifted children delight in humor and their pleasure can also become a source of your own enjoyment.

Cherie also displayed her giftedness at play. She had an enormous attention span. We salvaged many a Sunday morning by allowing her to entertain herself. One of us would respond to her 6 A.M. call by placing her Fisher-Price playschool or playhouse in the crib. At the age of two, she could sit there, absorbed with it for an hour or more, singing nursery rhymes, humming, and talking to herself.

Of course, when I was busy with dinner or needed to study and wanted Cherie to occupy herself in her playpen, she would have none of it. When I complained to my mother that other babies seemed content with that arrangement, my mother wisely noted that Cherie was no dummy: She wanted to be where the action was.

Cherie's ability to engage in complex imaginative play flowered as she grew. At the age of five, she and her best friend, a child of similar temperament and abilities, constructed entire Barbie doll villages on her bedroom floor, improvising linens, furniture, and buildings with shoe boxes, tissues, cotton balls, paper clip dispensers, wooden blocks, Legos, empty oatmeal boxes, and whatever else the two of them could scavenge from the toy box or my kitchen closet and desk.

The girls would engage in their building activity for hours. Usually by the time the city was erected, it was time for dinner and bed and I had the unenviable task of asking them to clean up so that we wouldn't step on the toys and break them or our toes. This, as you can imagine, was met with howls of displeasure. "But we just started to play," they protested. It never occurred to them that the creation of these towns was a wonderfully imaginative and expansive play experience, in and of itself. It truly was a joy to watch.

THINKING ABOUT YOUR OWN CHILD

For most parents the label of "gifted" does not come as a surprise. Educators of gifted children have found that we identify our children as being unusual long before schooling and testing are considered. We're so good at it, in fact, that when we err, it tends to be on the side of *underestimating* our children's abilities.

How do we have this uncanny ability to know that our children are gifted? I believe that our youngsters' abilities reveal themselves to us in the little things that they say or do. In our family, Cherie's imitation of her simian friend, Curious George, her unusually advanced vocabulary, her creative play, her long attention span, and her sense of humor all contributed to our intuition that she was indeed gifted.

Your child may display his giftedness in other ways. Watch for:

- Spencer's invention of his own secret alphabet and number code
- The long sentences that Jennifer masters at a very young age along with a certain capacity and willingness to carry on "adult" conversations
- Mark's seemingly endless attention span
- Adrian's use of unusual and sophisticated vocabulary
- Max's fascination with numbers, weights, clocks, and puzzles
- Mara's interest in puns and wordplay
- Paul's physical dexterity that allows him to throw a ball farther, run faster, and climb higher than his friends
- Carla's sense of humor and flexible thinking
- Michael's boundless curiosity
- Julie's memory of exact detail
- Heather's ability to draw a surprisingly accurate likeness of an object
- Frank's facility in memorizing and "reading" stories before his peers have mastered these skills
- Janie's perfect pitch

- Josh's adroitness at pulling together seemingly disparate ideas to create a new sense of order or reality

In addition to providing valuable clues to your child's abilities, these little everyday events infuse your interactions with your youngster with a certain delight. Gifted children can be great fun to have around because they are interesting, vital people.

PRECOCIOUSNESS VERSUS GIFTEDNESS

As I explained earlier, Cherie was an early reader. I took this as evidence of her giftedness. I was wrong. On a superficial level we might consider the early acquisition of skills such as reading or writing as indicators of giftedness. But experts are quick to point out that precocity (early or premature development) and giftedness are not necessarily synonymous. Researchers have found, for example, that within a group of bright preschoolers, the best readers are not necessarily the children with the highest IQ scores and that, conversely, not all children with high IQ scores learn to read early.

Anne-Marie Roeper, headmistress of the Roeper Lower School in Bloomfield, Michigan, explains in an article in the *Gifted Child Quarterly* that people often confuse giftedness with precociousness. She points out that giftedness comprises a child's ability to think, to generalize, to see connections, and to discover alternatives. The gifted child is not necessarily ahead of others academically. A precocious child, on the other hand, is ahead of others in development, which means that this child will be more able or mature at a particular time. "Other children catch up with the precocious child later."

It's important to realize, therefore, that teaching your baby to identify different species of birds or stuffing your four-year-old's head full of math facts will not "make" him gifted. Facts won't do it, but his ability to think will.

THE LEARNING CHARACTERISTICS OF GIFTED CHILDREN

The late UCLA professor of education, May V. Seagoe, compiled a list of learning characteristics of gifted children that expands on these notions. The following have been gleaned from daily classroom observations. While Dr. Seagoe's emphasis is on teaching and learning, these attributes can also clarify for you the small, everyday ways that your children exhibit their giftedness. I feel this list best conveys why having such a child in your home is a joy.

A gifted child will have:

1. Keen powers of observation; naive receptivity; sense of the significant; willingness to examine the unusual.
2. Power of abstraction, conceptualization, synthesis; interest in inductive learning and problem solving; pleasure in intellectual activity.
3. Interest in cause-effect relations, ability to see relationships; interest in applying concepts; love of truth.
4. Liking for structure and order; liking for consistency, as in value systems, number systems, clocks, calendars.
5. Retentiveness.
6. Verbal proficiency; large vocabulary; facility in expression; interest in reading; breadth of information in advanced areas.
7. Questioning attitude, intellectual curiosity, inquisitive mind; intrinsic motivation.
8. Power of critical thinking; skepticism, evaluative testing; self-criticism and self-checking.
9. Creativeness and inventiveness; liking for new ways of doing things; interest in creating, brainstorming, and freewheeling.
10. Power of concentration; intense attention that may exclude all else; and long attention span.
11. Persistent, goal-directed behavior.
12. Sensitivity, intuitiveness, empathy for others; need for emotional support and a sympathetic attitude.
13. High energy, alertness, eagerness; periods of intense voluntary effort preceding invention.
14. Independence in work and study; preference for individualized work; self-reliance; need for freedom of movement and action.
15. Versatility and virtuosity; diversity of interests and abilities; many hobbies; proficiency in art forms such as music and drawing.
16. Friendliness and outgoingness.

EVER-WIDENING CIRCLES

As our understanding of intelligence has changed over the decades, so has our appreciation of giftedness. It's not so much the acquisition of knowledge as what a child does with it that has been found to be important.

Gifted children are innovative: They dream up and solve problems; they invent new ways of thinking; they take apart their radios and make fire using magnifying glasses. Gifted children think deeply and make connections between disparate bits of information; they analyze and hypothesize; they turn a problem around and look at it from a new angle. Gifted children try to make meaning out of the chaos that surrounds them; they wonder and experience wonderment. Gifted children have minds of their own that they use abundantly. This perhaps is the best definition of what it means to be gifted.

CHAPTER 4

How Does a Child Become Gifted?

Inside the child, everything is moving.
Harmoniously. The eyes remain wide open,
passionately involved. The arms, the legs, continue
their ballet. The hands endlessly explore.

—FREDRICK LEBOYER
(QUOTED IN *THE METAPHORIC MIND*, BOB SAMPLES)

RECENTLY, MARJORIE, A GOOD FRIEND OF MINE, WAS DESCRIBING HER experiences with her two highly gifted daughters, now ages sixteen and eleven. She talked with special excitement about her youngest daughter's development during infancy.

"My earliest joy," she asserted, "was watching Jessica's intelligence emerge. At ten months she had an expressive vocabulary of ten words and a receptive vocabulary of more than thirty.

"Jessica was so interesting! It was as if she were a big person in a small person's body. She had a personality and a great sense of humor. She made jokes! And she was so sensuous—she was easily stimulated and got pleasure from all of her senses. She was really entertaining.

"I felt extremely competent at nurturing infants," my friend continued. "I believed that I could make any child talk. The whole experience was so gratifying because she responded so well!"

Marjorie's comments about her parenting skills reminded me of a fascinating study conducted by a team of psychologists headed by Dr. M. B. Karnes, a specialist in giftedness. The team compared parenting activities in ten families of gifted preschoolers with similar practices in families of ten nongifted preschoolers.

The team found that two groups of parents varied in several respects. While both sets read to their children daily, for example, the parents of the gifted children spent an average of twenty-one minutes a day at that activity, whereas the parents of the nongifted kids spent only seven minutes. This disparity was even more evident when the

34

researchers examined minutes spent daily at schoollike activities: twenty-three minutes on average as opposed to four minutes.

In addition, while both groups reported that their children watched television for an hour and a half daily, the children in the gifted group experienced much more parental involvement in fantasy play such as block building, making up rhymes and songs, or going to the museum and on nature walks. Mothers of the gifted children more frequently reported consciously promoting language development in their children. They also tried to expose their youngsters to diverse experiences and encouraged their autonomy.

Research studies such as these seem to point to the conclusion that intensive parental involvement enhances intelligence. That may well be true.

There also may be another, related explanation: Because a child is gifted, she responds positively and enthusiastically to her parents' efforts. Her responsiveness reinforces her parents' desire to interact with her. As in the case of little Jessica and her mother, Marjorie, the greater the child's delight in learning, the more motivated the parent becomes to teach. It's the giftedness itself—the child's thirst for understanding—that may elicit a high degree of parental involvement.

This reciprocity between parent and child brings forth the question of the origin of giftedness. Is giftedness a hereditary trait that is fixed at birth, or does it result from external forces (such as parenting style) operating on the child once he's born? Will reading to your child twenty-one minutes a day, for instance, render him a candidate for the gifted program at school? How do children become gifted, anyway? Is it *nature* or *nurture*? Or is it both?

NATURE VERSUS NURTURE: THE CHICKEN OR THE EGG?

In the past, scientists generally agreed that a person's intelligence was a result of his heredity and was fixed at birth. In 1905, French psychologist Alfred Binet and his colleagues constructed the first IQ (intelligence quotient) test as a way to predict school success among Parisian school children and to identify those who were mentally retarded. The test Binet created seemed to accomplish this purpose (see chapter 5).

Early researchers found that IQ scores from intelligence tests such as the Binet (which in 1916 was revised by Dr. Lewis M. Terman and his associates at Stanford University and renamed the Stanford-Binet) changed only minimally when a child was retested a week, a month, or even two years later. Thus, it was assumed by all that IQ was relatively constant, changing only in small increments and in relation to a person's growth from childhood to adulthood and then old age.

This view of an unvarying IQ eased decision-making for parents, educators, and psychologists alike. If the IQ remained constant, caregivers and teachers would be able to classify a child according to his intellectual potential. Parents could plan his education, educators would know what to teach, and social workers could make better foster home placements.

While this strict view of a fixed intelligence has fallen by the wayside, genetic behaviorists, who analyze and interpret the influence of heredity on development, continue to investigate how genetics help to determine intelligence.

These studies have yielded some fascinating conclusions. According to Dr. Robert Plomin, an expert in behavioral genetics and a faculty member at the College of Health and Human Development of Pennsylvania State University, long-term investigations that have included more than 100,000 twins, and both biological and adoptive parents, "make it difficult to escape the conclusion that heredity importantly influences individual differences in IQ scores." Dr. Plomin explains, for example, that genetically related individuals adopted apart show significant resemblance, and identical twins are substantially more similar than fraternal twins.

Yet Dr. Plomin also makes the point that "children growing up in the same family are not very similar." Most of us probably already know this, judging from our own experiences with our siblings and our children. Indeed, in Dr. Plomin's words, research has shown that "siblings show greater differences than similarities for the major domains of psychology."

Why should this be true? It's easy to see that other factors can affect how children fare within a family. To begin, the inheritance of intelligence is most probably a highly complex matter involving many different genes rather than a single gene, in contrast to the inheritance of simpler traits such as blood type or hair color. Second, outside factors may also have influence such as:

- Position in the family (birth order)
- Relationship with siblings
- Gender
- Differential treatment by parents

- Socioeconomic status of parents at the time of the child's birth (which may vary from sibling to sibling)
- Unique sets of friends and peers
- Accidents, illnesses, or other trauma
- Unstimulating, painful, or disturbing situations at school or highly stimulating, exciting school environments

Finally, a child's own temperament may influence how he responds to his environment. As British psychologist Dr. John Radford explains in his book, *Child Prodigies and Exceptional Early Achievers*, children within the same family react differently to the same situation. Dr. Radford quotes the famous psychologist Gordon Allport's folk wisdom, "The same fire that melts the butter, hardens the egg."

In short, a child's experiences in the world ultimately help to shape how his hereditary gifts manifest themselves. And that brings us to our second point: the importance of environment or *nurture* as a factor in intelligence.

ENVIRONMENT: *HOW TO HAVE A SMARTER BABY*

In 1982, I interviewed Dr. Susan Ludington, a professor of maternal-child health at UCLA's School of Nursing, for a *Los Angeles Times* article on how fetuses respond to conditioned learning. Shortly thereafter, Dr. Ludington and I collaborated on a book entitled *How to Have a Smarter Baby*. The central idea of the book was that when parents appeal to a fetus's or a newborn's *preferences*, they can actually augment their child's IQ over time while also establishing a deeper bond with the child. That was when I first researched how parental involvement—*nurture*—can influence a child's potential intelligence. I'd like to share with you some of the more salient points from that book along with more recent findings on this fascinating subject.

Brain Growth

The creation of brain cells begins at the moment a baby is conceived and continues for only five months. Therefore, the number of brain cells is determined before a child is born. At birth, a baby's brain has all the cells it will ever have (100 to 200 *billion* brain cells) and it has reached 25 percent of its eventual adult weight.

Since no new brain cells are added, how does the brain complete its growth? Obviously, it does not depend on the addition of brain cells but rather on how well and with what complexity the existing cells develop. Stimulation causes the individual cells to grow increasingly more elaborate systems of interconnecting branches. The greater the complexity (and therefore weight) of each cell, the higher the potential for connections with other brain cells, the heavier the brain, and the greater the capacity for intelligence.

By the time a child has reached his first birthday, his brain will have achieved 70 percent of its eventual adult weight. During that first year 70 to 85 percent of the brain cells will be completely developed.

It is clear, then, that a baby's first twelve months of life is a stage of tremendous development. Dr. Ludington calls it the period of the "brain growth spurt." During this time, brain cells are extremely sensitive to their environment and respond to both positive and negative conditions. But brain development does not begin at birth. Rather, it starts while the child is still in utero.

Life in the Womb

In my work with Dr. Ludington, I was surprised to learn that newborns don't suddenly start functioning in the delivery room, as if a hidden switch were pulled the moment the umbilical cord is cut. Researchers recognize intrauterine responses by using fetal monitors and ultrasound exams to document changes in the fetus's movements, heart rate, and brain waves. Fetuses become sentient beings the last two months of pregnancy. They respond differently to their mother's heartbeat and voice than they do to loud noises such as approaching airplanes and rock concerts, or to gentle, soothing music such as the tinkling of bells or Brahm's "Lullaby." By thirty-six weeks, the fetal ear is open and fully functioning.

Indeed, up to six weeks before birth, fetuses actively use their sense of hearing as well as their other senses such as taste, touch, sight, and movement. They even exercise their limbs by pushing against the uterine walls. They have a sense of taste: Thirty-four-week-old fetuses swallow more sweetened amniotic fluid than distasteful fluid. They suck their thumbs, swallow and make facial expressions that resemble crying. This stimulation helps their nervous system develop. By the time the fetus is twenty-seven weeks old, it responds to movement, touch, and light.

Newborn Capabilities

Far from being a quiet, dark, muffled environment, the uterus during the last trimester is a lively, stimulating place. In a way, it prepares the child for his entrance into the "outside" world. This is important to know because usually we think of newborns as being capable only of eating, sleeping, and excreting. It is truly a fallacy. Researchers have found that newborns' senses are quite developed at birth.

Exhaustive studies have confirmed that a newborn:

- Sees clearly within 13 inches of her face
- Identifies her mother's face by four days of age
- Can follow appealing objects (especially black and white geometric shapes) that are held 10 to 13 inches from her eyes
- Discriminates the loudness and pitch of sounds and turns her head to find sounds
- Differentiates between speech and nonspeech sounds only twelve hours after birth
- Recognizes parents' voices by one week
- Has a keen sense of touch and very sensitive skin
- Tastes everything and can distinguish among sweet, sour, and bitter
- Distinguishes the scent of her mother's breast milk from all others within hours of birth
- Recognizes the scent of clothing and perfume or aftershave by one month of age

These findings are significant, because until the age of six months, babies learn primarily through their senses. They have not yet developed the memory capacity to create their own thoughts. And so, by stimulating a young baby's senses, you are bound to increase that child's use of his brain cells.

Structure and Development of Brain Cells

Brain cells (*neurons*) store, send, and receive information through a series of electrical impulses called *synapses*. The electrical currents travel from the center of the neuron (*cell body*) along a long thin extension (*axon*) to the next neuron. Each cell body is composed of a nucleus surrounded by a complex network of branches, called *dendrites*.

The dendrites pick up messages from the neighboring axons. The greater the complexity of the dendrite network, the more connections are made and the more messages are transmitted. According to Dr. Barbara Clark, in *Growing Up Gifted*, "We can, through changes in teaching and learning procedures, affect the growth of dendritic branching and increase . . . the complexity of the network of connections among neurons."

Think of the brain as an extraordinarily dense tangle of electrical wiring. Just as the wires for your lamps or refrigerator require insulation in order to transmit electricity properly, so do the neurons in the brain. Neurons are coated by a sheath of material called *myelin* that protects the neuron and amplifies the signal being sent from one cell to the next.

Myelin is produced by *glial* cells. Dr. Clark explains that these unique cells also "provide the brain with nourishment, consume waste products, and serve as packing material actually gluing the brain together." The increased production of glial cells is quite significant. According to Dr. Clark, as we increase the glial cells in the brain, we accelerate the speed of learning. Indeed, researchers analyzing sections of Albert Einstein's brain found that it had substantially more glial cells than sections of brains belonging to people of more average abilities.

Obviously, the number of glial cells is significant for a child's intelligence. How do we increase that number? According to Dr. Clark, "We influence the rate of glial cell production by the richness of environment we provide." It's a chain reaction: Stimulation from you and the environment increases your child's glial cell production, which in turn helps to insulate his neurons with myelin. These myelinized brain cells transmit information more rapidly and efficiently than uninsulated cells. Thus, you and the environment influence myelin production and the speed at which synapses occur.

Appealing to Babies' Preferences

Based on these findings, it seems clear that environment and stimulation help the development of brain cells. Newborn babies actually have preferences as to the kinds of stimulation they enjoy and they are capable of choosing one kind over another.

In the early 1960s, for example, Dr. Robert Fantz, a developmental psychologist at Case Western Reserve University in Cleveland, Ohio, developed a sort of "peep box" that surrounded a baby sitting in an infant seat. Placing a black and white checkerboard card and a plain gray card in front of the child, he watched through a peephole to see which card the baby would look at. Invariably, the baby's eyes traveled to the more interesting design—the checkerboard.

Later studies determined that babies preferred black and white geometric designs over plain brightly colored cards and that their eyes traveled to the edge of the design where the black met the white. Why black and white? Apparently, these colors create the most contrast and are, therefore, the most appealing to youngsters. Babies even lose interest in a pattern if they have observed it for too long and prefer designs of increasing complexity as they mature.

In *How to Have a Smarter Baby*, Dr. Ludington describes her own research study in the same field:

> I devised a [motor-driven] mobile for newborns that incorporated all the features researchers had shown were important for visual stimulation: black and white for contrast; checkerboard for pattern; cross for geometric shape; and a simple motor to control the mobile's movement.
>
> I used this mobile in a study to determine how fast newborns could learn to manipulate their environment. . . . I attached a string from the mobile to the infant's toe. The baby's kick tugged the string which, in turn, activated the motor, producing a one-quarter turn of the mobile. During the twenty minutes of this kind of activity, the babies' kicking rate increased an *astounding 200 percent.*

The virtues of this kind of stimulation (you wouldn't have such a mechanized mobile yourself but you certainly could use a purchased toy or a checkerboard design that you've drawn on a paper plate) are multiple. The babies in this study had the opportunity to focus and learn about something that interested them. They spent time concentrating on the design: The more time concentrating, the longer was the attention span. (When was the last time you thought of a newborn as being able to concentrate?) Finally, this experiment helped these children to feel that they had some power to manipulate their environment.

According to Dr. Ludington, "Stimulation accelerates a baby's mental ability and increases a child's skills in finding ways to stimulate himself. Studies have shown that with continued and consistent stimulation over a two-year period, IQ can be boosted by 15 to 30 points, when IQ measures are taken at four or five years of age.'' Such a statement is a far cry from the concept that intelligence is fixed at birth.

THE GIFTED BRAIN

According to Dr. Clark, by the environment we provide we not only change the behavior of children but also their brain structure on a cellular level. ''In this way,'' she explains, ''gifted children become biologically different from average learners, *not at birth* [italics added], but as a result of using and developing the wondrous, complex structure with which they are born. At birth nearly everyone is programmed to be phenomenal.'' Unfortunately, the converse is also true. If a child's environment lacks appropriate stimulation, his ability to learn will suffer.

Based on scores of research studies into animal and human brain/mind research, Dr. Clark postulates that the brains of gifted individuals are biologically different from those of average intelligence. To paraphrase her findings, in gifted individuals:

1. There is an increase in neuroglial cells, allowing more nourishment and support for neurons.
2. The neurons become biochemically richer, allowing for more complex patterns of thought.
3. Dendritic branching increases, thus increasing the potential for interconnections between neurons.
4. The number of synapses and the size of the synaptic contact increase, allowing more complex communications within the system.
5. The part of the brain involved in future planning, insightful thinking, and intuitive experiences (the prefrontal cortex) is used more frequently.
6. The ''alpha state'' of relaxation occurs more frequently, allowing for more relaxed and concentrated learning and higher levels of retention. (The alpha state is a slowing of the brain waves that gives the sense of a floating state of consciousness. During such a state, the brain's ability to focus is heightened.)
7. Brain rhythms are more coherent and synchronous, allowing

for heightened concentration, focused attention, and in-depth probing and inquiry.

So, to answer my initial question—Are intelligence and giftedness the result of nature or nurture?—clearly the answer must be that it is both but not as separate entities. Rather, it is their *interaction* that is important.

CHAPTER 5

Testing: The Good, the Bad, the Ugly

The creative and gifted students reach out beyond the amassing and recall of facts. They are at home with the overarching concepts involving the great unitive themes. They strive for a coherent view of themselves, the world, and of human destiny. Indeed, it is by this quality, more than by standardized tests that we can identify them, for they are ever seeking the interrelations that lead to a higher synthesis.

—ELIZABETH MONROE DREWS
(QUOTED IN *GROWING UP GIFTED*,
BARBARA CLARK)

MY FRIEND PHYLLIS IS ADAMANTLY OPPOSED TO IQ TESTS. SHE believes that children who do not score well enough to be admitted into gifted programs feel as though they have been marked for failure. "It becomes a self-fulfilling prophecy," she declared to me. "The score goes in the file and every teacher reads it and prejudges him. The child is labeled for life.

"Besides," she added, "those tests are not valid. Schools haven't caught up with that yet. I think the school district should use its money to improve general programming for all children rather than single out a few for special treatment because of how they did on *one* test *one* morning in the third grade. I'm boycotting testing altogether for my children. I don't want them to be hurt by it the way your daughter Aimee was."

Yes, my family has had both good and bad experiences with IQ testing, as I'll explain later. But even though I respect my friend's point of view, I cannot agree with her wholeheartedly. At this point in time, I regard testing as a sort of necessary evil. In today's schools, the IQ test is the most frequently relied upon tool to determine if a child should be placed in a gifted program. According to a recent *New York Times Magazine* article by journalist Elizabeth Stone, forty states recommend or require its use to identify gifted children. These tests govern an estimated 90 percent of all gifted programs in the United States. "The IQ test," writes Stone, "still has the weight of a CAT scan."

Innovators such as Howard Gardner, Robert Sternberg, and Joseph Renzulli are making inroads into altering the status quo, as I'll explain below, but their impact is far from universal. I wish that there were a more equitable way to separate the children who would gain from the special programming of a gifted class from those who would feel intimidated by the heavy work load and intense competition. Certainly, *all* children would benefit from enrichment and instruction that emphasizes more complex thinking skills of the kind the best gifted programs offer.

Unfortunately, I agree with my friend's assertion that schools have not caught up with the new views of intelligence, but since educators continue to rely heavily on IQ tests alone to determine placement in gifted programs, it behooves us as parents to understand what these tests can tell us about our children—and, perhaps even more importantly, what they can't—so that we may make informed decisions about our children's future.

THE TESTING DILEMMA

The lack of consensus regarding what exactly constitutes intelligence and giftedness has spawned a parallel controversy about appropriate scientific ways to identify gifted children for placement in specialized school programs.

Testing, or the "study of individual differences," as it has been called among psychologists, began early in the twentieth century with the Binet intelligence test. For decades thereafter, the IQ test reigned supreme as the single method for ferreting out genius in our midst. Today, as our notions of intelligence and giftedness have widened to incorporate creativity, leadership abilities, and artistic achievement, among other attributes, the old workhorse IQ test has increasingly come under fire from parents, school personnel, and research psychologists for being too limited and limiting.

You may have been caught in the cross fire of this controversy. Should you have your child tested or not? Will it hurt or hinder his options in the future? Do the risks of his taking the test (and possibly scoring below the "gifted range") outweigh the benefits of his being placed in a gifted program? Should you advocate for that placement?

None of these questions are easy ones, yet you may have to answer them to the best of your ability, given your child's particular needs and talents, and your community's resources. My best advice is to put your child first. Consider who he is and proceed with care. One of the hallmarks of parenting is that none of us can predict or control the future consequences of today's choices. We can only do our best in the moment with the information we have. Fortunately, often we're pleasantly surprised by the outcome.

On behalf of IQ tests, I must say that they do serve a function: They assess certain valuable traits. But they must be used with caveats: They must be administered correctly and scored correctly. And those scores must be taken for what they are, not inflated or endowed with a greater evaluative power than they have. The tests themselves are useful only when they are *one part* of an assessment process that takes into account many other abilities, as well as your child's emotional health. This is why, ultimately, you must look at your child and let him be the deciding factor in getting into a gifted program.

In this chapter we will consider four questions: (1) What are intelligence tests? (2) How accurately do they measure what we now consider to be giftedness? (3) What is the most equitable way to place children in gifted programs? (4) Should we, as parents, advocate to get our children into these programs?

WHAT IS AN IQ SCORE?

After all this talk about IQ, you may be wondering what IQ scores actually mean. IQ, or intelligence quotient, is based on how well a child performs school-related tasks when compared to other children. As originally formulated, IQ was established as the ratio between a child's mental age (MA) and his chronological age (CA). The initial formula looked like this:

$$\frac{Mental\ age}{Chronological\ age} \times 100$$

An eight-year-old who performs exactly like other eight-year-olds would have an IQ of 100: His mental age and chronological age are identical. On the other hand, an eight-year-old who performs like a twelve-year-old would score an IQ of 150.

Today this formula has been altered. Instead of comparing mental age with chronological age, the child's performance is compared to a national standardized sample: Psychometrists look at how well the child performed in relation to other children his age who also took the test. Again, the average score is 100.

Fifty percent of all IQ scores fall between the range of 90 and 110. Ninety percent of the population has IQ scores between 70 and 130. The higher or lower the score, the more rarely it occurs in the general population. On the Stanford-Binet or the Wechsler, which I discuss more fully below, the scoring levels look like this:

SCORE	MEANING	FREQUENCY
90–109	Average	50% of population
110–119	Bright-average	11–27% of population
120–130	Superior	3–10% of population
140	Very superior	7 out of 1,000
150	Very superior	9 out of 10,000
160	Very superior	1 out of 10,000
180	Very superior	1 out of 1,000,000

One of the inherent problems with using IQ scores alone for placement in gifted programs is the arbitrariness of the "cutoff." Some schools require an IQ of 125 to make a child eligible for gifted programs, whereas others may require an IQ of 132. A child who scores 128, for instance, would be admitted to the first program but excluded from the second. The issue gets cloudier when you consider that the score of 128 is not carved in stone: On any given day, a child's IQ score could be 3 to 5.6 points higher or lower. What's more, if the child isn't well or has had an emotional upset the morning he was tested, the score could be further affected.

Nevertheless, IQ scores have become exceedingly and inappropriately important to parents (perhaps because parents haven't been fully informed about the implications—or lack thereof—of the tests). As Jacqulyn Saunders, co-author of *Bringing Out the Best*, puts it, "It's been said that you may forget your anniversary or your mother's birthday, but once you know your child's IQ score it is burned on your brain forever."

THE MOST COMMON IQ TESTS

The two tests most frequently given to assess IQ are the Stanford-Binet and the Wechsler. Research has found that brighter students tend to score higher on the Stanford-Binet than they do on the Wechsler. Older people tend to do better on the Wechsler and younger people tend to score higher on the Stanford-Binet. In addition, the Wechsler scale has less "floor" and "ceiling," meaning that it doesn't discriminate as well as the Stanford-Binet in the highest and lowest ranges of performance. You should be informed of these scoring issues when you receive the test results from the psychometrist.

The Stanford-Binet

The Binet-Simon scale, as it was originally known, is the granddaddy of all modern IQ tests. Albert Binet developed his test in France in 1905 after trying scores of approaches to measure intelligence including analysis of handwriting, physical traits, and palm lines. In 1904, the minister of public education in France appointed a commission to study subnormal children in Parisian schools. Dr. Binet and his colleague, Dr. Simon, created a test of thirty items of increasing complexity to assess which children were too slow to be included in the normal curriculum. Dr. Binet was looking to measure judgment, comprehension, and reasoning.

Since its inception, the Binet-Simon has gone through many revisions. In 1916, Dr. Lewis M. Terman of Stanford University completely reworked and expanded the test and introduced the idea of IQ. At that time, the test became known as the Stanford-Binet. A second even more comprehensive revision was undertaken in 1937 and others were undertaken in 1960 and 1976. Those tests are called the Stanford-Binet L-M form. The most recent version—the Stanford-Binet IV—was published in 1986.

Today the Stanford-Binet is composed of a series of tests grouped according to a child's age level. The tests meant for younger children, for example, include toy objects such as cars, dolls, blocks, pictures, scissors, and little dogs. Within each age level, the tests are of approximately the same difficulty and measure abilities such as:

- Verbal ability
- Ability to understand analogies and abstractions
- Skill at solving problems
- Aptitude in perceiving cause and effect relationships
- Adroitness at classifying objects

The examiner administers tests within a range of several ages: The lowest level at which all "tests" are passed is called the *basal age* and the highest level at which all "tests" are failed is called the *ceiling age*.

Great skill, training, and experience are required of the person who administers and scores the Stanford-Binet because the test is rather complicated. If the tester falters or gropes for words, he may ruin the rapport between himself and the child. In fact, if he inadvertently changes some of the wording of the test, even slightly, he may modify the difficulty of the test and even invalidate the score. In addition, each "test" must be scored while it is in the process of being given in order for the tester to know if he should continue to the next "test." Perhaps it is for these reasons that today's educational psychologists administer the Wechsler tests more frequently than they do the Stanford-Binet.

The Wechsler

The Wechsler comes in three forms:

WPPSI: Wechsler Preschool and Primary Scale of Intelligence (for children ages three years ten months sixteen days to six years seven months fifteen days).

WISC-R: Wechsler Intelligence Scale for Children—Revised (for children ages 6 years to 17 years).

WAIS: Wechsler Adult Intelligence Scale (for people age 16 and older).

Each of the Wechsler tests is divided into ten subtests. Some measure verbal ability and others measure performance in tasks such as manipulating designs, completing mazes, and repeating series of numbers. These are not offered in sequence but are alternated to help hold the child's attention. Performance tests seem to be more fun than verbal tests.

If your child were to take the WPPSI, he would encounter the following subtests:

VERBAL SUBTESTS

- *Information:* Questions relate to factual information about the world—money, parts of the body, the environment. Children demonstrate their curiosity, memory, and alertness during this test.

- *Similarities:* Questions measure the "ability to abstract and generalize." Children are asked to name similar items to ones presented or to explain why two items are similar. The more abstract the answer, the higher the score.
- *Vocabulary:* Questions measure the ability to understand and use language. Words become more abstract as the test progresses.
- *Arithmetic:* Questions are asked verbally and must be answered in the same way. This subtest measures your child's understanding of number concepts and his ability to solve problems in his head.
- *Comprehension:* Questions asking "What would you do if . . ." involve everyday problems that test your child's ability to make social judgments in creating solutions.

PERFORMANCE SUBTESTS

- *Picture completion:* Your child will be asked to point to the missing part in a series of increasingly complex drawings. This exercise tests his ability to pay attention to details.
- *Geometric design:* Your child will be asked to copy geometric shapes—the more accurate the drawing, the higher the score. This exercise measures visual-perceptual-motor skills.
- *Block design:* Your child will be asked to duplicate designs (either demonstrated or pictured on cards) using red and white blocks. This exercise measures his ability to analyze a problem visually, breaking it into its component parts.
- *Mazes:* Your child will be asked to complete a series of mazes—the faster and more accurately, the better. This exercise measures his ability to plan in advance.
- *Animal house:* Your child will be asked to place colored pegs in holes to match a pattern. This exercise measures his ability to learn a new task quickly.

The WISC-R substitutes several other subtests for the ones listed here. For example, rather than the mazes subtest, the WISC-R contains a *picture arrangement subtest*. It not only measures a child's ability to plan ahead but also indicates his adroitness at interpreting visual clues; he must put the pictures in the proper order so that they tell a story. Such a skill also requires social awareness. In addition, the WISC-R contains a *coding subtest*, in which your child is required to reproduce a sequence of numbers and symbols on paper. This test measures his level of fine motor coordination.

It's important to bear in mind that an IQ score on a Wechsler is a composite of verbal and performance scores. Two children with an identical IQ could have very different profiles of ability. In fact, a child with a gifted or bright-average IQ may show a wide disparity between the verbal and the performance scores.

When the IQ score of the WISC is reported to you, ideally you should receive a breakdown of the subtest results and at the very least you should be informed of both components so that you clearly understand your child's areas of strength and weakness. While it's normal for the verbal and performance scores to differ to some degree, an IQ that is extremely high in one area and extremely low in the other would warrant further testing and evaluation, since this variance could indicate an error in the testing procedure or a potential learning problem.

QUESTIONS YOU SHOULD ASK

Your child's educational future may depend on how she fares on an IQ test. Certainly, you'll want your youngster to have the best testing experience possible—one that will most accurately reflect those abilities measured on the IQ scales. In her book, *The Baby Boards*, early childhood educator Jacqueline Robinson suggests the following helpful guidelines in evaluating the examiner:

- *How has the person been trained?* You'll want someone who has taken graduate courses in intelligence testing and measurement and who has given many IQ tests under the supervision of a psychologist. I would prefer someone with years of experience rather than months.
- *Does the person have experience with young children?* Young children have shorter attention spans and may feel intimidated by strangers. Familiarity in working with these youngsters is essential, especially if your child is a preschooler.
- *Does the examiner have access to other professionals when he or she is interpreting the tests scores?* This is most important if your child's score is unusual.
- *Before the test appointment, ask for a brief meeting with the person who will be administering the test.* This is your opportunity

to assess the tester's demeanor. If you bring your child along she may be able to establish an early rapport.

- *Be with your child when you meet the examiner at the test appointment.* According to Ms. Robinson, "Good rapport between the examiner and your child is considered so essential for obtaining valid test scores, that collectively the authors of the major intelligence tests . . . recommend discontinuing the test if rapport cannot be established or maintained." If you are present during the first few minutes of the test and notice that your child is anxious or unhappy, you can ask for the test to be rescheduled with another examiner.
- *Where will the test be given?* The room should be comfortable, free of distractions, and if it's in your child's school, not imbued with negative connotations (for example, it should not be a room used for disciplining).
- *How many children is the examiner scheduled to test that day?* Depending on the child, it takes one to two hours to administer an IQ test. According to Ms. Robinson, three tests a day should be the examiner's maximum.
- *Will the examiner be responsible for interpreting the scores and writing the evaluation?* Computer programs cannot be as accurate as the examiner in evaluating your child's behavior. I would insist on a report written by the examiner.

If your child is taking one of the Wechsler tests, make sure that the full test is being given. The school district may want to save time and money by administering only the verbal portion of the test. This would give an incomplete picture of a child's abilities, as was our experience with our daughter Aimee. In addition, once the evaluation is written, I would also ask for a final meeting to discuss the findings and what they mean. Make sure to request a copy of the written report. Otherwise the score may simply appear alone on the cumulative record without any further explanation of the school psychologist's concerns and findings.

THE PERILS OF GROUP TESTING

Group tests are inexpensive (and therefore popular) for school districts to administer since they need not be given by a trained psychologist.

Many experts decry the fact that these tests do not measure IQ as accurately as do individual tests. In their book, *Your Gifted Child*, educators Joan Smutny, Kathleen Veenker, and Stephen Veenker explain that group intelligence tests are flawed because:

- The advanced child may hurry ahead and miss details of the questions.
- The creative child might examine all aspects of multiple-choice questions, overlooking the obvious answers.
- The perfectionist child might go back over answers, reconsider, and change correct answers to incorrect ones.

In addition, children are likely to be highly distracted in a classroom setting. Smutny, Veenker, and Veenker cite a study among junior high school children that found a child who scored 120 on a group test could possibly score 140 on an individual test.

Most experts advise that if group tests are to be used at all, they should be viewed as only a very "coarse" screening device to single out children for more extensive individual testing. Some suggest a score no higher than 115 on a group test as a cutoff for admission into a gifted program so that more children will be included rather than excluded.

SHOULD YOU COACH YOUR CHILD FOR IQ TESTS?

While Cherie was still a preschooler, her dad was studying for his Ph.D. in psychology. He was, at that time, required to take a course in measurement and testing for which he purchased a WISC test kit. That small suitcase is still collecting dust on a shelf in our bedroom closet, since Mitch specialized in clinical work and does little psychometrics. If a client needs testing, Mitch refers him to a specialist.

But that kit, much like Pandora's box, beckoned to me for many years. I would have loved to have had my husband take it down and let Cherie and Aimee play with the puzzles, blocks, and pictures. I would have been even more excited had he administered the test to our kids, just to satisfy my own curiosity. This, I'm happy to tell you, never happened, for at the mere mention of such treachery, my good husband almost took my head off.

"You can't let them play with the test," he fumed. "That would totally invalidate the results. Besides, I'm their father. They would respond differently to me than they would an impartial tester. Forget it."

Oh well, I thought, good try. In truth, few are the parents who would have access to their own IQ test. Yet, today, books have appeared that purport to teach parents how to coach their kids for these tests. My husband and I covered the phenomenon of test coaching in one of our recent books, *Kindergarten: It Isn't What It Used to Be*. We make the point that training children for these standardized tests has little meaning. Discrete bits of information or skills have little value and make little sense when they are not integrated as a part of the child's full development.

We explain:

In addition, your coaching would, for all intents and purposes, invalidate the test. The scoring for all such tests is based on all children being in the same boat. The test is constructed with the expectation that the test-takers have never seen it before. Any score that your child would receive as a result of your coaching would not truly reflect his abilities or his developmental maturity. And that could be detrimental to your child in the long run because his teachers' expectations may be based on an inflated and invalid perception that he actually understands the developmental concepts reflected in the questions and not on the reality—that he has been coached.

THE SHORTCOMINGS OF IQ TESTING

IQ tests do not give a complete picture of any child. In fact, numerous experts in intelligence and child development have vociferously argued against using these tests exclusively to place or exclude children from gifted programs.

The question of the value of IQ tests actually revolves around one's definition of intelligence. In the past, when intelligence was viewed as a fixed, indivisible feature of one's character, the IQ test was perceived as the most appropriate way of discerning that intelligence. Today, however, the professional literature leans toward the "splitters" (see chapter 2) such as Drs. Gardner, Sternberg, and Renzulli—those who view intelligence as composed of multiple components. These researchers believe that IQ tests measure only one aspect of intelligence—analytic reasoning—but do little to assess the learning process, creativity, insight, or other factors now thought to be a part of intelligence.

Dr. Michael A. Wallach at Duke University, for example, believes that IQ is not a criterion for measuring giftedness at all. He cites national studies in which other researchers found "no correlation between IQ scores and awards or prizes for out-of-school accomplishments in the fields of creative writing, science, music, the visual arts, drama, dance, or in group leadership."

Experts' criticisms leveled against IQ tests include arguments such as:

- IQ tests tell you only how good a person is at taking IQ tests (right-brain dominant and creative, divergent thinkers may not have "good" test-taking skills).
- IQ tests have little power to predict how a child will fare in the future and can only predict school performance (which is no guarantee of success in life, as we all know).
- IQ tests can be inaccurate, especially if administered under improper conditions with many distractors. Even nervousness, lack of motivation, lack of sleep, an earache, minor family problems, or the examiner's demeanor can skew the results.
- IQ tests measure intelligence in the middle ranges. The most difficult questions have been eliminated. This factor penalizes people who can solve highly complex problems that require more time.
- IQ tests are biased against certain racial, cultural, and socioeconomic groups. Children who speak English as a second language, for example, are at a decided disadvantage when taking an English-language test, as are those who come from economically depressed homes.
- IQ tests may stigmatize low scorers and establish self-fulfilling prophecies.
- As a child grows older, it becomes more difficult to score well on IQ tests. They are more like achievement tests—a measure of what information a person has learned, not a reflection of his innate abilities.
- IQ tests put late-bloomers at a disadvantage.
- IQ tests measure what people know rather than their capacity to acquire knowledge.
- IQ tests measure analytic ability but don't measure creativity—what some experts call the pinnacle of intelligence—or the ability

to apply intelligence to real-life situations and adapt to the environment.

In her book, *Growing Up Gifted*, Dr. Barbara Clark quotes gifted education specialist Elizabeth Monroe Drews who explains that gifted children do not necessarily amass and recall facts, which is one of the subtests on an IQ exam. Their talents lie in their ability to think about "the overarching concepts involving great unitive themes." In truth, IQ tests do not measure the capacity to think about such large questions. In a survey of 661 social scientists and educators who specialize in testing, conducted by Dr. Mark Snyderman of Harvard University and Dr. Stanley Rothman of Smith College, of the nearly 60 percent of professionals who felt that creativity was an important component of intelligence, more than 88 percent felt that IQ tests inadequately measured this trait.

Many experts believe that IQ tests are overused and relied on too heavily to make important decisions about children. Robert Sternberg, professor of psychology at Yale and one of the strongest current proponents of multiple views of intelligence, has said very clearly, "Identification of the gifted based exclusively or primarily on the basis of IQ is a mistake. . . . The bottom line is that in identifying the gifted through IQ, we are falling into the age-old trap of a little bit of knowledge being a dangerous thing."

It is for these reasons, among others, that specialists in the field of "individual differences" now believe that IQ testing is an inadequate way to identify gifted children. They feel that IQ scores must be *combined with other information* in order to more fully represent a child's true abilities.

HOW SHOULD YOUR CHILD BE SCREENED FOR A GIFTED PROGRAM?

If IQ tests are not the key to placement in gifted programs, what criteria should be used? Actually, experts are opposed to these tests being used as the *only* basis for placement. They recommend many other methods of screening kids that should be taken into consideration *in addition to* the IQ test.

In *Growing Up Gifted*, Dr. Barbara Clark devotes an entire chapter to exploring how teachers should identify gifted children within the school setting. These criteria include:

- Nomination from teachers, principal, counselor, psychologist, and others (forms used to report potentially children can be filled out after the school personnel have had an opportunity to closely observe the child in action).
- Teacher reports of student functioning, including intellectual, physical, social, and emotional functioning; learning style; level of motivation.
- Family history and student background, including health and medical records of child and family; developmental data; parents' education and occupation; description of family unit, activities, and interests; child's out-of-school activities.
- Recommendations from the child's classmates.
- Student's own inventory of himself and his values, interests, and attitudes toward school and out-of-school activities gleaned from his own report or discussions with a school psychologist.
- Student work and achievements.
- Scores on achievement and intelligence tests.

Ideally, according to Dr. Clark, these indicators would be used by the coordinator of gifted programs to develop a profile of the child. The profile would take the form of a case study and would be submitted to a committee for screening. The decision for placement and the kind of educational environment recommended would depend on the committee and the parents.

Admittedly, this process is rather lengthy and complex, in addition to being costly. As I recall, when it was a question of Cherie's placement, her first-grade teacher recommended her to the school psychologist, and she was tested and accepted with no further ado. Yet Dr. Clark's more cumbersome system also takes into account those children who may be gifted but who do not perform as well on IQ tests. It also may present a more well-rounded and more equitable assessment.

There is a danger of abuse, here, however. In recent article in the *American Psychologist*, Dr. Sally M. Reis warns that parents can be beguiled by misuse of such a comprehensive system of assessment. Certain school districts use the multiple criteria of group testing, teacher recommendation, parent nomination, grades, student interviews, and so forth as a screening device to decide to whom the school psychologist should administer the IQ test. Dr. Reis explains:

If the student's score is below the predetermined state or local cutoff score, the youngster is refused admission to the gifted program. This practice is logically flawed. If the youngster has extremely high scores or recommendations on all or many of the other criteria, the multiple criteria are being ignored in favor of a single indicator. . . . This practice often eliminates students who may not perform well on standardized IQ tests.

Other researchers have suggested alternative approaches. Some, like Dr. Robert Sternberg at Yale University, are developing new intelligence tests that are "more sensitive to varying kinds of intelligence and intellectual giftedness." Unfortunately, these tests are still a few years away from completion.

On the other hand, Dr. Howard Gardner and his colleagues at Harvard University suggest mapping out some twenty competencies (such as taking apart and reassembling gadgets, throwing a basketball accurately, observing and systematically exploring scientific phenomena, or writing a poem), many of which cannot be assessed in "paper and pencil tests." Children would be evaluated over a period of time in the security of their own classroom. This approach would also broaden the base of assessing who is gifted. Dr. Gardner's ideas on testing have been put into practice at the Healey School in Somerville, Massachusetts.

Dr. Renzulli suggests that identification of gifted behaviors should include direct observation by people who are well acquainted with the student while he is involved in a variety of activities. These activities should include ones that the student chooses himself as well as those that are required. How can a teacher know that one of her pupils is a talented poet unless she gives the child the opportunity to express himself in any way that he feels comfortable? Renzulli's approach is currently being used in individual school districts in all fifty states.

WHAT SHOULD YOU SHARE WITH YOUR CHILDREN?

Should you tell your child the purpose of the testing? That would depend on his age and his temperament. A preschooler or a child in the primary grades might just be told, "Justin, you're going to play some learning games with Mrs. Johnson." To inform a child that he's taking an IQ test to see if he's "smart enough" for a gifted class would create anxiety or possibly even a stress reaction during the test.

An eight- or nine-year-old, on the other hand, may already know about the test and the gifted program. In this case, it would be best to talk in advance about the meaning and validity (or lack thereof) of the test. You could explain, for instance, that the test measures certain ways that people think—but not others.

Should you tell your child her score once the results are in? Again, for young children, there is little point in doing this. An older child, however, might be curious. In the past, the IQ scores were guarded like the gold bricks at Fort Knox and I still think that's not such a bad idea. Curious or not, most children are not equipped to interpret all of the complex criticisms leveled against the test. An IQ score isn't accurate in and of itself and is only used as a benchmark along with other determinants. Knowing the score could inflate or deflate a child's sense of self, and ultimately, it could be self-defeating. My children still don't know their scores, although they are aware of who has been designated "gifted" and who has not.

A CAUTIONARY TALE

My friend Phyllis' mention of our younger daughter's experience with IQ tests reminded me of how painful and arbitrary testing can be. Aimee was born nearly four years after Cherie. I had made the conscious decision to be less intrusive in her early play than I had been with our first child. I thought that it would be psychologically healthier in the long run for her to be free of such a symbiotic relationship with me.

Certainly, I read to Aimee and played with her and took her with me to the market. In fact, during the first two years of her life, I stayed at home as a full-time mother to both children. What I did do, however, was to withdraw from structuring the games. I let Aimee take more of the initiative. Besides, I reasoned, she also has a sister in the house who gives her plenty of nonstop stimulation.

Aimee grew up with a very different character than Cherie, as siblings often do. Whereas Cherie was highly verbal, Aimee was physically robust, athletic, and outgoing—succeeding at soccer and Little League baseball. Whereas Cherie could think of nothing better than to crawl into bed with a good book, Aimee was extremely social. She had little patience for activities that required solitude, especially reading. Whereas with minimal effort Cherie excelled as a student (in elementary school, at least), Aimee worked hard for her grades and earned B's more often than A's.

I felt that Aimee belonged in the gifted program at school. Despite her less-than-perfect academic showing, she was enthusiastic about learning, curious, bright, and vivacious. She was among the class leaders.

Each year, I brought up with her teacher a possible recommendation for testing. Each year, a discussion ensued about Aimee's difficulty in organizing herself and her work. During parent-teacher conferences, Aimee expressed her concern that her friends were learning faster than she was—it always seemed to her as if she were looking over her shoulder, measuring herself against their achievements. She lamented that they were pulled out for "special class" twice a week while she was left behind with "the dummies."

We believed that since Aimee was quite young in her grade, part of her lack of focus was due to her being slightly out of sync with her classmates, and a late bloomer, to boot. "It's maturational," we were told. "She'll grow out of it."

By the sixth grade, Aimee's teacher finally recommended that Aimee be tested for the junior high school gifted and talented program that also included children who were high achievers. One morning, Aimee was called to the school office for the test. The psychologist administered the verbal portion only of the WISC-R and phoned me that afternoon quite agitated and perplexed:

> Mrs. Golant, I can't seem to make sense of Aimee's score. Clearly, from our conversations before, during, and after the test, she seems gifted. She has a sophisticated vocabulary and an excellent understanding of what's going on. Yet, Aimee's scores on the IQ test don't match my impression of her. They show her to be very high within the average range, and no matter how I manipulate the data, I can't get a different result. Because this test obviously doesn't convey who Aimee is, however, I'm going to recommend that she be accepted into the junior high gifted and talented program anyway, as a high achiever.

My husband and I had a mixed reaction to this news. On the one hand, recognizing that the older the child when tested, the more difficult it is to obtain a high score on an IQ test (Cherie's phenomenal score, for example, could have been influenced in part by the early administration of the test), we felt that we had placed our daughter at a disadvantage.

I, in particular, was upset that I hadn't pushed harder for Aimee to be tested when she was younger. On the other hand, we felt reassured that Aimee would, at least, be placed in a stimulating environment despite her score. It wasn't the score per se that I was worried about; I was most concerned that she be placed in a classroom where she would feel motivated and challenged. The test score seemed like her only ticket into such an environment.

How did Aimee take the news? At first, she was crestfallen, feeling stigmatized by the fact that she had taken the test and "failed" it. Her reaction was understandable. Yet the blow was softened by her admission into the gifted program the following year. We were going to have to wait and see how well she did.

The junior high program suited Aimee well. She worked hard and her grades hovered between A's and B's, as usual. We were relieved in that regard. But the school itself turned out to be a rather rough-and-tumble place. Eventually, Aimee felt intimidated by the constant undercurrent of violence and begged us to change her school. When she entered the eighth grade, we moved her, at her insistence, into a program that had a national reputation for excellence—if you were a highly verbal or logical child.

But Aimee was and is a bit of a free spirit. She is creative and physically adept. A spatial and right-brained learner, Aimee found it difficult to adjust to the lockstep, hidebound curriculum. Her best efforts were met with grades of C or lower. Despite the fact that her English teacher praised her poetry-writing project as one of the best she had ever received (and saved it as a sample for the following year's students) Aimee got a C in the class because she wasn't up to snuff in grammar—a subject that hadn't been taught as rigorously in her previous school.

Our daughter began to feel that no matter how hard she tried, she would never succeed. She expressed real doubts about herself and talked of "just giving up." "Why bother studying?" she lamented. "I'll only get a C." The only two classes Aimee excelled in were woodworking and softball.

My husband and I grew frustrated and then frantic. After numerous conferences and phone calls with teachers and counselors, we realized that the school was more interested in its reputation than in the welfare of its individual students. By the beginning of the tenth grade, we saw no choice but to move Aimee again. She agreed to the move grudgingly at first, since she didn't want to break into yet another new group of kids, yet she also saw the need academically. Aimee's new high school has worked out well, but the damage to her self-esteem was already done. Aimee felt "stupid."

Now in her junior year in high school, Aimee is back to A and B work with an occasional C. She is not currently enrolled in any advanced or honors courses. And recently she approached me with the thought that she might have dyslexia, a learning disability that involves number and letter reversals. (For example, she complained of reading "cowbeds" instead of "cobwebs" and as a result couldn't make sense of a reading passage.) She found reading difficult and tiresome.

This time, we decided to get to the bottom of things. We took Aimee to UCLA for testing. After administering a full battery of IQ, reading, and perceptual tests, the educational psychologist determined that Aimee was not dyslexic but actually had an attention deficit disorder. It was difficult for Aimee to retain information, so she did poorly on reading comprehension tests and on certain parts of the IQ test that require concentration and memory. Some of her other skills including verbal abstract thinking and spatial relations, however, were excellent.

Aimee's subtle undiagnosed disability has served to depress her achievement in schools for years (as if she were trying to swim with one hand tied behind her back) and can explain her initial incongruent IQ score. Unfortunately, in the process, it also undermined her self-esteem. To deal with the problem, we sought an ophthalmological exam to make sure that some undetected visual problem had not contributed to Aimee's difficulties, and we hired an educational psychologist who tutors Aimee in learning strategies to help her compensate for her disability. In addition, we have had Aimee receive some psychological counseling to bolster her feelings of self-worth.

HINDSIGHT AND SECOND THOUGHTS

Reading this story about Aimee, you might think that I might be as adamantly opposed to IQ testing as is my friend Phyllis. The truth is, however, that in Aimee's case, the initial test did exactly what it was supposed to do: It located a problem in Aimee's cognitive development. Unfortunately, neither we nor the school psychologist followed up on it!

The IQ test did not, however, give a fair assessment of our child's full abilities. The sixth-grade screening included only the verbal portion of the WISC—an area in which Aimee is weak due to her learning problem. And the UCLA educational psychologist noted on her report that Aimee has "other skills and talents which IQ scores and achievement results do not assess." Certainly the tests were mute on Aimee's creative talent in woodworking and athletics and on her emotional insightfulness and tremendous social skills.

Should we have done anything differently? Yes. I deeply regret that I didn't pursue Aimee's first IQ results or insist on a full battery of tests from the start. I didn't think that I had to, because she was admitted into the junior high school gifted program anyway. Perhaps if we had demanded further explanation and testing, we would have discovered and corrected Aimee's learning problem earlier, thereby saving her years of feeling inadequate and "stupid." In truth, she had been compensating for her disability on her own all these years. Imagine how less stressful school would have been for her had we pursued the inconsistency five years ago when we first had had an inkling that a problem existed.

Would we have been better off, however, never to have had Aimee tested, as my friend advised? I think not. To me, the waste of potential would be too great. I risked the possibility of my child being "stigmatized" by an average score for the opportunity of her receiving the rich learning environment of a gifted program. It felt that important to me.

As Dr. Lynn Fox, a psychologist involved in the Study of Mathematically Precocious Youth at the Johns Hopkins University, put it, "In the case of the academically talented, it might be wise to risk identifying students as gifted when they are not and give them the opportunities for special or individualized educational programs rather than to err by overlooking many talented students who are bored, frustrated, and unchallenged in their classes."

SHOULD WE ADVOCATE PLACING OUR CHILDREN IN GIFTED PROGRAMS?

The IQ test dilemma and experts' disagreement over other means of screening for giftedness put a heavy burden on us, the parents. As you can see, the current system is flawed, but until alternative methods are fully developed, it is the one with which we are going to have to deal. It is one of the inherent challenges of parenting a gifted child.

If your child is tested and scores within the gifted range, and seems eager and amenable to the program, then your decision is made easy. How should you respond, however, if your obviously bright and/or creative child is denied admission to a gifted program because of a single IQ test score that is below or just on the borderline of the cutoff? Should you push?

Again, it would depend on your assessment of your child: his needs and abilities, his strengths and weaknesses, his motivation and persistence, his temperament and emotional resilience. You should thoughtfully weigh the pros and cons and listen to the school personnel's feedback. Be careful not to let your own agenda or ego gratification cloud your judgment of what is best for your child (see chapter 13). In Aimee's case, for instance, we got what we desired by having her placed in the gifted program, but we missed what her deeper needs were.

If you do decide to pursue the gifted issue further, you might seek outside evaluation. Yes, it is costly, but it is possible that your child will perform differently on a privately administered test than on one given in the school environment. (This is especially true if group testing was involved.) You need not share the results with the school unless you so choose.

If, upon retesting, your child does obtain a higher score, that second score should be considered valid. In their book, *Your Gifted Child*, educators Smutny, Veenker, and Veenker explain that, "If your IQ tests at 140, you might have even superior ability but not lower. If your . . . IQ is 100, you can't get a 120 by fluke or strategy."

This approach, however, presupposes your accepting the notion that IQ tests are a true measure of intelligence. If, on the other hand, you agree with the many experts who express the view that IQ tests give only a limited picture of a child's abilities, then it is up to you to advocate for a broadening of the definition of giftedness (citing Howard Gardner, Robert Sternberg, and Joseph Renzulli's research) by working with the teacher, counselor, school psychologist, and principal. If you still have no satisfaction, you could approach your school system's coordinator of gifted programs and even the school board, if need be, to change the criteria for defining giftedness and acceptance into gifted programs. And, for goodness' sake, follow up on inconclusive or conflicting results!

But what if academics and IQ scores indicate that your child belongs in a gifted program when, in fact, she is emotionally unready for the experience? We have to use common sense in these instances. You may have your youngster enter the program on a trial basis. If she hates it, lacks motivation, or finds herself constantly struggling to keep up, there is little sense in continuing. The gifted program would seem more like a punishment than an educational opportunity.

In addition, not all gifted programs are created equal: Some may be boring or may simply require a greater volume of the same work (such as longer or more difficult vocabulary lists) without challenging a child's thinking skills. In that case, or in the instance that your capable child simply is not thriving in a program, you might seek out-of-school pursuits, tutoring, and mentor programs (see chapter 6).

How can you judge whether a program suits your child's temperament and needs? You'll know a problem exists if she exhibits signs of stress (see chapter 13) such as sleep disturbances or frequent stomachaches or headaches that lack an organic origin. Keep the lines of communication open among you, your child, her classroom teacher, the school psychologist, and the gifted program coordinator to monitor the appropriateness of the program.

Finding the setting that matches your child's needs is important, but sometimes your research followed by simple trial and error is the only method possible. Approach your task with the spirit of adventure. You'll find a discussion of the many educational options available to the gifted in the following chapter.

Finally, we must use our heads and our hearts in advocating for our gifted children. We *don't* want them inappropriately screened out of or inappropriately included in a program. We *do* want to challenge them without overstretching their minds or emotions. Finally, we want to tune into *their* needs, not *our* needs, for a full and challenging life.

PART III

Your Gifted Child in the World and at Home

CHAPTER 6

School Programs: Of Decisions, Choices, . . . and Elitism

True democracy demands that every child,
whether superior, average, or inferior in ability,
be given the fullest opportunity to develop
to the limit of his mental capacity.

—LEWIS N. TERMAN
(CITED BY MAY V. SEAGOE IN *TERMAN AND THE GIFTED*)

If you don't have high aspirations for your gifted,
you don't have them for anyone. Why does "gifted"
produce such shudders?

—JEROME BRUNER
(*NEW YORK TIMES* INTERVIEW, MAY 6, 1990)

RECENTLY I HAD A CONVERSATION WITH A FRIEND WHO IS A TEACHER at a public middle school that had just converted to "mainstreaming" its gifted population. (The children were put in "regular" classes but were to be given "enrichment" by teachers who had had *no special training* in dealing with the gifted.) The parents of the gifted children demanded the return to a discrete classroom setting for their children, threatening to withdraw their kids from the school.

My friend was baffled by the furor, stating that the school district policy required the new system because *gifted classes created elitism*. But I understood the parental outrage well. These kinds of programs are often inadequate and they don't serve our children. Gifted children have special educational needs, much like the learning disabled. Yet many in our society give the gifted short shrift, claiming that school systems should redirect monies spent on gifted programming for the benefit of all children. Perhaps this comes from a cultural bias against exceptional individuals. We'll explore the "elitism" fallacy a bit later in this chapter.

As parents, our odyssey in finding appropriate education for our children can sometimes be long and arduous. I have read many articles in which parents describe how they had to move from school to school, argue with teachers, principals, and school districts—sometimes even resort to court hearings—in an effort to secure for their children the kind of education that they surely deserve and need. Yet, once you have found the proper setting for your gifted child, you can't help but feel elated. The kind of emotional energy that goes into this search can be a paradigm for the whole experience of raising a gifted child: It is a joy as well as a challenge.

To help you understand the choice that you are facing regarding education, I would like to share with you our own experiences: first mine as I made my way through the public schools of New York City and Los Angeles in the 1950s and 1960s, and then my daughter Cherie's in the 1970s and 1980s. Our example is instructive, because between the two of us, we have encountered many of the educational options that may be available to you in the 1990s.

MAKING LEMONADE

In chapter 1, described to you my "bladder troubles" in the second grade that led our family doctor to discover my feelings of utter boredom in school. Perhaps surprisingly, I did not become one of those sullen, frustrated gifted children who acts out or turns off to education. When handed lemons, I decided to make lemonade.

As a child, the one place where I felt truly successful was at school. As I progressed from grade to grade, I flourished under the appreciative encouragement of my teachers. I worked (sometimes not so hard) and earned my A's. The good grades made me feel happy about myself. Eventually, I became an A junkie. Nothing else would do. I was always the first one with her hand up when a question was asked. I knew that I had the right answer and was impatient with those who didn't.

If things didn't go well for me socially, if I was the last one chosen for the basketball team, if the boys thought that I was always trying to show off, if I felt different and "weird," at least I knew that I always had my school successes to fall back on to bolster my feelings of self-worth. If nothing else, I figured I had that going for me.

SP: SPECIAL PROGRESS OR STUPID PEOPLE?

Somewhere toward the end of the sixth grade, my beloved teacher administered a group IQ test to the class. I loved tests. I saw them as a challenge and as a way to prove my worth to myself and those around me once more. I attacked this exam with vigor and qualified to be admitted into a program for gifted children at the junior high.

As happy as this made me feel, my nomination raised some problems in our family. The SP Program (*SP* for *Special Progress*) actually entailed two separate branches. On the one hand, I could choose to accelerate my education, doing the work of seventh, eighth, and ninth grades in only two years. Or, I could go through junior high in the normal three years but follow a program of enrichment: foreign language beginning in the seventh grade, advanced mathematics, and other extras.

The choice was complicated by the fact that my sister, only fourteen months older than I was and one grade ahead in school, had not qualified for the program the year before. She had missed out by an IQ point or two. If I were to choose the two-year track, I would graduate from junior high and, eventually, high school with her. We all feared that it would have a harmful effect on my sister's self-esteem. Besides, I was eager to start learning French: the enrichment program sounded enticing.

On the other hand, I was always in a hurry to achieve. The thought of skipping a year played right into that need. Why should I spend an extra year in junior high if I can better use that time in a university, I reasoned. My sixth-grade teacher reinforced this choice by sharing a story from her own life. Her dad had died while she was in college. "If I had not accelerated a year myself," she explained during a conference, "I never would have been able to finish my education."

I was sorry that I would miss the early introduction to French, but my ego craved the recognition I imagined I would receive for having been so clearly identified as gifted. My parents and I made the choice that I skip a year. And what about my sister? I dismissed her concerns, saying that I couldn't stop my own progress for her sake. She was just going to have to learn to live with the decision. I was ecstatic. I was also, most likely, insufferable.

As we were readying ourselves for sixth-grade graduation, I recall that my best friend at the time asked me, "If you're so smart, how are you ever going to find a man smarter than you to marry?" I worried all during that summer of 1959: How *was* I to do that, indeed?

At the beginning of junior high that question was answered swiftly and deftly, and I was painfully disabused of my illusions of grandeur. I discovered that although I was gifted, I was definitely *not* the smartest person who walked the face of the earth. Indeed, I found myself somewhere in the middle of my class—a humbling experience, but one that was most likely necessary, nevertheless.

I found the program itself challenging and interesting. I remember studying the evolution of language (starting with the Sumerian and Phoenician alphabets), the anatomy of the heart (we each brought in a beef heart to dissect and somehow the boys saw fit to send theirs sailing around the room, much to the horror of our excellent but hapless science teacher), the workings of the stock market, and three years' worth of junior high math and algebra in two years' time.

In 1960, our class organized a mock political convention and held a straw poll (Kennedy won!) for the whole school. We even debated current affairs issues during a school assembly as if we were United Nations delegates. I struggled through Shakespeare, despairing that I would never understand ''literature,'' and Dickens, which I savored.

One of the joys of inclusion in this SP program was the social network created among the students. No longer impatient with the slowness I perceived around me, I felt stimulated by the ideas that ricocheted among us. Bobby was a ''genius'' in math—how did he know so much? And Barbara wrote beautiful stories that had denouements and poignant endings while I was still trying to figure out what a *theme* was. Peggy seemed destined to become a doctor—she just loved biology—and Thomas could debate the best of them. My classmates became my friends and we all learned from one another.

As enjoyable as this program sounds (and it was), I found myself working harder than I had ever imagined I could or would. Looking back on it now, the whole experience seems like one endless term paper. In fact, I labored more in junior high than I ever did in high school, often staying up past midnight to do my homework. With the exception of shop and physical education, the forty or so students who were skipping the year were kept together for all subjects—there was no recognition that as individuals we had distinct areas of strength and weakness—and so the competition among us was as intense as the demands placed upon us.

In addition, as a group we were somewhat unsettling to the other students. Socially, we felt separated from the rest of the school. When we reached the ninth grade, for example, we were a year younger than other members of our graduating class. Most didn't take kindly to that.

They taunted us with epithets such as, "SP? That means *stupid people*, doesn't it?" As a social unit, we mostly kept to ourselves.

I reasoned that once we reached high school and were all mixed together in classes people would forget who had skipped and who hadn't. In effect, that was true. But it didn't make up for the social stress of being a year younger than one's classmates *and* a late bloomer, too. I thrived academically, taking honors as well as advanced placement classes, but I had difficulties socially, all through high school. I just didn't fit in.

When I graduated from high school, I was still sixteen while many of my classmates were already eighteen. I hadn't had a real boyfriend or a certifiable date. I sincerely thought that there was something wrong with me. (This, of course, threw me back into my studies with renewed vigor. After all, although I didn't do well socially, I knew I could do well in school.) I graduated seventh out of a class of more than 800 students. It never occurred to me that my age could influence the rate of my maturation.

THE JOYS OF COLLEGE

It wasn't until I was a college freshman, at seventeen, that I finally came into my own. My body had finished growing and I had reached the same stage of maturity that my peers seemed to have taken for granted. College also offered me the opportunity to spread my intellectual wings and fly. I loved it!

With my class rank and high SAT scores, I probably would have been accepted at the institution of my choice. But my parents had a hard time letting go of me. And I, a dutiful daughter, had even more difficulty hurting them by insisting that I was entitled to a life of my own. As Holocaust survivors, they had experienced so many losses in their lives that I simply felt incapable of inflicting what they perceived as yet another. Even UCLA seemed too large and alien to my parents. They were afraid that they would lose me there, and so I attended a suburban state college.

Despite my initial disappointment, I discovered that this school was not a bad choice for me. The college had relatively small classes, all taught by full professors. I got to know my instructors personally and again gained the recognition that I so desperately desired.

I became a big fish in a small pond. I was selected as a Rotary leadership scholar, elected president of the foreign language honor society, and eventually won, among other honors, one of only six scholarships nationwide offered by Air France for summer study at the Sorbonne. During the turbulence of 1969, at the age of twenty, I graduated magna cum laude, with an almost perfect grade-point average.

Do I regret my decision of skipping the year in junior high? It's hard to say. Crossroads such as those have a way of determining the direction of one's life. On the one hand (despite research findings to the contrary that I'll share with you below), I believe that I did suffer socially as a result of being younger, especially in high school. It deeply affected me for at least three years. On the other hand, in college my relative youth made little difference to my classmates.

As a freshman I met Mitch, my husband-to-be, in a health class (studying sex education, of all things). He was a "mature" sophomore of 19, at the time. Had I not skipped the eighth grade, our paths might never have crossed and our family or even this book might not have come into being. Besides, today I feel grateful to have had the opportunity to experience the intense stimulation and involvement of the gifted program. It helped me to form my identity as a competent intellect among other intellects. I wasn't the "best," but I learned that I could hold my own. Who is to evaluate the ultimate effect of such an experience?

CHOICES, CHOICES

I suppose it's inevitable that to some degree, as parents, we replay with our children what we encountered during our childhoods. After all, we only have our own lives to go by. Sometimes we attempt a correction, swearing we will make our children's lives better than our own—and we do. At other times, however, consciously or unconsciously we find ourselves repeating the past. As we help our children through each of their development stages, we remember how life was for us.

Thus, you can imagine that my children's education was of tantamount importance to me. I vowed that I would not let my kids languish in elementary school classes where they would experience acute boredom, as I had. My worst fear was that they would become turned off to education and not enjoy the full flower of their own abilities.

Cherie was a verbal, adult-oriented, precocious preschooler. It seemed to us as if she were four going on twenty-four! I knew that she would need some kind of special program once she started elementary school. The thought of her having to proceed lockstep with the class was intolerable. I was determined to find a better way for her.

My first option was to advance her entrance into elementary school. Cherie was born in February, so she was among the oldest children in her grade. (The kindergarten entrance cutoff in Los Angeles was December 10.). When she was four and a half, I placed her in the private preschool's kindergarten, fully expecting her to start the first grade the following year once we settled on an elementary school. After all, she was reading well already.

At about the same time, we began looking for our first house. I evaluated neighborhoods according to the reputation of the local elementary schools: The better the school, the more interested I was in an area. Then, as fate would have it, I ran into an old high school friend whom I hadn't seen in years. She had a daughter Cherie's age and had just moved into an area I hadn't really considered. She spoke glowingly of the school. "It's an open structure plan," Pam explained.

"What's that?"

"The kids move ahead according to their ability," she replied.

Music to my ears! "How can I find out more about it?"

Pam explained that the school was a model for the rest of the state. Dignitaries and teachers from all over the country visited to see how it ran. "They hold open house twice a month. Why don't you drop by?"

I attended the next open house and was overjoyed. The principal explained that children were placed in clustered classes: K–1–2, 3–4, 5–6, or in individually graded classes. Within each classroom, the teacher created learning centers. The centers covered a specific topic—say, at the kindergarten level, families—at various levels of difficulty. In such a unit, for example, a child could:

- Re-create his family by cutting out magazine pictures and pasting together a collage
- Draw his family and write the names of the family members and even dictate or write a story about them
- Make a family tree showing immediate family as well as grandparents, uncles, and aunts

At other centers, such as ones involving reading and math, the activities were built upon each other in difficulty and each child could move through the material at her own speed.

The school sought to encourage independence. On Mondays, each child set up a "contract" for work to be accomplished during the week, be it reading, math, science, or art. The teacher gave some group instruction, and then the children were set free in the room to fulfill their contracts, each moving from one learning center to the next at his own pace. The classroom was filled with the animated chatter of children learning cooperatively. If a child finished his week's assignment early, he could "check himself out" and go to the library, the resource room, the math lab, or the computer lab for more advanced work, or, weather permitting, to an outside patio where he could dig, plant flowers, or saw and glue together wood.

The teacher and student evaluated each contract at the end of the week and the teacher planned accordingly. Parent and community volunteers assisted the teacher in implementing the program.

This open structure seemed perfect. It also presupposed a real commitment from the teacher and a good deal of work on his part to devise the various activities and to individualize the program to each child's needs. In addition, it required a certain level of maturity on the part of the children. Some were better equipped to handle the open-endedness of the approach; others felt safer with more structure and direction from the teacher. The latter were placed in traditional rooms with more orthodox teachers.

After a visit to the classrooms, I was sold. My husband and I bought our first house in this neighborhood soon after Cherie's fifth birthday. Shortly thereafter, we felt triply blessed, for not only had we found a home and an appropriate school, but we also were thrilled to discover several other "older" five-year-olds on the street with birthdays in December and January. They seemed as bright as our daughter, and one little girl became Cherie's fast friend.

After Cherie's graduation from the preschool's kindergarten program, I placed her in summer school at our new elementary school. At that time I began to have second thoughts about accelerating her within the open-structure program. I remembered my own pain in feeling like a social misfit. I saw that the program was structured so that Cherie could advance as she needed to. If placed in a K–1–2 cluster, for example, she could do third-grade work in areas in which she excelled and grade-level work in areas where she was more average. The need for skipping a year seemed to wane.

Besides, our daughter's new friends were also quite talented, yet their parents were not pushing them ahead. I knew how important Cherie's friends had become to her. After much thought and discussion, we decided to keep Cherie with her peers.

Only later did we appreciate what a wise decision that was for our daughter. Cherie was quite precocious intellectually, but in terms of physical maturation she followed in my footsteps. In the sixth grade, for example, when her classmates were interested in more adolescent pursuits, she was still playing with her Barbie dolls in the backyard. Puberty was only a distant shadow on the horizon. We realized how much harder junior high and high school might have been for her socially if we had pushed her ahead when she was only five.

For the most part, the elementary school lived up to its reputation. I discovered along the way, however, that, innovative program or not, a school is only as good as its individual teachers. While most were absolutely outstanding, there were a few clunkers in the group. These we tried to avoid, but it wasn't always possible.

Cherie made good use of the resources and flexibility that the school had to offer. In the first grade, she became a peer tutor, helping kindergarten children learn to read. After she was tested for the gifted program, she began her years of involvement in a pull-out "special class" several hours a week. During the second grade, her teacher sent her out during reading group time to a fifth-grade class where she participated in a program that more closely matched her abilities. A parent volunteer offered a "Great Books" miniclass that Cherie was thrilled to attend once a week.

The academics went just fine, but after her best friend moved away when they were both in the third grade, Cherie began having social problems. Bereft of her kindred spirit, Cherie felt that she just didn't fit. She began seeing her attendance in the gifted class as a "brand." Giftedness did mean feeling different—some gifted children simply refused to go. Yet, paradoxically, Cherie also liked the class because she found it interesting and safe.

That need for safety sprang from troubles Cherie was having interpersonally. When she became involved in a conflict with another child, she wanted to talk about it, to "work it out." The others didn't understand what she was after. They teased her for being too sensitive, for not being "cool." "Can't you take a joke?" they jeered. She was at a loss to know how to deal with children who bullied her out of their own lack of emotional maturity. Recently she confided that she enjoyed her participation in the pull-out program because the children who "terrorized" her weren't there.

The difficulty culminated in the sixth grade when Cherie saw herself as a social outcast. The late onset of puberty was somewhat to blame (especially since hers was a particularly precocious class in that regard) but I couldn't stand by and watch my child put herself down. All of my protestations that Cherie's giftedness caused her to see the world differently from her classmates, all of my assurances that she would outgrow this awkwardness—after all, I had been there too—fell on deaf ears. My daughter felt isolated.

We couldn't envision Cherie going to junior high with the same group of children who had eroded her sense of self-worth. I began investigating alternatives. I spoke to the teacher of the gifted program at the elementary school. Had she any suggestions for us? I was feeling desperate.

WALTER REED JUNIOR HIGH SCHOOL

Have you ever experienced your child coming home from school singing with joy? Have you ever heard of an adolescent so excited for school to start in the fall that the *summer* seems like an interminable bore? How about a preteen who hates weekends? That was the quality of Cherie's experience at Walter Reed Junior High School's Individualized Honors Program (IHP) for highly gifted children.

This IHP program was an anomaly in the Los Angeles City School system. It was established in a public junior high of about 2,000 students. The program consisted of 150 highly gifted children (about 50 in each grade, all with IQ scores over 145 and a record of school achievement) and three superior teachers of math/science, English, and social studies who fully understood the particular needs of these children. The students took their required academic classes with these teachers and then mixed with the rest of the school for foreign language, shop, physical education, music appreciation, and so forth.

The children were all required to study Latin and logic (out of a book I remember using in college). They read the *Odyssey* and *Oedipus Rex* and learned history by studying the original documents, not textbooks. They kept poetry notebooks and creative writing journals; they created newspapers and extraordinary science projects.

Those highly capable in math had the opportunity to take algebra 1 and 2, geometry, trigonometry, math analysis, advanced placement physics, chemistry, and calculus for college credit—remember these are junior high students, not high schoolers. More average math students such as my daughter followed a program of individualized instruction in a math lab. The IHP program, written up in *Time* magazine as "perhaps the most successful junior-high curriculum in the U.S.," has produced an inordinate number of award winners in national math and science competitions.

Cherie thrived in this environment. She was endlessly happy—

stressed by the work load—but happy nonetheless. She had found a large group of girlfriends. They were "smart" but they still loved rock music and were interested in clothes and boys. They viewed the world in the same complex way and they were unbelievably verbal. Their slumber parties were a riot!

Looking back on it now, Cherie says that what made the IHP program so exceptional was its sense of acceptance. "It was okay to be who you were. You didn't have to hide your giftedness. Sure, kids picked on us for being in the IHP but we were part of a group of 150 people. We had a community. It's easier to be an individual in a group that is supportive than in one that is not supportive."

The one flaw in this system was that the city did not provide a follow-up program in high school. After this very intense experience, the children were left to tread water until they began college. Some went to private schools, but we had always believed in public education, so we did not consider that option. The majority matriculated to a neighboring high school and Cherie went along with her friends. Despite that school's provisions for large incoming groups of highly gifted adolescents (including honors and advanced placement classes and concurrent high school and college enrollment for those advanced in math) and a smattering of excellent teachers, the experience was just not the same.

Once in high school, Cherie again felt the pressure to hide her giftedness. "It wasn't cool to like school," she explained recently. "Besides, much of it was stupid and a waste. Anyway, the conventional wisdom said that you're not supposed to like school, or spinach, or hanging out with your parents . . . and so I didn't."

This is not to say that Cherie dropped out, but she didn't achieve at the level that she had in the past. She went to parties, became involved in community projects, worked part time, and carried on the normal, uproarious life of a teenager. She did enroll in advanced classes and, as a high school senior, even studied psychology at the local state college where my husband and I had met. Nevertheless, her grades became less stellar and our hopes of her attending an Ivy League college slowly faded. Yet Cherie couldn't wait to go to college.

Today, at twenty, Cherie is happily ensconced at a University of California campus and once again she feels that old excitement about learning. "There's a lot of personal freedom, here at school," she explained. "There's no pressure to conform because there's nothing to conform to. It's okay for me to be happy to learn." Once more my daughter feels fully challenged, in gear, and eager for more stimulation. I only hope that she uses this opportunity well.

YOUR CHILD'S EDUCATIONAL OPTIONS

As you can see, between the two of us, Cherie and I have experienced many of the educational options available to gifted children, with varying degrees of success and satisfaction. One or the other of us has been in:

- A regular class (without enrichment)
- A pull-out program
- Individualized instruction with a multigraded classroom
- A self-contained gifted class
- An acceleration program
    Advanced placement classes for college credit
    Concurrent high school and college courses

Why are there so many educational options? Well, if the experts find it hard to agree on what constitutes intelligence and/or giftedness and how to screen for it, is it surprising that they can't agree on a uniform educational policy?

Philosophical issues aside, how a school district chooses to deal with its gifted population also may depend on federal and state mandates, funding, availability of qualified teachers, and community pressure or hostility. According to Drs. Lynn H. Fox and Jerrilene Washington at Johns Hopkins University, "The real barriers to good programs for the gifted are probably rigidity, apathy, and ignorance on the part of educators and the general public." That's not a pretty picture. But let's take a brief look at some of what *is* available around the country.

The Regular Classroom

As I can attest from personal experience, placing your gifted child in a classroom in which everyone is taught the same material at the same pace and depth is the least effective (if not the most destructive) approach to education. In such a situation, most children will simply hide their giftedness in order to fit in with the rest of their peers or they will become bored and frustrated or underachieving as a result of no real stimulus.

According to extensive research findings, classroom teachers have a relatively poor track record identifying which of their pupils are gifted.

Dr. Margie Kitano, associate dean of the School of Education at San Diego State University, explains:

> Although teacher accuracy can be improved with specific training, evidence exists that, even after years of training, teachers frequently overlook their brightest students and rank them in the middle. . . . The teacher may expect the young gifted child to speak, read, write, calculate, play, cooperate, and socialize at high levels. Yet young gifted children may exhibit uneven development, disinterest in reading, nonconformity, dislike of detail, or sloppy work habits.

If your child has already been identified as gifted, perhaps even more destructive is that her talents may dissipate in a regular classroom setting. In her book, *Growing Up Gifted*, Dr. Barbara Clark explains that learners in the upper ranges of intelligence need as much special instruction to continue their growth as do students at the lower end. "Because all students must adjust to the average classroom program, the gifted student loses most," she laments. "This situation leads to loss of ability . . . as regression toward a more average ability level is the observed outcome."

To counteract this possibility, the teacher may attempt to cluster gifted children for enrichment. This approach is better than nothing at all, especially if the gifted learners can interact with one another. To be most effective, however, the gifted cluster would have to receive what are called "differentiated" assignments, as I will outline a bit later.

Pull-out Program

My daughter participated in a pull-out program in elementary school: Several hours a week she left her regular class and joined a multigraded group of gifted children for special instruction. Any program is only as good as its teacher, and for the first half of her elementary school career, Cherie's gifted teacher was merely adequate. She was eventually replaced, however, by a dynamo who had two highly gifted daughters herself and who truly understood gifted children's needs. Cherie felt "safe" in this program and had the opportunity to explore ideas with her peers.

Pull-out programs are not without their shortcomings. Other students may complain that the gifted kids are being singled out for the goodies. Those left behind may feel inadequate, "dumb," and eventually hostile; those going off to the program may feel ostracized and "branded" as different. In addition, the gifted children may be required to complete the regular classroom work they missed while attending their program, which may make the pull-out feel like a burden or even a punishment. Sometimes Cherie complained that being gifted only meant that she had to do double assignments!

What's more, despite the extra stimulation several hours a week, gifted children in this type of program must rein themselves in for the "regular" curriculum during the vast majority of their school experience unless they are lucky enough to attend an open-structure school. What a waste of talent and time! As one researcher put it, "Pull-out programs are a part-time solution to a full-time problem."

Individualized Instruction with Multigraded Classrooms

Individualized classrooms are by nature more flexible than regular classrooms. In an individualized setting, the teacher designs a program to suit each child's needs. Children work independently and in groups, according to their abilities. When several grades are grouped together, the gifted child can move into more advanced material without upsetting the balance of the classroom.

In this open-structure setting, the gifted child is more likely to work at his own level and to feel good about himself. In *Growing Up Gifted*, educator Barbara Clark explains that "If all students are valued and allowed to meet their needs, no students will feel that they must do what every other person does. The gifted can meet their needs without envy from others. Such a program has continuity and allows each student's needs to be met all through the week." As I mentioned earlier, this type of environment requires a committed and well-trained teacher who is willing to put out the extra effort to reach all of her students.

Self-Contained Gifted Classes

These classes (especially when children mix for nonacademic subjects) are most often used in middle school, junior high, and high school. It has been our experience that such self-contained classes meet the needs of the gifted most efficiently. When we took such classes in junior high, both my daughter and I felt challenged to the maximum of our abilities. And while I had never been tempted to hide my giftedness in order to be accepted (rather, it was my habit to display my abilities to seek approval from teachers, if I couldn't receive it from students), Cherie did fall into this trap during elementary school and high school. Her IHP program gave her the opportunity to shine.

A recent front page *New York Times* article on the difficulties that the highly gifted face in obtaining an adequate education confirms our experience that self-contained classrooms are the best way to educate children whose IQ's are 145 or higher. Journalist Sarah Wernick quotes Dr. Linda K. Silverman, director of the Gifted Child Development Center in Denver, as saying, "Sixty years of research shows that special classes make a difference for the highly gifted. They learn faster, learn more, develop better self-concepts, and have more friends."

These classes can have some limitations, however. Whereas Cherie's program allowed for differences in math ability among highly gifted children (the originators of the IHP realized that all children are not created equal), my SP program, on the other hand, lumped us all together: the gifted with the highly gifted, the math geniuses with the math "strugglers." This did a disservice to youngsters on both ends of the spectrum: Those who could do more felt held back while others barely hung on by their fingernails.

Self-contained classes must individualize instruction, as well. Highly gifted children are as different from moderately gifted as the moderately gifted are different from average learners. In addition, each child, individually, may not be strong in all areas. If instruction is not individualized, you may find tutoring a helpful way to bolster your child's areas of weakness or it can supplement his already burgeoning excitement about learning above and beyond what is being taught in class.

Acceleration Programs

Acceleration programs can mean:

- A single child entering kindergarten early
- A single child advancing at his own pace with a mentor
- A single child skipping one or more grades
- A whole gifted class skipping a grade
- Advanced placement classes for college credit

- Concurrent enrollment in high school and college
- Early college entrance program

Acceleration programs are often quite successful in meeting the needs of the gifted. Most researchers are positive about the results. In a recent article published in the *Gifted Child Quarterly*, Dr. Linda Brody at Johns Hopkins University and Dr. Camilla Benbow at Iowa State University explain that accelerated students performed as well as their older classmates and "exceeded the achievement of nonaccelerated students of the same age and ability by almost a year." I can affirm at least the first part of their statement: Even though was a year younger than my graduating class in high school, I still finished in the top 1 percent. My relative youth made no difference in my academic achievements. Dr. Barbara Clark explains that "for the highly gifted, opportunities for acceleration are essential."

One of the chief arguments against acceleration is the fear of social problems. Research shows that this fear is not justified. Many gifted children prefer socializing with older children, anyway. Nonetheless, I do know that I suffered socially during high school. Of course, I also can't ignore the fact that my delayed puberty, the subsequent stresses of adolescence, my complex home life, and the sensitivity that often accompanies giftedness might have contributed to my insecurity. At this point, it's difficult to place blame on any one factor. We'll delve deeper into social adjustment and ways to compensate if your child is socially unhappy at school in chapter 9.

Despite researchers' overwhelmingly positive assessment of acceleration programs, they are not welcomed universally. According to Dr. Barbara Clark:

> In general, teachers and administrators are opposed to acceleration, while parents and students, especially those who have experienced acceleration, are for it. Some possible reasons given for the negative attitudes of some educators are the convenience of lockstep, chronological grade placement, ignorance of research, discredited belief in social maladjustment, and state laws preventing early admission.

Other Alternatives

A popular alternative to gifted education has been developed by Dr. Joseph Renzulli, professor of educational psychology at the University of Connecticut. This "revolving door" model seeks to reach a wider band of children. It is based on Dr. Renzulli's view that giftedness is composed of the interaction of three character traits: above-average abilities (IQ of 120 or over), high levels of motivation and commitment to a task, and high levels of creativity.

The school creates a "talent pool," a group of students—between 15 percent and 20 percent of the school's population—who are tops in general ability or in any specific performance areas that the school might consider important, including high levels of creative input and motivation. (The usual gifted program, according to Dr. Renzulli, narrows its population to the top 2 percent to 3 percent.)

These children participate in a pull-out program that is established in a resource room. There, the kids are exposed to new ideas and fields of study that might not be available in the regular classroom. The resource room experience is supplemented by field trips, visiting speakers, and learning centers. Dr. Renzulli views these new topics as "invitations" for further study. Individual children choose from among the subjects presented. They learn necessary skills and then carry out research, creative work, or intensive investigation in the field. In effect, the students "revolve" in and out of areas of study depending on their own interests and ability. Dr. Renzulli's "revolving door" model is in use across the country and has been adopted by the New York City Board of Education as their accepted approach to gifted education.

Some schools offer other alternative solutions such as mentors, special tutors, internship programs (spending time in a hospital or at City Hall), and independent study. These programs can stimulate your child's interest in a certain field. However, they do have drawbacks in that often they are part-time. They are better than nothing but they cannot substitute for a fully integrated program of "differentiated" learning, as I'll explain below.

In addition to these school-based programs, there are a variety of extracurricular acceleration classes that meet during the summer or on weekends. The Johns Hopkins University, for example, conducts a yearly talent search (via administration of the SAT to seventh graders) to locate extremely able math students for its Study of Mathematically Precocious Youth (SMPY) program. Children attend an eight-week accelerated math program at the university during the summer where emphasis is placed solely on abstract, complex material. No time is allotted for drill. Johns Hopkins has also established an accelerated program for language arts.

Other universities and museums (such as museums of art or natural science) around the country offer special weekend and summer programs for the gifted (or for children who are interested), as well. If programs do not exist in your local school, you may want to take advantage of these alternatives.

A word of caution, here: Depending on the youngster and the flexibility of his school district, children returning from accelerative summer programs may proceed to more advanced courses in the fall. Unfortunately, others run into roadblocks set up by school administrators who require children to follow preordained class sequences, regardless of their skills and abilities. Make sure to inquire about school policy regarding credit and advanced placement before you sign up for a special program.

THE BENEFITS OF DIFFERENTIATED EDUCATION

What's the best way to teach gifted children once you have established a gifted program? Most educators of the gifted agree that teachers should follow a program of "differentiated" education, which refers to a distinction in the *quality* of the work and thinking demanded of gifted students as opposed to the nongifted. A child's thinking processes are taken one step further from skill-building and information-gathering into the realm of analysis and creative synthesis, and judgment.

Differentiated education is based on University of Chicago Education professor Dr. Benjamin Bloom's view that people learn in a series of stages, moving from remembering specifics to knowing how to deal with those specifics, to ultimately understanding universals and abstractions in a particular area of interest. Dr. Bloom's concept, known as *Bloom's taxonomy* among educators, divides learning into six steps. Each successive step requires mastery of the preceding level:

- *Knowledge:* Remembering specific information, be it math facts or whole theories.
- *Comprehension:* Understanding the meaning of the material. (It's one thing to remember that Einstein's theory of relativity is $E = mc^2$ and another, entirely, to understand what that means!)
- *Application:* Using the information in a new or creative way. (A child can learn and understand a geometry theorem or postulate but does he know when and how to use it in a proof?)
- *Analysis:* Reducing material to its elemental parts so that its structure can be understood. (Memorizing a poem would be different from analyzing its themes, images, and sounds. The

student would understand the relationship among the parts and be able to recognize assumptions, fallacies, and inferences.)

- *Synthesis*: Creating a new whole from the parts. This may involve writing a poem based on a theme or structure discussed in class or coming up with an original idea for a science experiment.
- *Evaluation*: Making judgments about the value of the information. Reading and understanding a short story—even analyzing it—is different from being able to state what makes it successful. The ability to evaluate contains elements of the other categories coupled with an internal or external set of criteria for judgment.

How would differentiated learning work in the classroom? In a fifth-grade project on ancient Egypt, for instance, a typical learner might write a report gathering information on King Tutankhamen or on the significance of death and burial rites in the ancient Egyptian religion. He would be adding to his store of knowledge while he honed his research skills. These activities would follow the first two stages of learning according to Bloom's taxonomy.

The gifted learner, on the other hand, might apply her knowledge of ancient history and her research abilities to more analytic, creative, or evaluative purposes. She might, for instance:

- Create a board game based on King Tut's life
- Compare and contrast the form and function of Egyptian pyramids with those built by the Mayans or the Aztecs
- Hypothesize how those pyramids were built in the first place

Ideally, all school programs should teach children how to develop their thinking skills using the higher levels of Bloom's taxonomy. But since gifted children learn information more rapidly, and generally require less drill and repetition, they can move more deftly from the knowledge and comprehension to the application and creative levels. That's what makes learning fun!

Teachers in differentiated programs should help their students to analyze future implications of information they have gathered, to compare and contrast works of literature, and to imagine hypothetical outcomes (for example, "What if Gorbachev had not come to power in Russia?" "What would happen to life on our planet if the sun took a two-week vacation?"). They should also guide their students into asking questions that will lead to further synthesis and evaluation.

Be wary of programs that simply offer "enrichment," however. There can be a vast difference between such an approach and true differentiated education. Enrichment can mean, for instance, simply doing more worksheets, longer assignments, and increased drill work of the same type as the rest of the class. Such "enrichment" can turn off a gifted child, for often she learns skills rapidly and needs far less repetition than the average learner. Enrichment can also mean speeding a gifted child through the normal curriculum without pushing her to think more deeply.

Unfortunately, an enrichment program that is not based on differentiated curriculum can be ineffectual. According to Grace Lacy of the New York State Education Department, "Too often, such efforts are a hodgepodge of games, kits, puzzles, trips, and artsy-craftsy activities rather than qualitatively different programs based on the needs and characteristics of the gifted."

BEFORE YOU CHOOSE A PROGRAM

Differentiated or otherwise, no one gifted program is ideal for all children because all children are different. Only you know your child and your family's situation best and only you can make the decisions regarding appropriate placement. Before exploring your family's options, however, it's important to consider many personal factors that can come into play:

- Your child's special intellectual needs and temperament
- Your child's areas of interest, ability, and weakness
- Your child's age, size, and social maturity
- Your child's peer group
- Patterns of physical maturation in the family
- Public school programs
    In existence in your area
    Available in neighboring areas
- Private schooling for the gifted
- Afterschool or summer school programs including early admission to college classes
- Your own financial situation, available time, resources, and flexibility in providing transportation
- The availability of scholarships, where needed
- Your willingness to be your child's teacher

We all want to do the best we can in providing for our youngsters, but sometimes compromise is unavoidable. I believe that any contact with a gifted program, even if it's only a few hours a week, is better than none at all. There is no point in your feeling guilty if that's all you can provide. If you're stretched beyond your own physical or financial limits in creating educational opportunities, you may consciously or unconsciously communicate your stress or ambivalent feelings and resentment to your children. Such double messages can confuse and hurt them in the long run.

If you do have some choice in the matter and must decide between several options, how should you evaluate which gifted program best suits your child's needs? Be sure to ask questions regarding how the program provides a differentiated approach. For example:

- How much weight is placed on drill and how much on application of knowledge?
- Are the students encouraged to analyze and form judgments?
- What opportunities exist for creativity and originality of thought?
- Does the teacher pose hypothetical questions or encourage the class to grasp implications and universal abstractions?
- In observing a classroom personally, can you sense the palpable excitement that fills the room when real learning is going on?

In *Gifted Children Monthly,* Gina Ginsberg-Riggs, the executive director of the Gifted Child Society in Glen Rock, New Jersey, gives additional suggestions for questions to ask program administrators:

1. *What is the educational goal of the program?*
2. *Is the program individualized for the special abilities of the students?*
3. *What kind of cooperation is there between the regular classroom teacher and the teacher of the gifted?* (Ideally, the curriculum of a gifted pull-out program, for instance, should be a meaningful elaboration of classroom work and should be integrated into regular curriculum. If the regular class is studying the American Revolution, the gifted class could debate and then act out the writing and signing of the Declaration of Independence.)
4. *How much training in education of the gifted does the teacher of the program have?* (At least one graduate education course would help the teacher understand the gifted child's educational issues. Involvement in continuing education and yearly conferences is ideal.)

5. *How are parents involved in the program?* (You should have regular meetings with the school personnel and you should have ample opportunities to share your child's particular needs and interests with the staff. In addition, parent classroom volunteers can add much to what's being taught as well as free the teacher from rote tasks to do more creative planning.)

6. *Are children enthusiastic about the program?* (It's a great idea to observe the classroom.)

7. *If students have demonstrated understanding of the regular class curriculum, do they have to complete work missed while in the gifted program?* (If your child has gaps in his learning, he should keep current with regular class work. If he's up-to-date, completion of missed work would be a waste of time and energy.)

THE NEED FOR GIFTED EDUCATION

I'll defend to the end the necessity for specialized programming for the gifted. The gifted and talented are the future leaders of our nation. They are charged with carrying on the tasks of finding cures to deadly illnesses, creating literature and art, solving our enormous environmental problems, teaching future generations, exploring space, and maintaining world peace. To deny them the kinds of educational opportunities that would encourage deep, creative, and complex thought seems destructive not just to them but to everyone who may gain from their contributions.

Certainly, we wouldn't think twice if a physically handicapped or a learning disabled child required special schooling. The need is obvious and outwardly apparent. Yet, usually the argument goes that gifted children are smart enough to fend for themselves—they'll do just fine without special programs. Others claim that gifted education is a middle-class ploy that drains much-needed funds from the education of the economically disadvantaged. Attention should be turned, rather, to those in greater need.

This is simply untrue. Gifted and disabled children alike are categorized as "exceptional" in the professional literature. In the next chapter, I will delineate personality traits of gifted children that, at times, make them difficult to live with or teach. These traits constitute special needs. In addition, in *Growing Up Gifted*, Barbara Clark amassed a series of characteristics that render gifted children worthy of a school program that differs from that of the average learner. In part, these include:

- Extraordinary ability to absorb and retain a quantity of information
- Advanced comprehension
- Unusually varied interests and curiosity
- High level of language development and verbal ability
- High level of visual and spatial ability
- Unusual capacity for processing information
- Accelerated pace of thought processes
- Heightened capacity for seeing unusual and diverse relationships
- Ability to generate original ideas and solutions
- Large accumulation of information about emotions that has not been brought to awareness
- Unusual sensitivity to expectations and feelings of others and emotional depth and intensity
- Heightened self-awareness with feelings of being "different"
- Idealism and sense of justice
- High expectations of self and others that may lead to frustration
- Advanced levels of moral judgment and sensitivity to inconsistency between ideals and behavior
- Discrepancies between physical and intellectual development and avoidance of physical activity
- Early involvement in intuitive knowing
- Creativity

Specialized education is particularly important for highly gifted children. Although many highly gifted children do achieve in extraordinary ways, others don't perform well in school. Experts believe that underachievement may be due to a child's boredom and feelings of social isolation.

In the front page *New York Times* article mentioned earlier, journalist Sarah Wernick reports on a highly gifted fourth grader who was referred to the school psychologist because she had no friends, refused to pay attention, and created discipline problems. The psychologist, Melody Wood, recommended the child to an appropriate academic program and counseling. "The critical piece of making things better," Ms. Wood explained, "will be arranging for [the student] to be with children who think the way she does, who won't make fun of her and who value who she is."

If the needs of gifted children are not appropriately attended to, a child's talents may wither on the vine. As Thomas Jefferson once wrote, "There is nothing more unequal than equal treatment of unequal people." We would not water a rose the same way that we would tend to a cactus. Specialized education for gifted children takes into account individual differences.

THE FALLACY OF ELITISM

Many in our society today (including, unfortunately, the school board where my friend teaches) view gifted education as unnecessary or even "elitist." These attitudes may harken back to our society's historically negative views of people regarded as "geniuses" (see chapter 14).

I believe that *all* children in our nation deserve better educational opportunities than are now readily available, but why not answer as well the needs of the gifted? Are they not deserving children, too? As Barbara Clark put it,

> When human beings are limited and restricted in their development, when they are not allowed to move, or to reach beyond, they often become bored, frustrated, and angry. There is physical and psychological pain in being thwarted, discouraged, and diminished as a person. To have ability, to feel power you are never allowed to use, can become traumatic if continued.

The truth is, people fear that once gifted children are grouped together, the will become overbearing or patronizing snobs. Actually, I know from my own experience that just the opposite occurs. Dr. Barbara A. Kerr, the associate director of the Belin National Center for Gifted Education at the University of Iowa, interviewed by Dr. Lawrence Kutner for an article in the *New York Times*, explains that very bright children who are forced to remain in a regular classroom throughout their education are more likely to become contemptuous of people of average intelligence: "They become impatient and think that the other kids aren't really trying." Elitism occurs when a gifted child is the only bright child in the class.

Once placed within a group of their intellectual peers, however, these kids suddenly realize that they are not the only smart ones on the block. For some children it can be a shocking comedown, but it also is a sobering and humbling encounter with reality. Indeed, it helps gifted children to learn compassion and understanding of those who must strive hard to do well. In fact, in his 1972 report to Congress, the former U.S. Commissioner of Education Sidney P. Marland, Jr. made the same observation:

> The relatively few gifted students who have had the advantage of special programs have shown remarkable improvements in self-understanding and in ability to relate well to others, as well as in improved academic and creative performance. The programs have not produced arrogant, selfish snobs; special programs have extended a sense of reality, wholesome humility, self-respect, and respect for others.

Even though our family was fortunate in finding the proper educational setting for Cherie, probably circumstance, timing, and luck had a lot more to do with it than planning on our part. Yet, we *did* have a frame of reference in mind—we knew what we were looking for. In locating a program for your child, you will have to work within the framework of what is available to you in terms of public and private enrichment classes as well as consider the needs and specific abilities of your child.

In your quest, however, don't forget that just having the time to stare at a patch of lawn closely and see the extraordinary complexity of shoots, runners, and roots and the fantastic interweaving of ants, earthworms, soil, and clover are a part of a gifted child's education, too. It's important to pursue a differentiated education, but it's also important to allow your gifted child to be a child.

CHAPTER 7

The Complex Personality of the Gifted Child

You need a certain dash of inspiration, a ray on high,
things not in ourselves, in order to do beautiful things.

—VINCENT VAN GOGH

What is politely called curiosity in children
is greed. The objects of greed are shaped by
what we feel we have in short supply.

—LYNNE SHARON SCHWARTZ, *LEAVING BROOKLYN*

RECENTLY, I WAS CHATTING WITH TWO FRIENDS WHO HAD CONTACT with gifted children. One is a nursery school director and mother of a gifted seven-year-old daughter. The other is a substitute elementary school teacher who alternates between teaching in a gifted magnet school and a science magnet school. (Magnet schools were established by the Los Angeles Board of Education as a way to facilitate racial integration. A magnet school draws children from throughout the district who may be interested in or qualified for specialized education. The school population is racially balanced according to a predetermined formula.)

Both friends groaned when I mentioned the title of this book. "Gifted children?" said Marge, the preschool director. "I've got one of those at home. You're not kidding when you say challenges. . . . Her constant need for information, her questions, her intensity, her nonstop talking! Sometimes I feel that I can't take it anymore!"

Ah, I remember it well. Between ourselves, my husband and I had several pet expressions for Cherie's prodigious verbal abilities: When she was merely charming we used to say that she had a bad case of the "yaketies" (as in *Yakety-Yak—Don't Talk Back*); when she was insufferable, we called her "motor mouth"; and when we were really exasperated, we labeled her output "verbal diarrhea"—not a pretty picture, but you get the idea.

Not having a gifted child at home, but rather teaching them, the other woman, Francine, had a slightly different perspective. "You know," she confided, "most of the children whom I teach either are gifted or highly gifted, and I have to say that they *are* different from other kids. They seem somehow *older* and more serious, as if there's something else operating upstairs." She pointed to her head. "I'm sure that once they arrive home, they're just normal kids, but in school you can see that they march to the tune of a different drummer."

While it's true that gifted children are kids first and gifted second, it's also true that their giftedness does render them unique in some ways. And that difference can also make them hard to live with.

THE DOUBLE-EDGED SWORD AND THE TWO-SIDED COIN

In her book, *Bringing Out the Best*, Jacqulyn Saunders delineates how traits that we, as parents, cherish in our gifted child can also help to drive us and others crazy when taken to their furthest extreme. Their verbal abilities, for example, can make us feel as though they talk too much and certainly well above the heads of their peers. Their great attention spans may render them resistant to interruption. Their ability to learn quickly can easily degenerate into sloppiness. Their creativity may devolve into an escape to fantasy worlds and a rejection of what we parents may consider to be "normal" behavior. Their ability to learn independently may cause them to disdain help, even if they need it. Their critical thinking skills may elicit unreasonable standards for themselves or others. Finally, their preference for complexity may trigger needlessly convoluted solutions to simple problems.

Others have found similar potential problems, especially in the school setting. Roxanne Cramer, a parent and teacher of the gifted from Vienna, Virginia, and formerly Mensa's National Gifted Children coordinator, published the following list of character traits and potential problem behaviors in the *Gifted Children's Monthly*. It is based, in part, on work by May V. Seagoe. I'm certain that you'll recognize some of these positive traits that can have negative repercussions in your own children, especially at school. In place of "teacher" you can also read "parent."

Bear in mind as you read this list that each gifted child is unique, with her own special needs. Not all of the items pertain to all children. These points also may or may not apply depending on your own (or the teacher's) personality and needs. It's best to regard the following as helpful concepts, not as immutable facts.

CHILD'S CHARACTERISTICS	POTENTIAL PROBLEMS
	The child:
1. High verbal ability, unusually large vocabulary	Seems older or more mature than he or she is, leading to unrealistic expectations . . . has difficulty developing listening skills; uses this verbal gift to manipulate or dominate others.
2. Early reading	Presents problems to primary teachers who may not know where to begin to meet the child's language arts development.
3. A questioning attitude	Questions authority as well as rules, regulations, and generally accepted facts; teachers feel threatened, which could result in hostile feelings toward the child.
4. Keen powers of observation	Sees through sham and pretense; teacher must be secure enough to admit he or she does not know something.
5. Long attention span, persistence, intense concentration	Is unable to go on to a new activity; becomes oblivious to everything and everyone around, sometimes missing explanations, directions, assignments.
6. Ability to learn basic skills more quickly and easily and retain much information with less repetition	Resists drill and repetition; becomes impatient with those who do not learn as quickly; devours material almost as fast as the teacher prepares it.
7. Wide range of interests	Leaves activities incomplete.
8. Very narrow interests	Sticks to things he or she knows best, unwilling to risk trying new things; signals perfectionist tendencies.
9. Creativeness, originality, putting ideas and things together in novel ways	Is seen as being nonconformist or rebellious, even "weird."

10. Unusual, often highly developed sense of humor	Sees humor in situations that escapes others; sometimes leads to judgments of inappropriateness by others.
11. Ability to see relationships, make connections	Makes intuitive leaps that can exasperate the teacher who insists on step-by-step procedures.
12. Sensitivity	Is often overly sensitive, taking minor jokes or teasing too seriously; has feelings easily hurt.
13. High energy level	Cannot sit or wait quietly; is impatient; seems to have inherent need to be constantly engaged in activity; becomes bored, sometimes disruptive; can exhaust teacher.
14. Independence	Has difficulty working with others on group projects or activities requiring cooperative effort; usually prefers working alone, doing it his or her own way.
15. A "loner"	Does not develop appropriate social skills, which leads to more isolation.

FLASHES OF UNDERSTANDING

The first time I studied this list, I experienced many moments of recognition about my own personality and my daughter's. So *that's* where my feelings of impatience and my need to feel intellectually occupied at all times comes from. (I recall as a child reading the dictionary while I sat on the toilet—I couldn't let a minute go to waste!) So that's why Cherie is so sensitive and so intolerant of authoritarian attitudes and mediocre teaching in school. I'm sure that you experienced similar "Aha's!" yourself.

You can use this list to your gifted child's benefit. Suppose that Timmy hates to practice his multiplication tables and won't sit still in class. Once you identify the origin of Timmy's disruptiveness—his giftedness (he's bored and understimulated)—and realize that the problem is not purely a self-control or emotional issue nor an undiagnosed physical problem such as hyperactivity, you and your son's teacher can address the behavior problem from a more productive angle.

Rather than scolding the boy, for example, the teacher could provide enrichment for him (not additional drill, but math brainteasers requiring Timmy to use his knowledge of multiplication to solve increasingly complex problems) that will keep him happily occupied. Gifted children have a ravenous appetite for stimulation. Research shows that these kids don't develop behavior problems when they are actively engaged in learning that is appropriately challenging, meaningful, and complex.

Barring this kind of intervention, Timmy may come to believe the teacher's scolding: He will see himself as a behavior problem and a "bad boy." Not only would such an attitude be inaccurate but it would also lower your son's self-esteem. In fact, he could create a situation in which he acts out his own self-fulfilling prophecy. "The teacher says I'm disruptive, so I must be, and I might as well make a ruckus."

Such sad situations have been documented in research literature. In his book, *Giftedness, Conflict, and Underachievement*, J. R. Whitmore describes the case of Bobby, a six-year-old with an IQ of 153, who spent a second year in the first grade because of his disruptive behavior and his refusal to complete classwork. It is crucial that you communicate your child's abilities to his teacher because her underestimation of his talents can lead to his maladjustment.

In addition, when you as a parent can step back and say, "No wonder Timmy is acting this way . . . ," I believe it helps you to defuse some of the bite of these negative traits. You no longer take them personally. Placed within the context of giftedness, your child's problem behaviors may seem less formidable and more understandable. And once you are able to understand, you are better equipped to offer your compassion in helping to resolve the difficulties.

HEIGHTENED SENSITIVITY

It's never easy on a child when a sibling is born, and our family was no exception. Cherie was three years and nine months old when Aimee came along. At the time, we believed that she was old enough to handle the stress. After all, we reasoned, she was firmly ensconced in nursery school; she had lots of friends, her beloved books, puzzles, her *Wizard of Oz* record, and a "grown-up" world of her own. She seemed secure and happy. Besides, she was verbal enough for us to believe that she would let us know what was bothering her.

Boy, were we ever wrong on the first count! Of course, Cherie had her own world, but it didn't negate the fact that this very world was turned upside down by the arrival of a cute, seven-pound, squalling interloper. Cherie became demanding, tantrumy, clingy, whiny, needy, regressive, and mostly impossible. We were right on the second score, though Cherie did tell us what was bothering her: She wanted *attention* and she wanted her sister *gone,* right now!

We set about trying to help our daughter to adjust. I spent lots of time holding her and cuddling her. She especially enjoyed pretending she was a baby again. We bought her a punching bag to help her release her aggression and a "Cookie Monster" puppet that we dubbed the "Attention Monster" ("Me want attention!") that she used at will. We even purchased a newborn baby doll, crib, and high chair so that Cherie could feed her "baby" while I fed mine.

All of this was to little avail, for we hadn't acknowledged that Cherie—our first child and the first grandchild in our family—had been the apple of everyone's eye. She was unwilling to share the love she had received with *anyone* else. We also did not realize that as a gifted youngster Cherie's extraordinary sensitivity would cause her to experience the birth of her sibling with enormous pain.

The effects of this pain began making themselves clear to us several years later, when Cherie was about six years old. She continually complained that she was not receiving enough affection from me. She said that she was starving for some "loving." Yet when I held her in my arms and cuddled her in our favorite chair, she became stiff. She stared out the window and commented on my garden or passersby. The warm, melty feeling of intimacy that I had always experienced when holding and playing with her was suddenly absent. Cherie was right: She was not receiving enough affection, not because I was withholding it but because she had walled herself off from me. She became depressed and withdrawn while I became frightened.

I wasn't certain if this kind of depression or withdrawal was common among children, but it certainly didn't feel right to me or my husband. Alarmed, I began questioning my role as a parent. Had I contributed to Cherie's state? I feared that I had failed her in some way.

I brought my worries into a session with a psychotherapist. The counselor very wisely explained that children as bright as Cherie are like finely tuned precision watches. They are extremely sensitive to changes in their environment. She suggested that we seek a child therapist for our daughter to help her deal with the trauma of her sister's birth. I had to agree. If Cherie was pushing me away out of anger now, at the age of six, I couldn't imagine what she would do when she turned sixteen and would begin the process of separation in earnest.

Fortunately, the therapist we found helped our daughter work through this difficult time in her life. The therapist spent about six months engaged in play therapy with Cherie individually, gaining her trust and affection. Then, she asked us to bring Aimee (who was about three years old) to the sessions in order to reenact the original problem. Obviously, Cherie didn't take kindly to the intrusion of her sister. But Aimee's presence over the next three months did help Cherie to express and cope with her feelings of anger and abandonment. Finally, over the course of several family sessions, she was able to unshackle herself from her emotional armor and let us in once again.

In fact, one afternoon I found the children at play in the backyard. There was three-year-old Aimee, bedecked in Cherie's hat and shoes, pushing the stroller with all her might around the patio. And who was playing baby in the carriage? Why, Cherie, of course, waving a long-lost bottle, sucking her thumb, and gurgling mock baby noises. Both kids were deliriously happy in their fantasized role reversals and I burst out laughing at the sight of them. In acting out the role of her sibling, each child made peace with the other.

Although we succeeded in helping Cherie in this instance, it is still true that she is a highly sensitive individual. There were moments when we referred to her as Vesuvius—her feelings were so strong and so close to the surface that they frequently erupted—this in a family of other emotionally sensitive people. And there were times when she was deeply hurt by the childish and offhand remarks of her classmates. Indeed, as I explained earlier, she often sought to work out problems with her cohorts by talking things over when in truth the other kids didn't have a clue as to what she wanted from them. This disparity in communication ability and sensitivity frequently heightened Cherie's feelings of isolation and differentness.

Cherie's sensitivity is not unique to her. It seems that heightened sensitivity is one of the hallmarks of giftedness. In her book, *Growing Up Gifted*, educator Barbara Clark cites Walter B. Barbe, an expert in the psychology of gifted children, on gifted children's sensitivity to learning, to discovering or solving problems, or simply to other people's feelings. "It is so much a characteristic of giftedness," writes Dr. Barbe, "that it can almost be said that the two terms [giftedness and sensitivity] are synonymous."

Indeed, the more highly gifted the child, the greater the intensity of this sensitivity. This can create problems. Gifted children may have extreme reactions to the normal trials and tribulations of growing up, as our daughter did with the birth of her sister. Since they are so tuned in to social cues, they may also interpret thoughtless or silly remarks as rejection.

Researchers have pointed out that gifted youngsters may take their normal but intense (and different) response to mean that there is something wrong with them. Other children may tease a gifted child for her vehement reaction to a relatively minor incident, further amplifying the child's feeling of being weird. This was very much Cherie's experience.

FEELING DIFFERENT, FEELING BAD

Because they are so sensitive and aware, gifted children do understand that they are unlike their age-mates. This is true socially and intellectually as well as emotionally. In an article on the vulnerabilities of highly gifted children published in the *Roeper Review*, Seattle gifted education consultant Dr. Wendy C. Roedell points out that a three-year-old who expresses abstract ideas using the vocabulary of the average six-year-old may have a hard time being understood by age-mates. "Four-year-olds who enjoy playing monopoly and checkers," she explains, "have difficulty finding same-age playmates with similar skills."

Unfortunately, most children don't want to feel different: They prefer to fit in and "belong." Researchers point out that gifted children who perceive themselves as being distinct from their peers have significantly lower self-concepts than children who see themselves as part of the mainstream. When everyone else around them views the world differently, gifted kids begin to doubt themselves and their own reality. It is a natural human response that psychologists call *cognitive dissonance*.

A good friend of mine explained how this worked during her childhood. Today Leslie, who holds a Ph.D. in psychology, is the mother of two teenagers: a gifted son and a highly gifted daughter. Although she was never tested herself (there was no gifted or talented program in the small town in which she grew up), she was placed in "accelerated" classes for junior and senior high school.

Leslie always had many questions. She remembers, in particular, a seventh-grade math class in which her teacher was instructing the students about some of the fundamentals of geometry. He had explained that a circle has 360 degrees. Leslie's hand flew up. "Why that number? How did they decide on 360 degrees?'' Good question, but unfortunately Leslie's teacher didn't have an answer or wasn't willing to pursue the issue further. Even if he couldn't take the time from the class period to explain the origins of geometry to my friend, this teacher could have offered to answer her questions during lunch or after school.

Instead, he responded abruptly, ''You'll just have to take my word for it, Leslie.'' This response made Leslie feel that her question was pointless and unnecessary. In fact, in succeeding days, she generated many more queries that she then suppressed for fear of seeming even more inept. No one else had as many questions as she did and Leslie began to believe that her need to ask was a function of her ''stupidity''—and not her interest, her curiosity, her giftedness, or the teacher's poor preparation and attitude. Feeling different, she disparaged herself, rather than the situation.

I have been on both sides of this problem, first as a child, and then as a parent trying to salve my own child's wounds. I have found that *acknowledging the differentness* rather than denying it helps to mitigate some of its pernicious effects. Expressions such as ''I know that you want to be just like your friends, but there are times when you see things your own way, and that's okay, too'' can help your child adjust to and value the fact that she is a unique individual. In addition, I believe that locating a peer group of gifted kids in which your child feels ''normal'' is crucial. I'll have much more to say on this topic in chapter 9, which deals with meeting your child's social needs.

INTROVERSION AND INTROSPECTION

In their book, *Your Gifted Child*, authors Smutny, Veenker, and Veenker cite some startling research conducted by Dr. Linda Silverman at the Gifted Child Development Center at Denver University. According to Dr. Silverman, 75 percent of the population is composed of extroverts, but of the remaining 25 percent that are introverts, the majority—as much as 60 percent—are gifted. Whether or not your gifted child is an introvert, chances are he will want to spend a good deal of time alone, just to think.

In our home, we have one child who is an introvert and another who is an extrovert. Whereas Cherie craves times alone, Aimee is uncomfortable unless she is socially involved. Even as a toddler, Cherie entertained herself for hours whereas Aimee couldn't tolerate playing alone. Whereas Cherie usually has one best friend at a time, Aimee has scads of "best" friends, each one more "best" than the next. Cherie rarely ventures forth without a book in her hand, but when it is a question of what to do with free time, the phone receiver simply seems to grow out of Aimee's right ear. Cherie is often lost deep in thought, while Aimee is "out there" mugging for the camera, dancing, mimicking friends, fooling around, and generally entertaining herself and others around her.

Actually, it's rather nice having one of each. My kids' personality styles complement one another. In addition, since my husband is relatively more extroverted than I am (our careers show this, too: I work in my room, just me and my computer, day in and day out, whereas my husband's work as a psychologist cannot be accomplished without other people), we each have a child with whom we can identify. That's important because extroverted parents who have an introverted child may believe that she is somehow deficient if she is shy, reticent, or slow to jump into a boisterous group activity. Yet these attitudes are quite normal for an introvert.

According to Dr. Silverman's research mentioned earlier, introverted children may also:

- Become embarrassed in public and may act differently among others than in the privacy of their homes
- Hang back, thinking ideas through before sharing them, and observing people and situations before joining in
- Try to be "perfect" among strangers but act out at home
- Concentrate on one activity at a time and hate to be interrupted
- Hide feelings or feel reluctant to talk about them; they seem more preoccupied with their own emotions than those of others around them

Not all of these criteria apply to all introverted children. Cherie, for example, has never been reluctant to talk about her feelings. In fact, often the opposite is true. And she heartily enjoys a good party or a rowdy evening at a rock concert. Even though she exhibits elements of introversion, she is still quite social and values her many friends. Whatever your youngster's temperament, your acceptance of her character will help her to feel good about herself—introverted or otherwise.

Finally, the introverted child is often quite introspective. He looks inside himself to understand the meaning of life. This, too, is a characteristic of a gifted child.

A SEARCH FOR MEANINGFULNESS

As a child, I was always quick to cry. Whereas other children seemed to allow small hurts and slights to roll off their backs, I experienced my world, including all of its injuries, profoundly. Indeed, my family life was quite complex and I was often deeply troubled.

As I alluded earlier, my parents had survived Nazi labor camps and the concentration camps Dachau, Bergen-Belsen, and Buchenwald during World War II. They had emigrated to the United States in 1946 as refugees with exactly five dollars between them, a year before my sister's birth and two years before mine. In Europe, during the war, they had survived starvation, slave labor conditions, terror, humiliation, and disease, the likes of which are inconceivable to anyone who has not lived through the experience. They shared their stories freely with my sister and me.

The joy in our home was always tempered by the words, "Who would have believed that we have survived to witness this?" Indeed, more often than joy, there was much sadness in our home over incalculable losses. Frequently my mother broke down and wept for no reason that I could discern. As an adult I have come to see that we are all—parents and children alike—in some ways victims of the Nazis. Each of us in our own way struggled with difficulties in separation, survivor guilt, nightmares, lack of extended family, and fear of trusting others. For my parents there was the additional interminable mourning of lost siblings, relatives and friends, towns and businesses, faith in God—indeed the loss of a whole way of life.

At the age of five, I realized that the chances of my parents surviving and my being born had been rather slim, if not minuscule. I grew up feeling that my life was a gift. It was special—it had been imbued with a certain significance. I was to live for those who had lost their lives. I was to make some impact on the world, to effectuate some healing, some correction. Outwardly, my parents had little to do with this vision, although they may have communicated it to me subtly.

No matter what its origin, this feeling that my life was a gift had a dual effect on me. On the one hand, I felt that I could not waste what had been won at such great cost. I owed it to my parents who had suffered and to my family who had died so horribly. I had a potential to fulfill. On the other hand, I felt that I was always in a hurry. I was afraid that I would die young, before I had a chance to consummate that potential and manifest that significance. My days were filled with a restless urgency and an ever-present hunger to do more.

I felt different from the children around me, who were not troubled by such profound thoughts. It was hard for me to relate to my peers meaningfully or they to me. I never quite fit in socially.

As I come now to the study of gifted children, I find that many of the deeper thoughts that I had had about the meaning of my life, which I had attributed to my legacy as a child of Holocaust survivors also can be related to my giftedness—for it seems that many gifted children face similar questions about the purpose of their lives. From a very early age on, they struggle with what we could call existential questions.

In an article published in the *Gifted Child Quarterly*, Anne-Marie Roeper, headmistress of the Roeper Lower School in Bloomfield, Michigan, explains that one of the differences between gifted and average children is that the former loses his sense of innocence early. Most young children are insulated by their natural lack of awareness of what goes on in the outside world. On the other hand, "the gifted child loses this protection sooner as he/she eats from the tree of Knowledge at an early age."

According to Dr. Roeper, gifted children are able to think in abstract terms before they are emotionally able to deal with this understanding. "Magical thinking is lost," she writes, "and the child is confronted with the cold facts of the environment and what he/she sees may be frightening. This is why we cannot say that the gifted child is privileged over others for knowledge is not in itself a privilege or even an advantage. In some ways, the preschool gifted child requires more help and support than other children." Other researchers point out that the gifted child's sensitivity to society's injustice and hypocrisy can lead to precocious feelings of despair and cynicism.

GIFTEDNESS AND THE QUEST FOR HIGHER GOOD

Michael M. Piechowski, a professor of education at Northland College in Ashland, Wisconsin, has investigated gifted adolescents' development. In a study published in the book *Patterns of Influence on Gifted Learners* he discusses how some gifted children follow an introspective-emotional maturational pattern—that is, they are quite aware of their own internal needs and growth.

According to Dr. Piechowski, great emotional intensity and sensitivity combined with high intelligence make a youngster acutely aware of the precariousness of human existence and, in fact, of our world:

Gifted youngsters often ask basic, philosophical, and existential questions. Somehow they develop not only a sense of objective truth but of inner truth as well. . . . Emotional intensity joins with a superior intellect to create a genuinely moral person, someone for whom questions of personal responsibility engage both the emotions and the will.

Dr. Piechowski's work builds on theories developed by Abraham Maslow. The father of the human potential movement, Maslow studied people who were able to fulfill their potentials to a relatively higher degree than others around them. He found that these people enjoyed both physical and psychological health. He called them *self-actualizers*. Dr. Maslow was able to identify character traits that seemed to be associated with such "well" people. Interestingly, many of these attributes also coincide with those found in gifted children. In *Growing Up Gifted*, Dr. Barbara Clark gleans these attributes from Dr. Maslow's book *The Farther Reaches of Human Nature* and summarizes them as follows. Self-actualizers are:

1. More aware and in touch, more perceptive, more realistically oriented.
2. More accepting of self, others, and the natural world.
3. Spontaneous, natural, authentic.
4. More autonomous and self-directed; largely free of the need to impress others or to be liked by everyone; resistant to conformity.
5. Intrinsically motivated; having metamotivations (e.g., actualization of potentials, capacities, and talents; fulfillment of their life's mission or purpose; self-knowledge; self-acceptance; growth toward unity and synergy).
6. Seeking unity, oneness, integration, increased identification with humanity.
7. Working for a cause, devoted to a task or calling, viewing work and play as one.
8. Holding universal values (beauty, justice, truth) that are important to well-being. Working toward fulfillment of metaneeds (see number 5).
9. Capable of rich emotional reaction and freshness of appreciation.
10. Enjoying a high frequency of peak experiences (moments of highest happiness and fulfillment) and frequent mystic, natural, or cosmic experiences.
11. Capable of deep empathy and profound relationships with others; great ability to love and enjoy sexuality.
12. Seeking privacy on occasion for period of intense concentration.
13. Creative and have less constricted thought processes; they use a sense of humor that is not hostile.

14. More democratic in character structure.
15. Continually wondering about life; treating each day as new.

I began this chapter with a series of personality traits that can render raising a gifted child somewhat difficult and I conclude with this list that so clearly illustrates why the complex personality of a gifted child can bring such joy. The truth is that for most of us, although we visit each end of the spectrum with our kids from time to time, reality hovers somewhere in the middle. And even though we can't predict where our children will land from one moment to the next, I find it helpful to study the roadmap of potentialities in advance and to see that although the potential for striving is great, the potential for full self-actualization springs from the same seeds and is greater still.

CHAPTER 8

The Perils of Perfectionism

*Perfection is dangerous to achieve, usually
arriving as a disguise—and enaways flaws are
necessary as the escape route for inadvertently trapped
evil spirits.*

—WALTER HAMADY, *ANOTHER INTERMINABLE GAGGERBLABB*

*People seldom see the halting and painful
steps by which the most insignificant success is achieved.*

—ANNIE SULLIVAN (OCT. 30, 1887, QUOTED IN *THE STORY OF
MY LIFE*, HELEN KELLER)

AS A CHILD, I LOVED ALL THE MOST DIFFICULT PICTURE PUZZLES, crossword puzzles, mazes, and the like. I hated to lose at solitaire and would play compulsively until I won. Sometimes my need to achieve got expressed in the weirdest ways.

There was the time I took apart my radio because I wanted to see if I was smart enough to put it back together again like a giant puzzle. Guess what! I wasn't!

At the age of seven, I dropped a favorite "ruby" ring (the kind you find in a Cracker Jacks box) from the fourth-floor balcony of my grandparents' apartment onto a pile of construction debris just to prove to myself that I could find it. Right, again. Thirty-four years later, I still haven't forgotten it.

When I was about ten years old, I buried my gloves in the snow at the school yard, daring myself to find them. After the first two successful trials, I decided the challenge was too easy. On the third attempt, I circled the playground several times with my eyes closed before trying to locate the hidden treasure. Need I say more? I came home with cold hands and a red face that day. (I never did find those gloves, even after the snow finally melted.)

There were even occasions when I deliberately changed answers during exams to test myself. When I was certain that I had a perfect score, I would erase one of my correct answers (especially on a long multiple-choice test) and pencil in the wrong one. Later, I would actually feel vindicated when the wrong answer was marked with a big red X. Crazy, huh? Don't ask me why, but somehow I wanted to see what would happen if I let imperfection enter the system.

My favorite incident involved a staple. This was no ordinary staple, mind you, but a heavy-duty industrial-strength tin fastener—the kind that gets shot out of a staple gun at 40 miles per hour. I had found this gem on the floor of my great-aunt's dry-goods store on a visit there. In natural four-year-old fashion, I wanted to know how far I could push it up my nose. I found, much to my amazement and consternation, that I could get it up quite far—so far that I couldn't retrieve it with my finger. In fact, the harder I tried, the further I pushed it into my nostril.

Rather than tell my mom about my experiment—heaven forbid—I thought I'd just wait it out. Well, once cousins, great-aunt and great-uncle, parents, and sister were assembled around the dinner table, my nose decided that it had had enough of the foreign body. It gave a mighty sneeze and the staple flew from its resting place, making a loud "plink" as it landed on the linoleum.

"What was *that*?" demanded my astonished mother in front of the assembled family. I leave it to you to imagine the rest of the story.

In talking these incidents over with my sister, Henriette, who is both a teacher and a candidate for a Ph.D. in clinical psychology, she suggested that this kind of behavior was not only an outgrowth of my curiosity but was also an attempt on my part to prove my worth to myself. I was not competitive in the sense that I pushed myself ahead by keeping others down; rather, I did (and probably still do) have the need to continually assert to myself that I was okay. This behavior manifests itself most clearly in the form of perfectionism.

PERFECTIONISM: DISPARITY BETWEEN THE REAL AND THE IDEAL

According to Dr. Barbara Clark, education professor at California State University, Los Angeles, it is not uncommon for gifted children to hold an ideal of what they think they should be that does not match who they are. "Often their physical ability has not caught up with their mental ability," she explains in her book *Growing Up Gifted*, "and they cannot accomplish the things that they want to in the way they want." But that certainly doesn't stop them from trying and then feeling as if they're failures if they are unsuccessful.

Paradoxically, giftedness sometimes can contribute to those very feelings of failure. In an article on the vulnerabilities of highly gifted children, Wendy C. Roedell, director of the Northwest Gifted Education Center in Seattle, points out that our youngsters use their extremely capable intellectual abilities to imagine ambitious and detailed projects. Unfortunately, they then direct their similarly well-developed critical thinking skills toward finding fault with those projects. ''The inner drive to be perfect,'' Dr. Roedell writes, ''leads many gifted children to perceive themselves as failures even when external evidence indicates high-level success.''

Recently an incident occurred that reminded me of how the ideal doesn't always match the real in our family. Cherie, now twenty, is a psychology student at the University of California at Santa Cruz. She had just settled herself into her sophomore year at school when the 7.1 Bay Area earthquake violently shook the whole region. The university is but 10 miles from the epicenter, so you can imagine the force that was unleashed on the residents of that community.

Although Cherie is a veteran of many minor quakes in Los Angeles, and was physically unhurt by this huge temblor, she did suffer some emotional injury. As happens to all victims of such natural disasters, her feelings of safety were undermined. The world that she knew—indeed the ground that she walked upon—could no longer be trusted. Her sense of control over her life was literally and figuratively shaken. Strong aftershocks continued for weeks on end. With each shock, the terror, returned: Could this be the ''big one''?

Cherie found it hard to sleep at night, unable to let go for fear that another major quake would catch her unprepared and unaware. This, of course, played havoc with her ability to study. One day she called me, hysterically crying because she finally had fallen asleep at 6 A.M. that *morning*. She was about to take a difficult statistics midterm. She felt exhausted, unready for the test, and frantic.

''Why are you so hard on yourself?'' I asked her. ''You've just been through a terrible ordeal. You're entitled to have a bad quarter with poorer grades. You're smart. You'll make it up eventually. Why not give yourself a break? We love and support you no matter what.'' Then I read to her an editorial that had been published just that morning in the *Los Angeles Times* on the psychic aftershocks of the quake. Cherie finally understood that everyone was struggling with the same issues as she was, and she calmed down.

Although I was able to help Cherie get a grip on herself, I later realized that she seemed to be asking me for permission to fail, for once in her life—permission that I granted. Behind her tears and her words, I could hear her need for perfection and her terror at its absence. *What if I don't do well on this test? What if I fail it? Will you still love me? Will I still be a good person in my own eyes?*

MISCONCEPTIONS THAT REINFORCE PERFECTIONISM

Perfectionism causes an individual to crave tremendous control over his life. Of course, this kind of control is often impossible. Perfectionism also implies that an individual constantly struggles to be "the best" at whatever he undertakes: "If I'm perfect, then I'll finally be good enough; I'll finally be lovable." In light of the elusive nature of perfection, you can see how such an attitude could be self-defeating.

Not surprisingly, perfectionism is one of the greatest problem areas for gifted children because our youngsters can easily confuse their abilities and achievements with their estimation of their self-worth. If you're only as good as your last report card, then how do you define who you are? In *Bringing Out the Best*, author Jacqulyn Saunders explains that many high-ability children become "prisoners" of their own achievements. "They live in fear of making a mistake," she points out. "Often they are unable to distinguish between times when it's appropriate to give their all and times when it's a waste of emotional energy." As a result, they easily exhaust themselves in lost causes or unproductive relationships.

Gifted children may also misconstrue the notion of giftedness to mean that they must be the best in everything they do at all times or, at the very least, a prodigy in one field of endeavor. These unrealistic expectations can cause our children inordinate stress. Perfection becomes the devil nipping at their heels, goading them to avoid the moments of mediocrity and ordinariness that we all must experience as human beings.

HOW PARENTS PROMOTE PERFECTIONISM

I'm sure that over the years my own demandingness conveyed to Cherie some impossible expectations that she believed she had to meet at all costs.

My father, his father, and his grandfather before him were inveterate perfectionists. (My great-grandfather was apparently such a stickler for detail that word has it he used to polish the soles of his shoes!) My dad was of the school that preached, "It it's worth doing, it's worth doing well (read "right"), or don't bother doing it at all," which he intoned to me while I helped him to wax the car or hammer in a nail. Before his retirement, he was a tool and die maker by trade and his work demanded a high degree of accuracy. He saw no reason why this kind of precision and rigorousness should not mold all of life's endeavors. Not surprisingly, he was rarely satisfied.

I took his words to heart. I became a driven student. When I brought home A's, he asked if I could have done better—or if anyone else in the class had an A, too. (That would lessen my achievement.) I began striving for A + 's and became one of those students (the kind that most kids hate) who grew despondent over a B grade.

I equated C's with failure. After all, C meant average—and I couldn't tolerate the thought of being average. During my entire school career—junior and senior high school, college, graduate school—I received only four C's, mostly in math and chemistry courses. Although I ranked seventh in a high school class of 800, and graduated magna cum laude from college, because of those four C's, I decided that I wasn't smart enough to attend medical school. I thought that I had to be perfect.

TOO MUCH OF A GOOD THING

While unrelenting demands can lead to perfectionism, too much praise can also cause problems. Don't get me wrong—I'm not advocating that you withhold your kind words altogether, but they need to be applied appropriately and judiciously. If you laud every move that your child makes, she will become skeptical and suspicious: After all, if you don't discriminate between the great and the merely so-so, how can she believe you? Or, as my kids used to tease me, "Mom, how can I know if my picture is really good? You like everything I paint!"

In addition, too much praise can cause your child to internalize an unrealistic picture of himself. I recall one little girl on Cherie's soccer team whose parents screamed their approval every time she merely ran up or down the field. She didn't even need to come in contact with the ball for them to be pleased with her achievement! And she strutted around practice as if she were Pele incarnate, much to the disgust of the rest of the team.

Finally, children who are continually praised may come to believe that what they can *do* counts more than who they *are*. The danger, here, lies in the possibility that a project won't turn out as expected and the child will feel like a failure *as a person*. Children may believe that they are imposters and may live in fear of being found out. In addition, this attitude can cause children to become totally goal-directed. They lose sight of the pleasure and adventure of working at a task and eventually become the driven adults who must be admonished to stop and smell the roses lest a heart attack strikes. I'll share some strategies for avoiding these pitfalls a bit later in this chapter.

THE GOOD AND THE BAD OF PERFECTIONISM

A certain measure of perfectionism is not always destructive. It can push children to achieve at extraordinary levels. In an article on the vulnerabilities of highly gifted children published in the *Roeper Review*, Dr. Wendy C. Roedell, director of the Northwest Gifted Education Center in Seattle, Washington, explains that "the meticulous attention to detail necessary for scientific investigation, the commitment which pushes composers to keep working until the music realizes the glorious sounds playing in the imagination, and the persistence which keeps great artists at their easels until their creation matches their conception all result from perfectionism."

No one who is successful in a chosen area of endeavor is without at least a drop of perfectionism in his blood. The kind of "positive perfectionism" that Dr. Roedell refers to I like to think of as the pursuit of excellence.

On the other hand, when taken to its extreme, perfectionism can cut the other way. It may be a reason for a gifted child to underachieve. In *Perfectionism: What's Bad About Being Too Good*, Dr. Miriam Adderholdt-Elliott provides five ways in which perfectionism can manifest itself as underachievement:

- Procrastination that can come from a fear of success as well as a fear of failure
- Fear-of-failure syndrome, which renders a child reluctant to risk difficult challenges
- Paralyzed perfectionism that results in total inertia

- All-or-nothing mindset that can cause a child to do his worst or just give up if he can't be "the best"
- Workaholism since self-esteem is tied to performance (and no one else can be trusted to do as good a job)

When internally imposed standards for achievement become unreasonable, perfectionism can lead to depression among gifted children. It can also be the source of enormous impatience with others.

IMPATIENCE AND INDEPENDENCE

When Cherie was a junior in high school, she enrolled in an advanced placement American history class. Until that point, Cherie had been an excellent student of history. She loved, in particular, studying about the formation of our democracy and the writing of the constitution. She enjoyed this period of our history so much that at one point she had fantasized about becoming a constitutional lawyer.

Unfortunately, in Cherie's opinion, the teacher for this class was far from adequate. Whereas her gifted friends at neighboring high schools were studying the original documents and Supreme Court decisions that helped shape our nation's heritage in preparation for the AP exam, Cherie's class was treated to a daily fare of dittoed handouts that sported Peanuts cartoons in the upper right-hand corner.

Cherie became bored, impatient, infuriated, and then turned off. "If Mr. D. isn't going to do any work," she declared, "neither am I!" And she didn't. In fact, not only did she rebel at the classwork but she also became hostile and condescending toward her ill-prepared teacher. In looking back on this experience today, Cherie said, "Mr. D. killed my love for the period. He just didn't do his job."

At the time, I repeatedly pointed out to Cherie that she was only hurting herself with her attitude and performance: Her teacher certainly had no investment in how she fared. But having become accustomed to teachers instructing at a much higher level, Cherie simply would not tolerate mediocrity. Mr. D. rewarded her with a B in the class and a critical comment about her classroom comportment (both of which she deserved). And, of course, to add insult to injury, Cherie did not pass the AP exam at the end of the year.

The type of impatience and irritability that Cherie displayed is the handmaiden of perfectionism. People who are demanding of themselves are equally demanding of others. Indeed, that attitude contributed to my decision to leave the profession of teaching to become a writer. I held the unrealistic expectation that all of my students would be as motivated to achieve as I was in teaching them. When they weren't, I felt endlessly frustrated.

In fact, one of the most convincing arguments for specialized education for gifted children is the research finding that these kids, when chronically placed in an environment that they find boring and then frustrating, become intolerant of others (see chapter 6).

HOW TO AVOID AND/OR
DEAL WITH PERFECTIONISM

In our house, it's still a struggle! I have finally learned to accept myself with most of my warts. This was a tough pill to swallow, but I got lots of practice when I turned from teaching to writing. I could be as demanding of myself as I wanted but I also had to learn to tolerate editors' rejection letters—and believe me, I received plenty of them. At first these depressed me terribly. After all, I reasoned, I did my work and now I deserve my A—in this case, the sale of an article or short story. Then I became enraged. How dare they not like my work? Don't they know who they're dealing with here? It took me a while to appreciate how truly different real life is from school. Gifted or not, perfectionist or otherwise, no one owed me anything. I even learned to cherish the personalized, hand-signed rejection note over the pre-printed form.

My struggle to come to terms with my perfectionism, however, occurred only after I became a parent. As result, my children have their own insecurities to deal with. It's better to nip extreme perfectionism in the bud than to try to repair the damage later on. Several experts offer good advice on how to do so:

1. *Teach your child about losing.* In their book *Your Gifted Child* educators Smutny, Veenker and Veenker suggest that gifted children need to learn how to function in competitive situations and especially how to recover after losses.

    We parents have learned that losing a baseball game or doing poorly on one assignment is not the end of the world; next week or next season we'll get another chance. But children don't have our store of experience or sense of perspective, and may view any disappointment as an irreparable disaster. To help your youngster get unstuck from fixating on the catastrophe, you can validate her feelings by saying, "I know how hard it is on you to lose. You must feel really let down." This gives your child the opportunity to vent her emotions. But then you can gently remind her that even though the team lost, she did hit the ball when she was at bat. She is learning and improving and even enjoying the sport. The old adage, "It's not whether you win or lose but how you play the game," does apply here.

2. *Stress noncompetitive activities.* Smutny, Veenker, and Veen-ker also recommend that gifted kids should be involved in some noncompetitive activities that are intrinsically rewarding. What are noncompetitive activities? In *Finding Time for Fathering*, my husband and I explain that during noncompetitive creative play, parents emphasize the *effort* that their child makes, not the result. They dwell on the importance of the "process" of play (how one's child approaches a situation) rather than on the "goal." You can say, for instance, "Isn't it great to make up funny stories," or "I love the way your imagination works!"

In noncompetitive play, there are no winners and no losers—only people having fun. Activities such as creative story telling, gentle roughhousing, playing with clay, and abstract scribbling with crayons (without having to *make* anything realistic) are ideal. We'll explore these play ideas more fully in chapter 10.

3. *Remind your children that they are in control of their efforts but not necessarily the results of their efforts.* We often think of achievement in terms of quantifiable successes such as winning a prize at a debate contest but sometimes such distinct goals are difficult to reach for reasons that have little or nothing to do with our own labors or good intentions.

In the case of debate, for example, Kenny is in charge of how well he prepares the topic and how much time he puts into honing his debating skills, but he has little control over the judge's decision (and the fact that the judge argued with his wife that morning and isn't feeling particularly generous) or the kind of competitors he will face. Doing one's best rather than winning should be the goal.

In *Bringing Out the Best*, Jacqulyn Saunders expands on this idea. She explains that parents must praise their children's efforts as well as their successes. "Handling failure appropriately," she suggests, "also merits congratulations. For example: 'I see your plaster dinosaur foot fell apart. I like the way you set it aside and moved on to reading your book. . . .' In this type of situation, it should be made clear that *whatever* the child decides to do is all right. Choosing to try again will be a lesson in perseverance; choosing to toss the dinosaur foot in the trash will be a lesson in living with one's limitations.''

4. ***Offer appropriate support.*** In her book, *Growing Up Gifted*, Barbara Clark states that from her experience children don't benefit from being told that something they think is awful actually is very good, even if you think it is. Dr. Wendy C. Roedell, gifted education coordinator in Seattle, Washington, expands on this point. ''Years of hearing parents and teachers say *that's wonderful!* to projects that do not meet the child's own high standards leads to a distrust of feedback from those sources.''

Dr. Clark suggests that rather than protesting to the contrary when your child claims to have made a mess of things, you can say, ''I can see that you're not satisfied with the way that turned out. What would you like it to be that it isn't?'' Your child will feel more supported in this way and you can better understand the place where his thought processes became distorted into a perfectionistic mode.

5. ***Talk about your own perfectionism.*** Dr. Clark adds that since perfectionistic children usually have at least one perfectionistic parent, one of the best ways to help your child handle this issue is for you to share how you have dealt with your own self-criticism.

For example, if Michelle freezes up when she gets the second question wrong on a math test (and can't go on to complete the test, fearing that she's stupid!) you can explain to her how you used to be critical of yourself in the same way. Then share how you overcame this problem by quieting the negative voice in your head.

Eventually, perhaps, you learned to skip any questions that you couldn't do so that you could go ahead to the ones that you were able to figure out. Later, when time allowed, you went back to review the problems you were unsure of. In that way, you didn't waste your time feeling anxious or trying to solve an equation that just stumped you. This explanation will provide a valuable model for Michelle.

6. ***Be honest about your own normal limitations.*** Jacqulyn Saunders adds that you might also model a graceful acceptance of your own mistakes. You would say something like, '' 'Well that didn't go the way I wanted it to. But that's okay.'

Whenever the family prepares to enter a new situation, the parents talk about things that might go wrong and ways they might respond.'' When your gifted child notices that you accept your limitations, he will be more tolerant of his own.

7. *Recognize behavior that is unrelated to "accomplishments."* Saunders recommends giving praise for things that have little to do with achievement. ''Refraining from hitting one's sister even when she deserves it, sharing a balloon with a friend who popped his, playing with the dog when he needs exercise—are all acts of worthy praise. When care is given to reward these kinds of behaviors, as well as more glaring accomplishments, high-ability children will come to define themselves by reasonable internal standards.''

8. *Teach your child that "gifted" doesn't mean "perfect."* In an article on children's misconceptions about giftedness, Dr. Leslie Kaplan, an educator at the College of William and Mary in Virginia, advises that our youngsters need help to understand their abilities, personalities, and shortcomings. ''They can't do everything well nor can they do one thing well all the time. . . . Failure is often subjectively defined; doing one's best is what's important.''

9. *Accept your own limitations.* Finally, the solution to the perfection conundrum may lie within you. If you, like me, are a perfectionist, you might benefit from learning to relax your own very high expectations and unrealistic demands. What's wrong with being ordinary? If you give yourself permission to be average once in a while, you may also be doing your child a big favor.

We are all entitled to make mistakes or to just do a mediocre job from time to time. Think of mistakes as an opportunity for your child to learn and grow. Besides, it's excellence we're striving for—not necessarily ''perfection''—and excellence is often the product of trial and error.

TOWARD EXCELLENCE THROUGH SUCCESSIVE APPROXIMATIONS

One of my writing instructors, the late Robert Kirsch, was a book reviewer for the *Los Angeles Times*, a prolific author of fiction and nonfiction, and a truly gifted and spiritual Renaissance man. In the last course that I took with him before his untimely death, he spoke to the class about a fascinating subject. He asked us to identify where in our bodies we sensed excellence. It was Dr. Kirsch's notion that each of us has a special physical response when we feel ourselves in the presence of excellence—be it excellence of our own creation, someone else's, or even God's. He made the point that if we don't recognize what excellence "feels" like, we'll never know when we're finished with a project.

Some people in the class stated that they sensed excellence when the little hairs stood up at the nape of the neck. For others, it was goosebumps or the sensation of the stomach dropping as if riding a roller coaster. Excellence is a feeling of awe.

In this class, I realized that I experience excellence by crying. I cried in Paris when I stood in the Museum of Impressionism, absolutely overwhelmed by the beauty of Monet's room-length water-lily paintings, and I cried while listening to Vivaldi's *Four Seasons* in the exquisite but tiny Sainte Chapelle, surrounded by the panoply of scarlet and cobalt-blue stained-glass windows. I cried on the lip of the Grand Canyon at sunset and while watching a double rainbow shimmer over a waterfall in the early-morning mists of Kauai. And I have cried during the act of writing when feeling that I have captured and conveyed an essential truth.

How does one attain that moment of excellence? As a parent of gifted children, it's important for you to know that it doesn't occur all in one piece at once. Rather, excellence is most often the result of successive approximations: repeated attempts, failures, and reworkings.

I learned this in my early days as a writer of books. Of course, my expectation was that I would turn in a "perfect" manuscript the first time around but I soon (and very painfully) learned that there is no such thing as writing—only *rewriting*. With each version, and with the help of a demanding editor and publisher, I got closer and closer to the ideal until finally, at moments, I could feel the tears welling up.

Vincent van Gogh describes his first attempts at a painting as "absolutely unbearable" and Henry Miller characterizes the experience by saying, "I began in absolute chaos and darkness, in a bog or swamp of ideas and emotions and experiences."

Pablo Picasso, in his flamboyant way, explains his process of successive approximations as a series of destructions:

With me, a picture is a series of destructions. I make a picture, and proceed to destroy it. But in the end nothing is lost; the red I have removed from one part shows up in another. . . . When one begins a picture one often discovers fine things. One ought to beware of these, destroy one's picture, re-create it many times. On each destruction of a beautiful find, the artist does not suppress it, to tell the truth; rather he transforms it, condenses it, makes it more substantial. The issue is the result of rejected discoveries.

Even Mozart, who was reputed to write down whole symphonies and concertos in one piece, actually spent time humming and mulling over melodies and fashioning them in his mind before he approached the paper. "When I proceed to write down my ideas," he explained in a letter, "I take out of the bag of my memory . . . what has been previously collected into it. . . . For this reason the committing to paper is done quickly enough, for everything is, as I said before, already finished."

The process of successive approximations so necessary for the creation of a work of art or the distillation of a scientific hypothesis is the antithesis of perfectionism. The former presupposes a willingness to hang in there, to persevere even if an idea is half-baked and—perish the thought—imperfect, while the latter dismisses anything that doesn't fly on the first attempt with a dissatisfied grunt and an impudent wave of the hand.

As the parent of a gifted child, you would do your youngster a great service by valuing his fledgling attempts, imperfect as they may be. Each seemingly faltering step (backward or forward) is in truth a stride toward an openness to learning and the possibility of eventual excellence. You are teaching a process. As Henry Miller describes his experience as a writer, "Somewhere along the way one discovers that what one has to tell is not nearly so important as the telling itself." As parents, I believe the best we can hope for is not so much achievement vaunted over all else but rather that our children love the doing of their life's work, for from that love springs greatness.

CHAPTER 9

"You Gotta Have Friends . . .": Helping Your Gifted Child Meet Her Social Needs

*I always shrank in my skin on hearing that word,
"different." Not because I wanted to be like others—
I wanted others to be like me.*

—LYNNE SHARON SCHWARTZ, *LEAVING BROOKLYN*

I HAVE A PARTICULARLY SWEET MEMORY. IT'S OF TWO LITTLE girls—they're six years old, maybe seven—one with dark brown wavy hair and lively dancing eyes and the other with lovely long red tresses and a pixie-ish gap-toothed grin. They are hard at work, building. Sometimes it's a vast array of houses and stores for their Barbie and action figure collections. Sometimes it's horses, corrals, and barns— when they are playing Little House on the Prairie or Black Stallion. At other times it's some fantastic city of the past or future, complete with unicorns, dragons, king, queen, coach, horsemen, and castles.

The girls play for hours and accompany their game with song, shrieking with glee when mimicking Paul Simon's "Fifty Ways to Leave Your Lover," adding some salty original verses, swooning in unison over Shaun Cassidy. In quieter moments, they play *The Wizard of Oz* over and over and over again on the old record player.

These two youngsters were truly peers and best friends; the understanding that they had forged with each other was one-of-a-kind. Red-haired Sara, a whiz at math, painted lovely pictures. Cherie loved to read and create stories. Together they shared books, insights, and secrets. They followed each other into baton twirling, gymnastics, and drama classes. At school, they alternately competed with and helped each other. Wiry and athletic, Sara was more apt to scrape her knees; Cherie spent hours reading and thinking and wondering about things. These two intense children enjoyed an intense relationship.

TIMES CHANGE

During the third grade, Sara moved to a community about forty-five minutes away. Cherie suddenly found herself bereft and utterly lost. Certainly, she had other friends at school, but no one could replace Sara. Despite our families' joint efforts to bring the girls together at least one weekend a month, the lack of continuity in daily contact and the loss of shared experiences eventually served to distance these friends from one another.

I believe that the coincidence of Cherie and Sara's giftedness was also a factor in my daughter's feelings of loss. If one's abilities fall in the range of one out of a thousand—or even one out of a hundred—it can be awfully hard to find a kindred spirit in an ordinary classroom of thirty-five students. Given the fact that elementary school–age girls play mostly with other girls while boys tend to stick with their own gender, one out of a thousand can really mean one out of two thousand when you're looking for a friend in the third grade!

As the years went by in elementary school, Cherie came to feel more and more alienated from her classmates: They teased her for being too sensitive; they made fun of her extended vocabulary; at times they even scorned her achievements. They literally said to her, "You're different. You're weird. We don't want to be around you."

Cherie could find no one else to enter that special and complex world she had created with Sara. So she abandoned it as a place of refuge. By the sixth grade, she felt so intimidated by her classmates that she submitted to their abusive behavior in order to feel as if she belonged. Even if they laughed at her, she felt their contempt superior to simply being left out altogether.

As a parent and a former gifted child, this experience was enormously painful to watch. My daughter's difficulties evoked my own long-suppressed memories of similar taunting and rejection. I felt enraged at the children who teased or ignored her.

My husband and I had worked hard to nurture Cherie's feelings of self-worth in the hope that her internal strength would protect her from the kind of pain that we had experienced as children. Yet we felt powerless to counteract the damage we saw being wrought by these thoughtless classmates.

I sat with Cherie for many hours, hugging her as she cried and telling her that her giftedness allowed her to see the world in different terms than her classmates. It made her unique and special in her own way. "I know things are hard now," I said, "but don't worry. You'll have many more friends once you're in college."

This, unfortunately, was not advice that Cherie appreciated. At eleven years old, the dubious salvation of college seemed a lifetime away. Besides, Cherie didn't want to be *different*. She wanted to belong, and for reasons that were still unfathomable to her, she somehow could not. Even after conferences with her teacher about playground confrontations, she was unable to break the barrier that made her feel alien to her classmates. Coupled with the raging hormones of preadolescence and a high degree of sensitivity, Cherie was a very unhappy little girl.

The one argument that seemed to give Cherie some hope was my frequent reminder that she had developed many good friends at her religious school—friends who appreciated her and didn't disparage her abilities. Cherie encountered them, lamentably, only twice a week. Nonetheless, it was important for my daughter to recognize that away from the charismatic yet bullying group at school, she was socially competent. "Maybe it's not *you*," I offered. "Maybe it's just that clique of kids. . . ."

Looking back, Cherie remembers that I was her best friend during those tumultuous times—what a sad state of affairs. At Cherie's age, all the support in the world that my husband and I could provide paled in comparison to indigenous friendships. I also knew that it was inappropriate for me to intervene among her classmates—it would only increase their ammunition for derision.

The best that we could offer was to move her to an environment in which she would find herself more the norm than the exception. Placed within a larger pool of like-minded youngsters, we hoped that Cherie would no longer feel like a social misfit. We took a chance and moved her into the program for highly gifted children at Walter Reed Junior High School.

The gamble paid off, not just academically but socially, as well. The very first day at junior high, as Cherie sat alone somewhat forlornly during lunch, three girls approached. "Hi! You're new here, aren't you?" they greeted her. "You're in all of our classes. We thought we'd get to know you." She was dumbfounded, then delighted, and the rest is history.

WHAT IS SOCIALIZATION?

Socialization refers to your youngster's ability to get along well with others and be happy and comfortable in the company of other children and adults. You teach socialization in everyday conversations with your youngster. For example, reprimands such as ''Don't take toys that don't belong to you'' or ''Don't kick sand in that little girl's face'' during an outing at the park sandbox are an integral part of how your child learns to relate to others in his world. Socialization is evidenced by your youngster's actions in the world:

- Your child shares toys, fantasies, and books; ideas and information; materials, time, and space.
- He expresses his feelings in words and can acknowledge the feelings of others.
- He is capable of joining a group in the process of a game.
- He respects the rights and property of others.
- He clearly verbalizes his needs.
- He abides by the rules and limits (morals, if you will) of your family and culture and has learned right from wrong.
- He is generally courteous and considerate.
- He feels good about himself and others.
- He asserts himself but can also accept the leadership of others.
- He feels as if he belongs.

These are skills that most children acquire and refine throughout childhood and adolescence. You teach them at home while, ideally, his teachers reinforce appropriate behaviors during classroom interactions with peers and with other adults.

SOCIALIZATION BUILDS SELF-ESTEEM

Like our relatives, the apes, we are by nature social animals. According to philosopher/psychologist Abraham Maslow, after the basics such as food, shelter, and safety, the need to belong is paramount. Only when we feel we belong can we go on to turn inward and develop a strong sense of self.

Your child's sense of belonging begins during her early social interactions with you, her parents. At birth you pick her up and talk to and smile at her; you sing and make eye contact; you respond promptly when she is in distress; you create a warm and loving bond with her. You are teaching your child that the world is a friendly place and that she can trust you to be there in an affectionate and gentle way. She is a part of your family and she feels safe and secure. She smiles back and gurgles, causing you to laugh, talk, and play with her all the more.

When your infant sees that she has a positive effect on you, she feels valued and begins to feel good about herself. This basic sense of belonging builds the self-esteem that underlies your child's eventual success in school and in all other facets of life. That self-esteem helps to support her feelings of social competence, the key to her ability to form and maintain positive relationships with other children. From a sense of belonging to your family group, your child moves into the world to find other groups in which she can claim membership.

THE POWER OF SOCIAL GROUPS AND SOCIAL COMPETENCE

Social competence means that your child understands and abides by the rules and limits created by your family and society. These dictates are what transform your baby from a totally self-oriented being to a functioning member of our society. Every family in every culture has rules and limits of this sort (such as no fighting, no biting, shake hands, keep an appropriate physical distance when talking to people, say please and thank-you, stop at red lights). Without these limits, life would be chaos for us all.

At home, you teach your child about these rules by setting an example and by establishing limits and following through with appropriate consequences. Your guidance is necessary; otherwise your youngster will have a hard time keeping friends and getting along with others in her world. Playmates often shun children whose parents always indulge them, for example, because the former feel unwilling to put up with the latters' constant demands. Your role as a parent is to set the stage for and reinforce the social learning that occurs in the outside world.

Anthropologists and social psychologists have discerned thirteen areas in which all cultures create codes of proper behavior. These include eating, excreting, sexuality, aggression, dependence and independence, emotional development and attachment to others, achievement, competition and cooperation, sense of individuality, life and death, mating, pain, and of course, right and wrong.

Some of these social standards apply to groups of children, as subgroups of civilization. You would see this most clearly if you observed a large, well-integrated high school. Kids "hang out" or otherwise socialize in clearly definable clusters. They may identify with different types of rock music, for example. Those teenagers who enjoy "heavy metal" will walk, talk, dress, and act differently from those who follow The Grateful Dead or rap music. Each group of adolescents has its own set of socially acceptable mores. It is the rare, highly socially adept teenager who can move easily from one subgroup to the next.

Given her difficulties in relating to her sixth-grade classmates, Cherie's problems could have stemmed from a lack of social competence. Yet, I believe that Cherie's problems occurred largely because of a dissonance in social expectations. Whereas she was perfectly in sync with Sara, and found a fairly good rapport with her religious school friends, she seemed as alien as a martian to her sixth-grade classmates. Once we landed her on the planet that was populated with other children more like her, she fit in more or less perfectly. It is for this reason that I strongly believe that gifted children need to have at least one other gifted friend, if not a whole peer group, in order to meet their social needs.

By the time Cherie graduated from her large public high school, she had been elected senior class secretary; she participated on the prom committee and in the senior fashion show; she rode on a float during the homecoming parade; she played in the junior/senior girls' powder-puff football game; she sang in the madrigal choir; she edited a newspaper; she worked as a camp counselor; and she organized the youth division of a communitywide event that drew some 30,000 participants. Because of the change to a more comfortable environment compatible with her own personality, Cherie blossomed.

SOCIALIZATION AND ACADEMIC ACHIEVEMENT

You may be surprised to learn that socialization is even important in terms of your child's intellectual or cognitive development. Research has shown that preschool children who have problems with social skills such as working together, agreeing or disagreeing peaceably, taking turns, and sharing may also develop academic difficulties.

An April 1989 *Newsweek* article by Barbara Kantrowitz and Pat Wingert entitled "How Kids Learn" makes the point that youngsters' social development has a profound effect on their academic progress. Preschoolers who have trouble getting along with their classmates can fall behind academically. They may even experience a higher incidence of dropping out of school and have later difficulties adjusting to adult life.

Academic problems can ensue because preschoolers learn most effectively when they *interact* with one another. In the book *Early Schooling: The National Debate* professor of early childhood education at the University of Illinois, Lilian Katz, explains that in addition to learning through trial and error and observation, young children's cognitive and social learning is greatly enhanced during play interactions.

Consider a simple group activity like stringing colored beads. Children learn about sorting and counting, they distinguish colors and shapes (a precursor to math), and they practice eye–hand coordination during this activity. But best of all, as they engage in fashioning their masterpieces, they hoard, trade, or share beads; copy one another's patterns and designs; discuss and compare their results. In other words, they are learning through the process of socialization.

Such social interactions may be particularly beneficial among groups of young gifted children. In a research study presented during the 1978 American Psychological Association's annual convention, giftedness specialist Wendy C. Roedell reported following a group of thirty-two intellectually advanced preschoolers during a school year. She observed that by the end of the year these children were significantly more involved in cooperative interactions than could simply be explained by maturation. She hypothesized that when gifted preschoolers are grouped together for play, they may create a unique, mutually stimulating social environment among themselves that facilitates their learning and social behavior.

It is for these reasons that child developmentalists like Marie Winn, who wrote the book *Children Without Childhood*, have found that when too much early emphasis on academics supplants all-important playtime, it can slow or reduce a child's overall development. Play teaches your gifted preschooler essential lessons about his world and the people in it. It would be unwise for you to sacrifice his learning of social skills for the sake of academics. We'll explore this idea further in the next chapter.

HOW TO FIND OTHER GIFTED CHILDREN

The quest for a kindred spirit is not an easy one, yet it's not an impossible task, either. The truth is, gifted children, because of their sensitivity, intuit when they are in the presence of someone who operates on their own wavelength. They gravitate toward these other children naturally, out of their shared sense of interest, imaginativeness, awareness, curiosity, and wonder.

In talking with several other mothers whose highly gifted daughters had social experiences similar to Cherie's, I discovered that in each case the youngsters sought out other gifted children with whom they could create deep and intense friendships. This kind of ardent intimacy doesn't apply exclusively to girls. I recall two brilliant teenage boys who had been my French students in a small private high school in Los Angeles. Perhaps because of their subtle eccentricity, they had found and clung to one another in an otherwise hostile environment. I am certain that their friendship dispelled their loneliness and that their constant intellectual sparring warded off others who would belittle them. Alone, each was rather lost; together, they had forged their own social subgroup within the school.

Clearly, the way to help your gifted child find friends is to expose him to social contexts where many other children may congregate. In our case, a change of school expanded Cherie's social opportunities. That, however, may not be an option for you, given the educational programs offered in your community (see chapter 6). And, even in an entire population of gifted children, yours may not find a confidant, as in the case of my friend Leslie's highly gifted daughter Lisa. Lisa had attended a gifted magnet school (in which all of the children were gifted) for years but she still felt as if she didn't belong. Lisa finally found her soul mate at a summer daycamp that did not specialize in the gifted.

If your child is in a gifted population and still has no real friends, should you be concerned? That would depend on your youngster, his situation, and his temperament. As kids change and grow, it's natural for them to be "between friends" from time to time. If, on the other hand, your child seems to go for months on end without a playmate and seems depressed about it, you might want to consult with a child therapist. You should also bear in mind, however, that highly gifted children may simply have a harder time finding peers. You may have to widen your search to include neighboring communities. Look into a variety of likely programs, not just for what they have to offer academically but also socially, including:

- Art and natural history museums, children's museums, and zoo programs for the arts and sciences

- After-school child-care camps
- Summer school classes
- Day camp and sleep-away camp (including, but not limited to, those specializing in math/science, sports, performing and fine arts, or computers, depending on your child's interests)
- University programs for junior high and high school students (often offered in the summer)
- Religious school offerings (if you are so inclined)
- Sports activities and teams
- Clubs such as chess, science fiction, computer, choir, stamp or coin collecting
- Youth outings, art classes, and competitions organized by the local park or the YMCA

If you are at a loss for locating programs, talk to the coordinator of gifted programs for your school, school district, or state and get in touch with the gifted children's associations in your community or state. These individuals and groups are sure to have listings of activities as well as announcements of parent conferences (where experts and parents share information and resources relevant to the gifted), if not in your town, then at least in a neighboring area that will help multiply your child's social options.

Bear in mind also that your gifted child can develop unevenly. He may be two or three years ahead of his chronological age in math ability but merely average as an athlete. He therefore may have several groups of friends to suit his varied interests and talents.

HOW GIFTEDNESS HELPS SOCIAL RELATIONSHIPS

Many experts argue that gifted children are generally quite well adjusted, even more so than their nongifted counterparts. They point out, for example, that studies have shown that moderately gifted children compare favorably to their more typical age mates when it comes to self-esteem, family relations, and friendships. In an article entitled ''Psychosocial Development in Intellectually Gifted Children,'' Drs. Paul M. Janos and Nancy M. Robinson at the University of Washington write that ''being intellectually gifted, at least at moderate levels of ability, is clearly an asset in terms of psychosocial adjustment in most situations.'' (Highly gifted children have a more difficult time of it, as we'll see in a bit.)

These researchers, among others, point to many studies demonstrating that gifted children:

- Are more mature, persistent, energetic, self-sufficient, and independent
- Are more sensitive to the behavior of their peers
- Are more capable of coming up with theoretical solutions to social problems
- Exhibit more advanced moral judgment
- Prefer playing with older children
- Are trustworthy under stress
- Have a feeling of self-worth and a sense of personal freedom
- Like children and enjoy playing with them
- Participate in extracurricular activities
- Are less aggressive, less apt to withdraw during social interactions, less anxious, less defensive, and less neurotic
- Cooperate, take suggestions, are courteous, and are self-assured
- Feel as if they have some control over the direction of their lives
- Become leaders among their peers

SOCIAL DIFFICULTIES: CONFUSIONS FOR PARENTS AND KIDS

This research certainly paints a rosy picture. Yet, I know from my own experience that social problems can exist. Sometimes it's hard to feel special. The responsibility to do great things with one's life can create unreasonable expectations and perfectionistic tendencies with an associated impatience and demandingness of others. Gifted children may suffer from the jealousy of their peers, and girls, more than boys, may hide their giftedness in order to ''fit in.'' Feeling different, they may be attracted to adult company rather than that of other kids, or as the constant center of their parents' attention they may become demanding, bossy, and arrogant. Conversely, they may suffer the humiliation of name-calling and rejection such as being labeled an ''egghead'' or ''nerd.'' Even their teachers may become jealous and hostile toward them (see chapter 14).

Many gifted children typically prefer older playmates (or at least those who are of the same intellectual/emotional age). Although I would strongly disagree, among at least some child psychologists this preference is considered a sign of maladjustment. After all, if this is the only game in town, an older friend is better than no friend at all.

But mixed-age peer groups do pose some problems. Consider, for example, the liaison of a gifted eight-year-old with a more average ten-year-old. Although intellectually the children may be peers, socially and physically the gifted child would most likely be at a disadvantage. You would probably need to carry on continuing discussions with your youngster about each child's strengths and weaknesses along with explanations regarding why Johnny is permitted to ride his bike to the mall while your son is not.

A 1956 study by Dr. R. Miller published in the journal *Exceptional Children* concluded that high-IQ fourth graders prefer other high-IQ children as friends more frequently than those not identified as gifted. If that were true across the board, wouldn't it make sense to include *only* other gifted children as the appropriate, true peer group?

These confusions are compounded by the gifted child's own complex personality. In her book *Bringing Out the Best* Jacqulyn Saunders emphasizes a painful paradox in growing up gifted: The sophisticated thought patterns that render a child gifted and give her the ability to understand and exhibit behavior well beyond her years can also keep her from making sense out of the more childish actions of her age mates. It has been said of gifted children that they possess the mind of an adult trapped in the body and emotional perspective of a child.

This paradox certainly holds true in Cherie's case. When she was about two years old, she would clamber to the top of a playground slide and expectantly station herself there for as long as fifteen minutes while older children climbed the ladder and slid down in rapid succession, ignoring her. Cherie wasn't really interested in the physical activity—she was too frightened and perhaps even too little to take the plunge herself. Rather, she anticipated that every child came up the ladder explicitly to *talk* to her. She greeted each and every one with "Hi!" and then tried to start conversations. It was her way of playing.

This penchant for verbal interaction carried into elementary school. Cherie wanted to talk out her conflicts with her classmates, while they were only interested in bowling her over and going on to the next entertainment, leaving her totally bewildered about how to deal with them. Her desire to verbalize her feelings made her seem all the more bizarre to her classmates.

THE TRUTH ABOUT DIFFERENTNESS

In a scholarly article entitled "Commonalities Between the Intellectual Extremes: Giftedness and Mental Retardation," Drs. Edward Zigler and Ellen A. Farber of Yale University make the interesting point that both gifted and mentally handicapped children have uncommon socialization experiences because their levels of intellectual functioning significantly diverge from the norm. In addition, according to Drs. Zigler and Farber, "Both low- and high-IQ children are treated differently from other children by their parents, peers, and teachers." These differences are likely to create a certain amount of stress that may ultimately affect a child's personality and his social adjustment.

There is a distinction, however, between simply being different and feeling that difference. Studies have documented, for instance, that those gifted children who perceive disparities between themselves and classmates may suffer for that knowledge. One such investigation carried out in 1985 by Drs. Paul M. Janos, Hellen C. Fung, and Nancy M. Robinson at the University of Washington, and reported in *Gifted Child Quarterly*, involved asking a group of 271 gifted elementary-age children and their parents questions about the youngsters' social relations.

While parents filled out questionnaires concerning their children's behavior, social competence, and problems, the researchers queried the children about whether or not they had friends their own age, whether or not they had at least one good friend, whether they had "too few" friends, whether being smart made it harder to make friends, and whether they thought of themselves as being different from other children.

The team of researchers found that eighty-eight youngsters in this study (37 percent) felt that they were different from their age mates. Of the seventy-one kids who gave reasons for this difference, 50 percent were positive; they felt "stronger" and "smarter," and said that they could "read better." Only four children expressed the differences as negative. Their comments included, "I feel too smart for them to like me," and "Being in a different grade makes me out of place near them."

Interestingly, despite the fact that most of the seventy-one children saw the differences in a positive light, *the self-esteem scores for this whole group were lower* (although not dangerously so) than those for children who didn't express feelings of differentness. The research team concluded that *"conceptualizing oneself as being different from other children may be felt as more negative than positive."* These findings support an earlier study carried out in England by Dr. J. Freeman in which 51 percent of seventy high-IQ children described themselves as feeling different. Those kids had a higher incidence of problems including disturbed sleep patterns, hyperactivity, showing off, and peer maladaptiveness.

There is yet another painful paradox here. Sometimes the gifted and pull-out programs—the very institutions set up to give much-needed special attention to our children—serve to label them and heighten their feelings of differentness. Nevertheless, James Alvino, editor of *Gifted Children Monthly*, has written in an article directed to teachers and guidance counselors that "gifted children need an established context in which to develop friendships based on common interests and ability levels. . . . *[They] need to be homogeneously grouped at least part of the time."*

THE HIGHLY GIFTED ARE EVEN MORE VULNERABLE

The list of positive social attributes that I cited earlier applies specifically to moderately gifted children. There are fewer studies on the highly gifted because there are fewer of them around to study. Depending on the researcher, children are designated as highly gifted if their IQ falls above 140, 160, or 180.

The little research that has been conducted shows that the more highly gifted the individual, the greater his potential difficulties in making friends and adjusting socially. According to estimates by Drs. Janos and Robinson, difficulties may exist for 20 to 25 percent of highly gifted children as opposed to 5 to 7 percent of moderately gifted and 6 to 16 percent of average children.

In another study comparing thirty-two highly gifted with forty-seven moderately gifted eight-year-olds, entitled "Friendship Patterns in Highly Intelligent Children," Janos and Robinson found that while the majority of moderately gifted children had two or more friends, the high-IQ youngsters were characterized by having no more than one close friend. Sadly, at least a third had no close friends at all. Other researchers put the frequency of social problems for the truly intellectually superior as high as 71 percent.

If it's difficult to find one peer out of a thousand, imagine the challenge of locating another child who is one out of ten thousand. As Drs. Janos and Robinson put it, "For the highly gifted, the discrepancy between the child's abilities and the ordinary school environment, with its peer group of same-age children, is so strong that maladjustment is very likely."

Dr. Wendy C. Roedell, gifted education consultant in Seattle, Washington, has studied the special vulnerabilities of this group of youngsters. In *Roeper Review*, a scholarly journal dedicated to gifted children, she wrote that difficulties arise because intellectually superior children must deal with issues that affect their self-perception such as:

1. ***Uneven development:*** The large gap between a highly gifted child's intellectual capability on the one hand and emotional, physical, and social skills on the other can be enormous and may lead to overdemanding pushiness from adults and peers and frustration on the part of the child.

2. ***Adult expectations:*** Parents urging children to live "up to their potential" may overschedule their youngsters and leave them little time for normal play, thereby sacrificing the time usually devoted to learning social skills. At the secondary school level, teachers of various courses may expect excellence without taking into consideration the child's overall course load or his need for social time.

3. ***Self-definition:*** The normal identity crisis that comes with adolescence may occur earlier because of the child's unusually strong analytic abilities. In addition, with so many options available, a highly gifted child may have difficulty choosing what academic direction he wishes to pursue yet may be pressured to do so at an early age.

4. ***Alienation:*** Highly gifted children have a more difficult time finding compatible peers who can converse and play at their level. If the child tries but fails repeatedly to make contact with others, he may withdraw from social interaction, thus depriving himself of the opportunity to learn and refine additional social skills.

5. ***Role conflict:*** Highly gifted adolescent boys may suffer from the accepted view that the athletic star rather than the math genius is the school hero. Teenage girls may be caught between their internal need to excel and surpass others versus the traditional view of females as more passive caretakers enmeshed in a social network (see discussion of girls' issues below).

JEALOUSY, ENVY, AND HOSTILITY

Toward the end of Cherie's difficult sixth-grade year, she came home one day absolutely stung by her teacher's thoughtless remark. Cherie had already been accepted into the junior high program for highly gifted children, yet she still struggled with math. Mrs. L., in a moment of pique, buttonholed her in front of the class and said rather snidely, "Well, if you're as smart as they say you are, why can't you learn how to divide fractions? I don't know how you're ever going to make it at Walter Reed Junior High if you can't do this *easy* stuff!"

Given Cherie's other problems that year, you can imagine how her teacher's hostility threw her off balance. This disparagement gave additional permission to Cherie's classmates to heighten their animosity toward her. After all, if the teacher could be sarcastic with impunity, what was to stop the students?

How could such antipathy arise? Mrs. L. lacked training in gifted education. She did not understand that gifted children may not be exceptional in all areas.

I think that a deeper issue also was at work. In our society, despite our protestations to the contrary, intelligent people are often belittled (see chapter 14). I recall one of my college chums saying to me, "You may be smart, but you sure don't have any common sense." It's difficult to understand or to know how to react to this type of malicious comment. There may be some truth to the statement (gifted children may not be street- and people-smart if they cannot relate to how others think or if their intellectual development far outruns their emotional development, thereby limiting their opportunities to practice social skills) but it is always meant as a slight when said in such a manner.

In Cherie's case, I surmise that envy is at the root of these insensitive gibes. Let me make it clear that there is nothing inherently wrong with envy or jealousy, per se. They are emotions like any others such as love or anger, pain or joy. They are reflections of an individual's feelings of inadequacy and vulnerability. We can understand the pain of the envious one, even if he lashes out, but we must also pay close attention to the harm it can do to the person who is being envied—our gifted child. It's not the emotion itself but what one *does* with the emotion that is significant.

An envious playmate who lashes out at a gifted child because she guilelessly does what she loves best—and excels at it—can be awfully hurtful. A classmate who gloats at a gifted child's temporary setbacks (for we all have them) amplifies the latter's fears of being an impostor and a failure. A teacher who feels his authority eroded by a gifted child's relentless pursuit of knowledge, so that he unconsciously undermines and stymies the child's progress, may not only be punishing but also destructive to her future.

In her book, *Growing Up Gifted*, Barbara Clark, professor of education at California State University, Los Angeles, describes one of the most devastating misuses of power in this regard. A bright young man of her acquaintance who had spent four years in a special gifted program entered a high school in which gifted education consisted merely of enrichment during regular class time if the context permitted. This youngster did well with little effort, but rarely felt challenged or stimulated.

One day, he received an F on an exam. He went to discuss the grade with his teacher, perplexed because he was certain that his answers were correct. As he made his plea, the teacher just sat in his chair smiling, not uttering a word. The boy renewed his entreaties and became increasingly frustrated and upset. Finally the teacher blurted, "Oh, you didn't really get an F." Then showing the boy the A + in his grade book—the highest grade in the class—the teacher concluded, "I just wanted to see how you would take it if you got an F." This young man finished his high school education by attending college classes.

People who assail gifted children out of enviousness, then, must suffer some wound to their own sense of self-esteem regarding their intelligence or achievements. Gifted adolescents frequently complain of dramatic incidents in which insensitive teachers and peers push them to the point of doubt and despair. Thomas M. Buescher, professor of education at Wayne State University, and Sharon J. Higham, the associate director of programs at the Center for Talented Youth at Johns Hopkins University, write in an article on the developmental adjustment among gifted adolescents that high school teachers, in particular, try to disprove a child's talents. In effect, the teachers say, "Prove to me you are as gifted as you think you are," in very much the same way that my daughter's sixth-grade teacher talked to her.

HOW YOU CAN HELP

Dealing with envy or hostility directed toward your child can be tough. In the real world, where people often act out of their unconscious motivations, the possibility that your child might get hurt is indisputable. It may not be fair, but that's just the way the world is. The following are a few suggestions that may help you lighten the load.

1. *Talk it out.* Validate your child's feelings of hurt and loneliness by telling him you understand how difficult it is for him to feel different from those around him. Allow him to cry and to vent his feelings in a supportive environment. Although it was ineffectual with my daughter, you might also mention to Josh that as he grows older, he will come in contact with more and more people who see the world as he does.

2. *Explore the emotion of jealousy.* Explain that people do sometimes become envious of those whom they perceive as being different from or ''better'' that they are and that their malice grows from their own pain. You might mention instances in which you or even he experienced these emotions in relation to others. (''Remember when Jeremy won the swim meet and you felt angry. . . .'') While this approach doesn't eliminate the conflict, it may help your child to take it less personally.

3. *Meet with the teacher.* If the problem occurs at school, it might be advisable to set up a conference with the teacher. She may have her own point of view on the issues that could help clarify the situation. For example, she might reveal that classmates have scorned your child in reaction to his bossiness. Once she has been alerted to negative behavior exhibited toward your child, however, she might also be able to intervene among the warring parties or she might use the information to teach a lesson on tolerance of individual differences *without* using your child as an example. After all, each child is a unique entity with his own strengths and weaknesses.

    In severe cases, the teacher should quietly call aside the hostile child to find out from him what incident had triggered his behavior. If she digs beneath the surface she may find a youngster who is hurting. Often children act out with their peers problems that are occurring at home. For instance, if Marty's parents punished him for bringing home a poor report card by revoking his Nintendo privileges for a month, he may feel safer venting his rage at Josh—who always seems to have the right answers—then expressing it directly to his mother and father.

4. *Meet with the school/school district administration.* If the teacher herself is the problem, however, a conference with the school principal would be in order to help defuse the conflict.

Lacking success there, you might seek out a meeting with the gifted coordinator of the school district or even the superintendent.

5. ***Remove your child from the situation.*** If your child experiences little relief from these strategies—or if they serve to heighten the animosity because they have drawn attention to the problem without resolving it—then obviously, as in Dr. Clark's example, the best defense is to get your child out of a potentially damaging situation and into one in which he will feel appreciated, not maligned.

HIDING GIFTEDNESS, ESPECIALLY DURING ADOLESCENCE

One of my worst fears as my children entered school revolved around their losing interest in learning. I imagined that they might become bored and that it would snuff out that spark of excitement so essential for continued growth. If that happened, I feared that their giftedness would eventually fade into a vast sea of indecision or mediocrity.

I'm happy to report that this fear was not realized—at least, not in the way that I had envisioned. I did find that once in high school, Cherie took pains to downplay her giftedness. It wasn't boredom that made her do this but rather her continuing need to be social and to fit into a more heterogeneous crowd. As she saw it, she had spent the first fifteen years of her life developing her academic self. Now it was time to even the score by being more social, at the expense of her academic life.

Cherie's attitude correlates with recent research showing that gifted children view their abilities as an asset in the realm of personal growth and academic achievement but as a *definite liability* in the area of social relationships. In a 1988 study by Drs. Barbara Kerr, Nicholas Colangelo, and Julie Gaeth at the University of Iowa, 90 percent of the 184 gifted high school juniors who participated in this investigation responded that the worst part about being gifted was the *social* consequence. In fact, girls viewed social issues as being negative more frequently than boys.

Hiding giftedness is a child's maladaptive way of coping with the painful feelings of differentness and alienation. Drs. Edward Zigler and Ellen Farber, whom I mentioned earlier for their work comparing mentally handicapped with gifted children, find that both groups try to camouflage their atypical abilities. Whereas the former adopt a "cloak of competence," the latter may cover themselves with a "cloak of incompetence." These psychologists give the example of a straight-A student who, when asked by her classmates how she did it, replied, "I cheat." During adolescence, peer pressure for conformity is a formidable force.

Some children simply refuse to "own" their talents. They may:

- Take unchallenging classes or avoid gifted programs altogether
- Lower their own and others' expectations
- Choose friends with lesser abilities
- Mask their giftedness by not applying themselves

Research has shown that adolescent girls are more likely to walk away from their giftedness than are boys.

THE GREAT DISAPPEARING ACT AMONG GIRLS

Studies conducted in the 1950s and early 1960s of gifted high school boys and girls found that high-ability boys were popular with both sexes but that bright girls, though well-liked by other girls, were significantly less popular with boys. A 1961 study by J. L. Coleman of 8,000 adolescents in ten diverse high schools, published in *The Adolescent Society*, found that while parents and teachers encouraged bright girls to achieve, peer pressure discouraged them from displaying their intellectual abilities. What a double bind!

Despite the enormous changes in our society in the last thirty years, our attitudes regarding women's achievement have not changed significantly. In an article on sex differences in education, Dr. Jacquelynne S. Eccles of the University of Michigan cites the following gender inequities gleaned from recent research at The Johns Hopkins University program for mathematically and verbally precocious children.

Despite the fact that gifted girls do as well as boys in high school math and science courses, they are less likely than gifted boys to:

- Enroll in accelerated or special programs
- Respond positively to an invitation to join a gifted program
- Enter college early
- Remain on an accelerated math track

- Enroll in math and science courses
- Major in science or engineering

Various other studies confirm how women are discouraged from pursuing education in mathematics and science. Indeed, as recently as 1984, less than 12 percent of the women entering the University of California system had the high school math prerequisites that would allow them to study 80 percent of the majors offered.

Unfortunately, this discrepancy carries into adulthood. Colette Dowling cites some startling statistics in *The Cinderella Complex*. Two-thirds of women with IQ's of 170 or higher are employed as housewives or office workers. Many take jobs as the ''power behind the throne,'' backing up the men in control but receiving none of the credit or remuneration for their contributions.

Although today many more women engage in meaningful careers, and even though studies show that girls get consistently higher grades in school than boys, the sex biases and double standards so obvious at mid-century are still with us, albeit more subtly.

Men still overwhelmingly surpass women in career achievements and financial reward. Studies have shown that male professors produce more research and creative work and men receive far more Nobel prizes and 70 percent of the National Endowment for the Arts Literary Fellowships (although both sexes agree that women excel in literature). Despite the fact that the number of women scientists and engineers increased 200 percent between 1972 and 1982, of the nearly 2 million American engineers, in 1982 only 3.5 percent were women. And according to John Tsapogas, science analyst at the National Science Foundation, in 1989, only 5.3 percent of our nation's engineers were women, an improvement but a paltry one, at that.

How is it that so many young women shun their giftedness on their way to adulthood? Much of the blame can be attributed to how female children are socialized and to the larger social context in which we live. Traditional sex role stereotypes abound in the media and advertising. Even your family arrangements at home may perpetuate a gender role model you hope your daughter will avoid.

At school, as well, girls are taught lessons about their ''proper'' place. They learn, for example, that if they speak up, if they are assertive—even aggressive—in pursuing information and achievement or in rejecting pat explanations, if they push to get their answers heard, they are sometimes considered ''bossy show-offs,'' ''obnoxious,'' and ''unfeminine.''

A fascinating 1985 study of more than 100 fourth-, fifth-, and sixth-grade classrooms in four states and the District of Columbia by researchers Myra Sadker and David Sadker reported in *Psychology Today* documents just one of the ways that these attitudes are formed. This team found that "at all grade levels, in all communities, and in all subject areas, boys dominated classroom communication." The researchers observed how teachers responded to students calling out answers. When boys answered without teacher permission, their responses were accepted; when girls did the same, they were admonished to raise their hands. According to the researchers, the message conveyed to both genders was "Boys should be academically assertive and grab teacher attention; girls should act like ladies and keep quiet."

A recent study at Wheaton College reported by Edward B. Fiske in the *New York Times* underlines how these sex role inequities continue even at the university level. The study by Catherine B. Krupnick, a researcher at the Harvard Graduate School of Education, relied on detailed observations of thousands of hours of videotaped classroom discussions. It showed that faculty members took male contributions more seriously than female ideas and allowed the college men to dominate the discussions.

According to Edward Fiske, these findings substantiate other researchers who report that professors are more likely to remember men's names, call on them in class, and listen attentively to their answers. In contrast, these same professors "feel free to interrupt women and ask them 'lower-order' questions," such as the date of a particular event rather than its meaning.

Other research has shown that girls begin to hide or "lose" their giftedness around puberty. As one team of Canadian educators, Sylvia R. Olshen and Dona J. Matthews, put it, "Girls cannot compete with and for boys simultaneously." During adolescence, the issue of belonging becomes paramount. As I explained earlier, girls are more apt to view their giftedness as a social liability that alienates them from their classmates.

In their developmental study of adjustment among gifted teenagers, Thomas M. Buescher and Sharon J. Higham outlined how social customs between boys and girls reinforce girls' rejection of their talents. At the age of twelve, both genders seek friends of similar abilities and build relationships in small groups. At thirteen, however, the genders diverge. Girls begin to widen their pool of friends and seek new labels for themselves such as member of student council or choir, dancer or athlete to counteract the "less desirable" designation of "gifted," while boys "dig deeper into these earlier, more familiar friendship patterns" and put their energies into solidifying their existing talents within their close circle of friends.

As the children go through school, the girls increasingly stretch the boundaries of their friendships and interests, seeking status outside the school, while gifted boys participate within the schools' structure, becoming members of the debate team and the school newspaper. Over time, some girls may feel the pull of "belonging" more strongly than the necessity to participate in classes that suit their abilities, so they "sacrifice their talent for acceptance." Boys also attempt to develop other labels in addition to "gifted." Yet, despite their extracurricular activities, they rigidly maintain their academic placement.

COUNTERACTING SEX-ROLE STEREOTYPES

One of the best ways to counteract these traditional sex-role stereotypes is through education. Heightened awareness helps render traditional sex-role behaviors more obvious to children of both genders. Even a preschooler can begin to understand how girls' options have been limited by our enculturation.

- Talk to your children about what they like *and* dislike about being a girl or a boy. Listen particularly for your youngsters' expressions of double standards. Emphasize how these standards impinge on girls' potential options.
- Point out sex-role stereotypes when reading storybooks, nursery rhymes, and comic strips. You can say, "Look how Snow White has to wait for her Prince Charming to save her. If you were Snow White, what would you do to help yourself?"
- Have your children rewrite (or retell) favorite fairy tales to reflect nonsexist characters and situations. (For example, Snow White could become Prince Magenta—and the Seven Sprites—who is eventually saved from the clutches of the evil King Mortimer by Princess Flora.) This is also an enjoyable exercise in creativity.
- Point out to your school-age child underlying messages in newspaper articles, advertisements, and television programs that are strongly biased.
- Make sexist or nonsexist collages from ads and articles cut from magazines.
- Read biographies of women who have struggled against adversity

to become successful. Movies such as the recent French film *Camille Claudel* underscore how poorly gifted women have fared in a man's world.

Many of these suggestions are based on a 1987 pilot study investigating ways to counteract the disappearance of giftedness among girls that was carried out in Ontario, Canada, by Sylvia R. Olshen and Dona J. Matthews. The fourteen gifted girls between the ages of ten and eighteen involved in this specially constructed "Women's Studies" course initially seemed unaware of the natural consequences of the double standards that they accepted without question.

In the course of discovering the sex-role biases evident in their daily lives, however, the girls became increasingly attentive to their own incongruent choices. This awareness strengthened their self-esteem and their resolve that "girls should have the same degree of choice academically, vocationally, and socially as boys have." Your daughters will benefit from similar consciousness raising, as well.

THE LIMITATIONS OF SCHOOL PROGRAMS

In our rush to provide a rich environment for our gifted children, we often place great weight on our own influence as parents and on our child's academic program. For example, placing Cherie in a flexible, open-structure elementary school environment made us feel as if we had taken care of all of our daughter's needs as a gifted child. True, the program was great for her academic self but, as it turned out, it was actually damaging to her social self. As you can see, these two aspects of our rather complex children don't necessarily coincide.

Finding the right academic program is all well and good, but it's important not to ignore *internal contributions* to giftedness. We must ask ourselves: Who is this person? What is his inner life like? What are his sensibilities? Gifted children possess a depth of understanding, intensity, and sensitivity to the world that can lie largely untapped by academic programs and projects. It also may be the source of rejection among less gifted classmates. As Michael M. Piechowski, education professor at Northland College, aptly put it in an article on gifted children's remarkably impassioned psychic lives, "People with less fire in their veins look upon those who have it as different, abnormal, neurotic. They avoid having such people as friends because they can neither understand nor appreciate them.''

When we don't value and nurture our children's sensitivity, close attachments, perceptiveness, heightened feelings of responsibility, self-examination, and deep empathy for others, they may come to believe that these facets of their personalities are unimportant, or worse yet, worthy of repudiation. Indeed, they may begin seeing their intellectual power as their only value.

Schooling may enrich the outer manifestations of giftedness—the achievements and accomplishments—but it may not directly support, foster, and enrich a child's emotional world. This can be one of your greatest challenges as the parent of a gifted child, for the fulfillment of your child's social needs is as integral to his future success and happiness as the fulfillment of his intellectual needs. Research studies have linked positive self-esteem (which emanates from a feeling of belonging) with academic achievement, psychological adjustment, successful social relationships, self-confidence, self-expression, effort, and leadership.

If your child is feeling that he doesn't fit in, it's time to help him *do* something about it. It's also important to have a little faith. Remember that although your child may have difficulties socially, he also brings to these problems his own enormous intellectual resources for solving them. What he needs is your understanding, your love, and your willingness to listen and help.

CHAPTER 10

The Importance of Play

There was a child went forth everyday,
And the first object he look'd upon, that object he became . . .

—WALT WHITMAN

ALL CHILDREN ENGAGE IN DIFFERENT KINDS OF PLAY. AMONG THEM are:

- Sports and playground activities, bike riding, and skating
- Painting, modeling with clay, papier-mâché, and other crafts
- Messing around with water, snow, sand, or mud
- Make-believe using dolls, toy trucks, Mom's old clothes, Batman capes, and cardboard swords
- Playing house, school, or doctor
- Puzzles, mazes, crosswords, brainteasers, riddles, and word searches
- Board games, tag, and hide-and-seek
- Construction kits including blocks, erector sets, and models
- Science experiments with plants, electricity, microscopes, and chemistry sets
- Reading, creative writing (or dictating), and story time
- Music and dance performance, puppet shows, and theater

Play is great fun. Yet, for children, play has a more important function, as well. Each of these preceding types of play (and I'm sure you have experienced many more) helps to teach your gifted child about himself and the world he lives in through many points of entry: social interactions, physical engagement, intellectual questing, and creative experimentation.

During playtime, your youngster learns about the laws of nature, cooperation, and esthetics; he develops a sense of mastery and learns to deal with disappointment and failure as well as success, thereby testing the limits of his own capabilities and the virtues of persistence;

he works out his emotions and his family drama (often in symbolic form) within the safety of a make-believe world; he experiences the thrill of creativity; he witnesses the ebb and flow of our animate and inanimate environment. Perhaps most important, fueled by his own intense curiosity, during play your child feels excitement and wonder about the world around him.

It has been said that play is a child's *work*. It is for this reason that I cannot overemphasize the importance of allowing your gifted child time to simply play.

It's likely that your child spends hours playing with other children. I have discussed the ups and downs of social interactions in the previous chapter. In this chapter, however, you'll discover your role as your child's first and permanent ''playmate'' as well as the importance of his experiences as he plays alone.

YOUR ROLE AS "PLAYMATE"

It may seem odd to think of yourself as your child's first pal, but that, in effect, is what you are. When you talk, giggle, and play peek-a-boo with your infant; when you stack blocks so your toddler can knock them down; when you roll a ball or read or introduce her to the strategies of the chessboard, you are engaging in play activities with her.

As I explained in the previous chapter, early interactions with your child help to develop her sense of belonging and her feelings of self-esteem that are essential for her later success in life. In addition, your play is a vital form of intellectual, physical, and social stimulation. Your input arouses her curiosity, elicits her verbal communications, excites her sense of adventure and creativity. Without it, your child may not grow and thrive.

Play is also useful as a teaching tool. My mother spent many hours playing with me, and I recall devoting similar time to Cherie as she pored over puzzles. At first we did them together, but as her hand–eye coordination improved, she was able to complete them herself. Your involvement in more complex tasks such as helping to find proper specimens to examine under a microscope or serving as an audience for a spontaneous puppet show help teach principles of biology or dramaturgy while demonstrating to your child that you value her intellectual and creative endeavors.

Perhaps the greatest gift of becoming involved in your child's play is that you are afforded a window into her soul. Children are most relaxed and guileless when hard at play. They share of themselves and their own perceptions freely and openly. Your involvement increases the feelings of intimacy between you, for not only are you drawn into your gifted child's world but by your involvement you also reveal your own world to her. This fosters your mutual love, and the greater the love and support, the greater your child's self-esteem.

QUALITY TIME—IN QUANTITY

"Quality time" was all the rage several years ago. Many of us came to believe that we didn't have to spend that much time with our kids as long as the time was well spent. And while it's true that what's important is not just the minutes but the interaction that occurs during those minutes (for example, a half hour of dozing next to your son while he's watching "Sesame Street" does *not* constitute quality time), it is also true that the more time spent together the better. Even if your child is in a top-flight school, he still craves contact with you. Five minutes each evening can't substitute for an hour. *Large quantities of quality time are the best.*

Quality time means paying attention to the kinds of interactions you have with your gifted child. Are you simply filling the minutes with activities? Or, do the activities work toward building your child's inquisitiveness, his creativity, his verbal abilities? Beyond that, do they enhance the intimacy between the two of you? The following activities can provide opportunities for quality play interactions.

USE NATURE AS A "PLAYROOM"

As my husband and I explained in our book, *Kindergarten: It Isn't What It Used to Be,* young gifted children have a refreshing and innocent sense of wonder about the world. They experience their environment as a mystery just begging to unfold. To them, everything is new and exciting. Since they are fascinated about the world around them, nature activities seem to be an ideal vehicle for exciting their minds.

You can spend time together planting carrots, radishes, or marigold seeds, even if your garden is only a large cup with a hole punched in the bottom, placed in a pan of water in the sunlight on a windowsill. Talk to your child about the growth cycle and how seeds need sun, water, and nutrients from the soil in order to flourish. Have her water the seedlings and watch as they sprout into mature plants. Let her experience the wonder of eating her home-grown vegetables or witnessing the opening and eventual death of a flower. (We had great fun one year when we grew a pumpkin that became our Halloween jack-o'-lantern and ended up shortly thereafter on the table as a delicious fresh pumpkin pie!) Harvest seeds for the next "crop."

Ask plenty of open-ended questions such as "What do you think would happen if . . . ?" You might even set up a tiny science experiment, contrasting seeds that were watered compared to those that were not, or plants left in the sun compared to others placed in a closet. Even the youngest children can be involved in these simple activities.

You can help your preschooler build a "nest" for a caterpillar she has found on the sidewalk. Rather than shouting "Yuck!" and squashing the green furry critter under foot, have her line a small plastic container or jar with leaves and flower petals and sprinkle some water within. Add a sturdy twig. Cover the container with plastic wrap with several air holes poked in it and secure it with a rubber band. You may be lucky enough to find a cocoon hanging from the twig several days later. Eventually, a butterfly may emerge. Our kids were thrilled with the miraculous transformation that we had observed. We then talked about the necessity of setting the butterfly free.

I remember as a young child spending hours observing and experimenting with different insects on my own. I loved to watch the ants parade in and out of their hill carrying impossibly heavy burdens and was always curious to see what would happen if I disturbed the anthill in some way. I was fascinated by a spider in a creepy corner of our outdoor covered patio. I watched her spin threads around and then devour ill-fated flies that had been ensnared in her trap. I found earthworms the most interesting of all, since I believed that I could pull them apart and watch the two halves wiggle away in opposite directions.

While my fascination with death and destruction seems rather morbid now that I commit it to paper (given my early, intensive exposure to accounts of the Holocaust, however, this is not surprising), I also was satisfying my own insatiable curiosity about nature and how the world worked. No class could have provided this kind of experience for me.

As you engage in nature activities—or even if you are just taking a walk—ask plenty of questions that require your child to think such as

"Why do you suppose this lawn is so yellow and that one so green?" "That's a pet store. What kinds of animals do you think are in there? Do you think we'll find some dinosaurs? Why not? What would you do if we met a dinosaur on the street today?"

A trip to the beach (if you're lucky enough to live near a large body of water) fulfills many of your child's play and intellectual needs. You can engage in swimming and a game of beach ball as well as a discussion of the origin of waves and tides. I'm certain your gifted child will be fascinated by the fact that the moon is somehow involved. You can talk about geography and geology. Where does sand come from, anyway? How did those pebbles become so round and smooth? What's on the other side of the ocean? What other countries, cities, or states touch on this same ocean, lake, or river? These questions provide excellent opportunities for joint research "projects" later.

You can also build elaborate sand castles and fantasize kings and knights. Then you can watch as the waves erode your handiwork. This provides opportunities for creative play while demonstrating to your child the inexorable rhythms of nature. Our family spent hours examining the flora and fauna of the tide pools at the beach. Sand crabs, starfish, sand dollars, sea anemones, and seaweed (especially the kind that has air bubbles you can pop) make fascinating playthings.

Such activities and conversations help to increase your gifted child's vocabulary, enrich his thought processes, and spark his own curiosity about the world around him. When you merely hurry through your tasks, you both miss out on so much!

ENGAGE IN NONCOMPETITIVE PLAY

In noncompetitive play, there are no winners or losers—only people using their imaginations to have fun. Emphasize the effort that your child makes and not necessarily the result. You can reduce stress for all of you by dwelling on the importance of the "process" (how your child approaches a situation) of play rather than on the "goal" (who wins or loses or is this a perfect job?). Such an approach is particularly important for gifted children because they can get stuck in a goal-oriented mindset due to accelerated schooling and parent/teacher goals.

If you engage solely in results-oriented activities with your children, you may be well on your way toward encouraging perfectionism. In addition, you may be robbing yourselves of opportunities to enjoy nondemanding, unconditional closeness. Below are some examples of noncompetitive activities that you can enjoy with your gifted child.

CREATIVE STORY TIME

As my husband and I explained in *Finding Time for Fathering,* during reading time, many parents feel compelled to finish the story, no matter what. They may even ignore their youngsters' questions and push ahead, losing sight of valuable missed opportunities for elaboration. Keep in mind that the discussion of the pictures and the ideas expressed in the story may be more significant for the enhancement of your child's reasoning abilities, creativity, and ultimately your closeness than actually coming to the end of the tale. The following suggestions, adapted from *Finding Time for Fathering,* can help make reading together more enjoyable and fruitful:

> *Make story time a fun time.* Set aside ten to fifteen minutes daily for stories. If you're not home in the evening at bedtime, this can take place in the morning, as well. Just make sure you're not interrupted—this time is special. Cuddle up together. Put your arm around your child. Story time should be a special part of the day when you share warmth and love, and it need not be abandoned once your child learns how to read on his own.
>
> *Use sound effects and different voices.* Don't be afraid to dramatize the story and bring it to life. This even fosters your child's creativity—and it's fun, besides! Age-old fairy tales such as "Goldilocks and the Three Bears," "Little Red Ridinghood," and "The Three Little Pigs" provide great opportunities for this kind of creative reading.
>
> *Get your child involved in the story.* Sometimes we become so caught up in achievement, we forget that interactions are important, too. Rather than fixing your sights on reading the story, you may want to just meander through it. Have your child look at the pictures and make up his own tale to go with them. This motivates him and activates his imagination. Or, stop reading when you get to an exciting moment and ask your child to tell you what he thinks is going to happen next. It matters not at all if his ending coincides with the author's. In fact, the more outrageous it is, the better.
>
> You may not finish the book, but so what? Your goal here is to have fun and liberate your child's mind. This approach has the

additional benefit of helping your youngsters think on their own and make choices.

Read with your child rather than to her. Encourage questions and comments. Even if she interrupts, your child is connecting with the story. Ask her why she has asked particular questions. Her answers will clue you into her thought processes.

When you engage your children in these kinds of conversation during story time or play:

- You help them to express their ideas and their feelings.
- You increase their vocabulary and enrich their thought processes.
- They learn how to struggle through complex ideas.
- They give free rein to their own imagination.
- Your kids feel loved, listened to, and valued.

ALLOWING YOUR CHILD INTO YOUR WORLD THROUGH PLAY

Finding Time for Fathering also suggests ways to use play to teach your children about your own life, thus enhancing family intimacy. Think of these suggestions as jumping-off points for your own ideas. Remember, it's not necessarily the activities themselves but the way you go about them that is significant.

1. *Story telling:* Story telling is one of the easiest ways to play with your children since it requires no special equipment and can be accomplished virtually anywhere at any time. Choose any event in your personal life that you want to share and change the characters to *animals.* Young children love to hear stories about their little furry friends. Bugs seem to go over well, too. Kids can relate to these creatures and they're usually captivated.

    Depending on your children's ages, you can even use story telling to teach your children moral lessons much like Aesop or La Fontaine did. Preschoolers still don't have a strong sense of right or wrong. They learn from the consequences of what happens to them. But a story can be a teachable moment. For example, you can use a tale about a hurt elephant to tell your child how to handle a skinned knee or how to call 911 in an emergency.

    Children are natural story tellers. Encourage your child to make up fables and tales of his own. If he's too young to write down his own words, he can dictate them to you. The story need not be grammatically correct. Your overattention to the mechanics of his language may curb his creative impulses. Write what he says, mistakes and all!

At the age of three or four, Cherie had already "written" several books in this way. I wrote her sentences down—one per page—and she proceeded to illustrate her tales. This activity also encouraged her to read what she had "written." Later we stapled her "book" together and she proudly reread her story to me. (Make sure that you save and date these creations. They're most entertaining to look at ten or fifteen years later!)

In creating these impromptu tales, you will find that you have shared some parts of yourselves with also having great fun. Kids love tall tales, even if you're not the best at imaginative story telling. They love it even more if the story comes from you, for you are letting them into your life in a profound way. If the story is their own creation, so much the better.

2. *Clay:* Playing with clay gets you and your children involved in textures and smells. Clay figures provide a great means of exploring your child's fantasy world: Characters can be created, altered, and destroyed in an instant. Clay manipulation is also a positive way to work off excess energy, anger, and frustration. When you pound, poke, and squeeze, you can all let off some steam!

When you play with clay, try to get away from the compulsion to sculpt perfect forms. Rather, with your gifted child, create unusual imaginative shapes. You can start your play simply by smelling, poking, pounding, and making sounds with the clay. Roll little clay balls and flatten them into pancakes. Coil snakes or worms into baskets. Move into more whimsical play, creating fanciful beasts.

In fact, the making of objects can lead to imaginative games. If you've made a sea serpent, for example, you can say, "The serpent is looking for more serpents to make a serpent family. Can you make a momma serpent and baby serpents? What should we name them? And now the serpent family is hungry; they're looking for food. Let's make serpent food. What do serpents eat, anyway? How about their house? What kind of a house do you think our serpent family lives in under the sea? Let's make one."

A practical note: Clay has the tendency to become embedded in carpeting and upholstery. We usually found it safest to do our sculpting on hard surfaces (such as the kitchen table or floor) covered with newspaper. Weather permitting, you can also play with clay outside where you won't have to worry about stray clay crumbs being ground into the linoleum.

3. *Crayons:* Crayons are a natural tool for the imagination, but coloring books tend to limit the scope of fantasy play. Why not draw

together on blank paper and make up stories to go along with your pictures? Again, it is a marvelous way for you and your kids to communicate with one another in a meaningful way. You need not be an artist—far from it. Indeed, scribbling releases tension and can also lead to creativity.

After you've both scribbled to your hearts' content, examine the drawings and identify any common objects, animals, or toys that are lurking among the scribbles (in the same way that you would visualize animals in cloud formations). Take a contrasting crayon and highlight whatever object you can see: cars, wheels, letters. The fun part of this game is that you as well as your children become involved in inventive play. You are creating something out of nothing and that activity carries with it a marvelous sense of discovery.

The scribble game also provides a way for you to observe how your kids think. Scribbling is a wonderful projective test—like an ink blot. You can look at a mass of tangled lines and see an ice cream cone, while your son will see flames shooting skyward from a wrecked airplane. While neither point of view is right or wrong, such disparities form the basis of some great conversations. "Gee," you may say, "what made you think about that?" It may be that the news report about a recent plane disaster had more of an impact on your son than you had realized. And that would be important for both of you to talk about.

Sometimes it's fun to make up stories combining elements and objects you find in your drawing: a puppy, a car, the letter C, grandpa, or a chair. This is also a wonderful way of making a connection.

The *squiggle game* is a variation on the scribble game. In this case, you make a squiggle and ask your child to follow your lead. You may fill up whole pages together. Each time you make a squiggle, it resembles more and more some real object. Or, your child can make a squiggle and you can turn it into something. Then you can make a squiggle and have her come up with a drawing. Again, the idea is to create something out of nothing.

OTHER WAYS TO ENCOURAGE YOUR CHILD'S CREATIVITY DURING PLAY

Aside from their purely enjoyable aspects, fantasy and creativity may have important consequences for your child's personality development as well. According to Jerome Singer, a psychologist at Yale University who has made a career of studying the importance of mental imagery, fantasy may form the foundation for serenity and purpose in our lives. In a *Psychology Today* article, he points out that children whose games lack fantasy have trouble remembering facts and integrating events. They may grow into adults who have impoverished inner lives and thus become aggressive, antisocial, or delinquent.

In a more positive vein, in his book *Education and the Creative Potential,* Dr. E. Paul Torrance explains that children learn more efficiently, become more successful in their careers, and eventually may help to solve society's ills when they learn how to use their creative abilities. Creative children become forward-thinking adults who are capable of coming up with new solutions to age-old problems.

Dr. Torrance outlines ways in which educators can give children a chance to learn and think creatively. I've adapted the most relevant of these for your use as a parent:

1. *Allow your children to encounter their toys on their own terms.* You may feel proud to have bought three-year-old Roger his first football and you may be eager to get to the park with him to show him how to toss that old pigskin around. Roger, on the other hand, may be fascinated by this strange ball that doesn't seem to behave like anything he has ever experienced before. He may want to throw, and spin and roll it in ways that a college coach would find blasphemous. He may even try to dig with it, sit on it, or smell and taste it! If you interrupt this multisensory exploration by attempting to give Roger formal instruction, he may rebel and refuse to play altogether.

   Children need time to explore playthings creatively and on their own terms. An authoritarian point of view ("No, hold the ball like this") can stifle your gifted child's learning process. Give him free rein to explore. After he has fully discovered what the toy can do, he'll be ready for a bit of instruction.

2. *Be careful not to interrupt your children's thinking time.* As responsible parents, we often give in to our natural urges to correct our children or advise them about the suitable approach to a play problem rather than letting them struggle to work out the problem for themselves. However, we subtly or overtly interfere with their creative learning experience when we impose our own point of view or help solve the problem for them.

   Dr. Torrance gives the example of a father who stopped himself as he was about to show his eighteen-month-old the proper way to stack blocks—big ones on the bottom, small ones on the top. Imagine how much more this little boy learned about the laws of gravity and the principles of construction when by his own process of trial and error he came to that conclusion himself.

3. *Provide opportunities for close personal observation.* Children are not happy observing from afar. They like to get right into things in order to satisfy their abundant curiosity. This is doubly true for gifted children. Microscopes, magnifying glasses, telescopes, front-row seats, and permission for hands-on manipulation provide outlets for your child's natural inclination to get up close. (Children's museums are great resources for this kind of play.)

Unfortunately, the need to investigate can sometimes spell trouble—I recall my own misadventures in radio reconstruction, described in chapter 8. Within the limits of safety, however, it would be best for you to perceive these sometimes destructive explorations as an outgrowth of your child's intense curiosity about the workings of the world rather than as mischievousness or purposeful misbehavior.

4. *Provide materials for exploration.* There is no limit to the number of toys that we can purchase for our children. There is, however, a limit to the budget. Having started our family at a relatively young age, we operated more in the mode of "starving students" than salaried providers. When it came to toys, often we improvised. Cherie spent untold hours, for instance, playing with an oatmeal box. She used it as a drum and a roller; as a container for other toys and as a stool.

The large box that contained your new washing machine can set the stage for hours of creative play. Together you can paint and decorate it to resemble a play house, rocketship, market, classroom, or car. The possibilities are limitless. Other great household items: nesting plastic storage containers, balls of yarn, tissue and wrapping paper, empty tissue and shoe boxes, toilet paper and paper towel spools, cotton balls, old clothes, different shapes of dried pasta and peas and beans (with which to make mosaics), cardboard, old magazines, magnets, magnifying glasses, leaves, stones, flowers, scissors, glue, and paper. Once Cherie and her friend Sara even made a collage from junk they collected on the way to and from school, which they proudly presented to their principal.

We found that toys whose functions was limited by their

highly specific nature often fell by the wayside, while those that could be used in many different ways enjoyed a long life. At Aimee's birth, for example, we bought for Cherie a doll that not only drank "milk" and "wet" her diaper but also ate "real food" and relieved herself at the other end. Although it seemed like a good idea at the time, Cherie played with this toy for about a month—just long enough for the novelty to wear off—while she continued to enjoy her good old brown Teddy with the shredded nose for years. Today's computer-driven toys that seem to play themselves also lose their cachet after a brief time.

Toys that go on forever are the ones that allow your child to project herself into them, taking on a different meaning each time she picks them up. From my experience, toys worth buying include books, magnetic alphabet letters, Legos, Tinker Toys, erector sets, doll houses (these can also include a play school, airport, and castle), crayons, water colors, finger paints, clay or modeling dough, sticky putty, the old-fashioned, noncomputerized, hand-operated trucks, airplanes, horses, boats, dolls, bikes, checkers/chess sets, and play kitchens.

5. *Encourage free expression.* I believe that it's important for you to let your children get good and messy when they play. Let them roll around in the mud so that they truly experience what mud means. (I've hosed my kids down many a time before I allowed them into the house!) Let your child choose her own wardrobe for school—so what if her socks don't match and her striped shirt clashes with her polka dot skirt. She is expressing her own autonomy.

Give your gifted child plenty of opportunities to brainstorm. Ask her open-ended questions such as "How many ways can you think of to use this empty tin can (or other common household object)?" She may reply, "A drinking or measuring cup, a wheel for a skateboard, a telephone, a home for a family of worms, tied on to my feet as high-heeled shoes, a bucket for sand, a toilet paper roll, a flower pot, a rolling pin for clay, a pendant, a dinner bell, a front door gong," and so on. The more outlandish, the better. Be careful not to limit her creative expression by posing your belief that a suggestion may be impractical. This is play, after all.

Be sure to reward your youngsters' imaginative ideas with praise and excitement while you withhold critical comments and judgment that inhibit experimentation. Finally, to encourage creativity, give *yourself* permission to be creative—*you* are your child's best model.

PLAYING ALONE AND THE VIRTUES OF BOREDOM

Have you ever been assailed by your child's whiny complaints: "I'm bored." "There's nothing to do!" "There's no one to play with." Often, we parents see this as a call to action. We may think, "Oh my god, Felicia is unstimulated. We must create some activity for her." Depending on my level of patience or the amount of work I had, however, often I would *not* respond in this way. Instead, I rather bluntly replied, "Go find something for yourself. It's not my job to keep you entertained."

This response may sound harsh or even uncaring, but my withdrawal was not out of disinterest or laziness. Instead, by taking a back seat when my children expressed boredom, I felt that I pushed them into taking responsibility for creating activities that *they* considered enjoyable. They became resourceful in making their own fun and they learned how to think for themselves.

I fondly recall, for instance, the hours Aimee spent constructing a "tent" city in the backyard. She hauled together two or three patio chairs as the supports for the tent. She threw an old beach blanket over these. Then, she dragged in chaise lounge pads for the floor and decorated the exterior with camellia petals she had plucked from the surrounding shrubs.

Finally, ensconced in her new "home," Aimee cooked up pies made of mud, berries from the privet hedges, and fallen leaves and blades of grass. These she would "serve" to us and to our poor dog, Kasha, who both relished and resisted all the attention being lavished upon her. From time to time, Aimee even brought her "blankie" outside and fell asleep in the cozy home she had built for herself in the yard.

No organized class in the world—no gymnastics, swimming, violin, ballet, or crafts and certainly no suggestion of mine—could command Aimee's attention to the degree that this spontaneous endeavor did. She continued to play this game in one form or another for many years. It increased her sense of creativity while it offered her an opportunity to construct a safe haven away from home.

I believe that such unstructured play is essential for gifted children. Too often we overschedule them into the many before- and after-school classes that we consider critical for their appropriate stimulation. Classes and parent-structured activities do have their place, but kids, like adults, also need the opportunity for downtime. They need time to simply think their own thoughts and come up with their own ideas about the world; they need time to pursue one or two favorite interests intensely to the exclusion of all others. When they are bored, and when their minds are freed of the demands of external activities, they have the opportunity to let their ideas flow.

In *Education and the Creative Potential,* Dr. E. Paul Torrance reminds us that "We are so accustomed to believing that the good child is a busy child, an industrious child, that we suspect he is up to some mischief if he is not visibly engaged in some approved activity." Dr. Torrance also points out that the poet Robert Frost was suspended from school because he was "daydreaming." I see no harm in allowing your child to stare off into space from time to time. I often find myself looking out the window or at a blank wall as I turn over an idea in my mind, and I'm sure you do the same.

WORD GAMES, MIND TEASERS, AND LOGIC PUZZLES

According to Dr. Torrance, one of the best ways to encourage a child to think creatively is to give him problems that he is capable of solving but of sufficient complexity to provide a real challenge. Fortunately, today, many resources exist to help your child exercise her mental muscles, all in the guise of play. Gifted children thoroughly enjoy these mind-teasing activities—I know mine did—and often they become engaged in these games when playmates are unavailable.

In an interview, Merrie Wartik, who teaches fifth and sixth grade gifted math at the Wonderland Avenue School's Gifted Magnet Program in Los Angeles, suggested a myriad of books with math-oriented puzzles and games to stimulate your child's thinking. She highly recommends the following resources (you'll fine full references in the Appendix):

- *Marcy Cook Math* series are recommended for grades three or four through eight, but depending on your child's interests and abilities, you may begin using these books earlier:
  Math Starters and Stumpers
  Think in Colors

Domino Dilemmas
Scavenger Hunt
Create a Number
Fraction Thinkers
Codecracker

- *Family Math* (University of California Press) has many activities that your child can engage in around the house.
- *Games Magazine* is chock full of riddles and puzzles.
- *Dynamath* (Scholastic Magazines) provides math play enrichment.

Other teachers of gifted children have recommended the following resources to me because they help stimulate creativity and intellectual thought. Gifted students just love these activities:

- *Good Apple* series of activity books (especially those by Bob Stanish):
  The Ambidextrous Mind Book (grades two through eight). Whole brain fun that combines learning with creative thinking and inventiveness.
  Mindglow (grades three through twelve). Creative activities built around Guilford's Model of Intelligence and E. Paul Torrance's theories on creativity (see chapter 2).
  I Believe in Unicorns (grades three through eight plus). Encourages fantasy play and creativity.
  Inventioneering (grades three through nine). Shows children how to create inventions.
  Calliope by Greta Barclay Lipson (grades four through eight). Helps children write their own poetry.
- *Good Apple* also publishes *Challenge,* a magazine that caters to parents and teachers of gifted children.
- *The I Hate Math Book* and *The Book of Think,* both by Marilyn Burns.
- *Puzzlegrams* By Pentagram (these include puzzles such as rearranging toothpicks to create new patterns).
- *Dell Book of Logic Problems* (this is a series) compiled by the editors of *Dell Puzzle Magazine.*
- *Dell Book of Cryptograms* (this is a series).
- *Dell Big Book of Crosswords & Pencil Puzzles* (this is a series of books that contain mazes, word games, logic puzzles, cryptograms, and other brain teasers) compiled by the editors of *Dell Puzzle Magazine.*

- *The Anti-Coloring Book of Masterpieces* (rather than coloring in the drawing, this book asks children to draw what they dream about).
- Books on the Japanese art of paper folding or origami.
- *Droodles* by Roger Price.
- *101 Amusing Ways to Develop Your Child's Thinking Skills and Creativity* by Sarina Simon (recommended for preschool to third grade).

When Cherie was in junior high school, her English teacher, Judy Selsor, gave her students weekly practice with word puzzles that come from the *Mind Benders* book by Anita Harnadek published by Midwest Publications. Cherie used to spend hours trying to figure out these increasingly complex logic puzzles and learned how to create and use a special grid to help problem-solve. Midwest Publications also puts out:

- *Figural Mind Benders* by Richard Bronniche.
- *Thinking About Time* by Randy Wiseman.
- *Connector Vectors: Creative Thinking Puzzles* by John H. Doolittle.
- *Think-a-Grams* by Evelyne M. Graham.
- *Math O'Graphs* by Donna Kay Buck and Francis Hildebrand.
- *Crossnumber Puzzles* by Anita Harnadek.
- *Challenging Codes: Riddles & Jokes* by Karen E. Morrell.

They also market a host of other books and computer software that encourage critical and creative thinking skills while they entertain.

Elementary school teacher Merrie Wartik also recommends extending the puzzles. She often encourages her students to create their own logic puzzles based on the games they play in class. She finds that these can be even more perplexing than the ones provided in the resource books.

Gifted children also love wordplay. Books such as *What's in a Word* by Rosalie Moscovitch and *Puns, Gags, Quips, and Riddles* by Roy Doty, and for older children *Vicious Circles and Infinity: An Anthology of Paradoxes* by Patrick Hughes and George Brecht, give kids new ways to look at words and ideas. Rich Hall's *Sniglets* encourages children to create their own fanciful language. If you can get your hands on some back issues of now out-of-print *Gifted Children Monthly* (or *Newsletter,* as it was once called), you'll find a section in the middle consisting of games and puzzles that will be right up your child's alley.

A marvelous new book by Susan K. Perry, *Playing Smart: A Parent's Guide to Enriching, Offbeat Learning Activities for Ages Four to Fourteen* is a compendium of new and useful play ideas for your gifted child. Ms. Perry is a true divergent thinker: She comes up with dozens of stimulating play suggestions, from creative use of photography to visits to a cemetery to games for distraction and fun during a long wait at the doctor's office. Among her suggestions for word and idea play are:

- Make up a Haiku poem (a Japanese verse form of three unrhymed lines that add up to seventeen syllables, arranged 5–7–5). For example:
  "Green-leafed plant in the
  still air of the waiting room,
  when is it my turn?"
- Show your child how to think up paradoxes such as "This sentence is false." or "This sentence contains exactly threee errors."
- Encourage your child to create a list of oxymorons—short paradoxical expressions such as a "loud whisper" or a "sad smile."
- Give your child a book of the drawings of the Dutch artist M. C. Escher.

Ms. Perry also suggests an excellent list of children's books written by famous authors as diverse and unlikely as Donald Barthelme, Truman Capote, William F. Buckley, e. e. cummings, Umberto Eco, Ian Fleming, Sylvia Plath, Gertrude Stein, Leo Tolstoy, and James Joyce. Perhaps the most intense kind of individual play is reading for pleasure.

THE CREATION OF AN INNER COSMOLOGY

Once finding an author she enjoyed, Cherie was in the habit of seeking out every other work that the author had ever written. Consequently, as a child she read whole series of books such as the *Black Stallion* cycle, *Little House on the Prairie* books, C. S. Lewis's trilogy, Madeleine L'Engle's tales of fantasy, and as she grew older, all of Tolkien, all of Judy Blume and Paul Zindel, all of Anne McCaffrey's dragon books, and as many of Agatha Christie's mysteries as she could lay her hands on. These series she wouldn't just peruse, but rather would seem to devour them whole. She read and then reread each book in sequence many times over, deriving great pleasure from the familiarity of the story and language.

During her childhood, each cycle of books influenced Cherie's play patterns. When she focused on the *Black Stallion,* for example, her imaginary play involved toy horses, which she asked us to buy for her in abundance. She alluded to equine lore in her everyday speech and began to understand the world from the point of view of the author.

I found this process fascinating to watch, yet I have not seen it written about in professional journals. Out of curiosity, I asked many of my friends who also parent gifted and highly gifted children if they experienced a similar phenomenon with their kids. All confirm that at least one of their children became totally absorbed in certain books the way that my daughter had. (I imagine that this activity may not be germane to gifted children, alone.)

I queried my friends about what they thought their children derived from this intense involvement. Some suggested that it was the familiarity of the characters and text that helped make their children feel soothed and secure. This certainly makes sense, as I remember Cherie always hauling out her favorite book series when she was home, recuperating from the flu. Often she would happily tuck herself in bed, engrossed in reading three or four volumes a day.

I suspect that another force was also operating in this interest in repeated reading. For with each group of stories, Cherie absorbed a whole world view that began to furnish her psyche with metaphors, images, and points of reference. Indeed, as she matured, Cherie's interest in science fantasy prevailed. Often these tomes spoke to her of the relativity of time and space, the secrets of life and death, the heights and depths of good and evil. In discussing her perceptions of existence, she eagerly quoted to us from her favorite authors and suggested that we read them along with her so that we could share her enthusiasm and her point of view.

Now that I think about it, I realize that Cherie's pleasure in reading was not so much an escape or a security blanket as it was an aid in the formation of what I like to call her inner cosmology—her sense of the order of the universe. Reading became for Cherie an entirely satisfying psychological, spiritual, and intellectual pursuit. When she was engaged in acting out the stories with her friend, Sara, reading took on social and physical benefits, as well. For Cherie, there was no more gratifying way to play.

CHAPTER 11

Siblings: Giftedness Is a Tough Act to Follow . . . Or Precede

If I am not for myself, who will be for me?
But if I am only for myself, what am I?

—RABBI HILLEL, *THE SAYINGS OF THE FATHERS*, 1:14

OUR FAMILY RECEIVED ITS SHARE OF SIBLING DISCORD. AS I MENtioned in chapter 7, Cherie did not take kindly to the arrival of her sister. Despite her attempts to impress us with great displays of affection whenever possible—there were the obligatory hugs (a little too tight) and kisses (a little too hard)—Cherie made a habit of cutting Aimee off in mid-sentence, belittling her, and swatting her away, as if she were an insignificant and annoying fly. And as a toddler, Aimee so wanted to play with and be loved by her older sister that she ignored the attacks and kept coming back for more, much like those weighted, round-bottomed dolls that instantly bounce back after you've knocked them over.

It hurt my heart to watch all of this. Like all parents, I wanted my children to love one another as much as I loved them individually. As irritating as Cherie and Aimee's fights were to me, I recognized that underlying it all, both children were in pain. Cherie felt displaced, while Aimee felt put down. In addition, I realized that my kids' bickering brought back painful memories of my own battles with my older sister.

I couldn't sit by and simply let nature take its course so I intervened whenever I had an inkling that Cherie was unleashing a barb against her sister. Sometimes I helped the children find a way to play peaceably together by inviting them to play side-by-side. If we were lucky, they launched into a cooperative game. Sometimes, if the hostility was too great, or joint play was inappropriate (after all, Cherie was entitled to her own time with her friends and special toys, as was

Aimee), I separated them. Unfortunately, I could not mediate all of their battles—some took place without my awareness.

Finally, when Aimee was about four, she realized that Cherie would never play with her in the way that she wanted. Growing angry at her older sister, Aimee withdrew from her and concentrated on other playmates who responded to her with more kindness and pleasure.

Although my daughters are friends today and have been since their preteen years, as is the case among many warring siblings, I believe that those early years of ridicule took their toll on both children. Aimee's self-esteem certainly suffered since it was Cherie's unconscious goal to annihilate her. And I do believe that Cherie also suffered, for she carries with her a certain measure of guilt for having harbored such negative feelings toward her sister whom she truly cares about.

SIBLING RIVALRY IS NATURAL

"Mother always loved you best." The Smothers Brothers made an institution of this age-old sibling complaint. Painful as it may be to you as a parent, sibling rivalry is one of the most natural and enduring emotions that your children will experience. We can trace our recognition of these powerful feelings of jealousy, competitiveness, and rage back to Cain and Abel.

Sibling rivalry often is shaped by the ages, birth order, and sex of our children. Youngsters close in age tend to be more rivalrous than those further apart. Two siblings who were born one after the other, as my sister and I were (only fourteen months separate our births), and who are of the same gender tend to struggle with even greater competitiveness. In contrast, sibling rivalry was a moot point for my husband: His brother is nearly ten years older than he.

Most of us would feel terribly displaced if we experienced ourselves being supplanted in the hearts of our most cherished loved ones by a young interloper. Authors and parenting educators Adele Faber and Elaine Mazlish give an excellent demonstration of how this works in their book *Siblings Without Rivalry:*

> Imagine that your spouse puts an arm around you and says, "Honey, I love you so much, and you're so wonderful that I've decided to have another wife just like you. . . . When the new wife finally arrives, you see that she is very young and kind of cute. When the three of you are

out together, people say hello to you politely, but exclaim ecstatically over the newcomer. . . . The new wife needs clothing. Your husband goes into your closet, takes some of your sweaters and pants, and gives them to her. . . . One day you find your husband and the new wife lying on the bed together. He's tickling her and she's giggling.

It's important to recognize that jealousy is a normal part of family dynamics. Gifted or not, *your children are bound to feel jealous of one another.* Jealousy is a normal human emotion that all siblings need to express rather than suppress. In a *New York Times* interview conducted by Lawrence Kutner, Dr. Wyndol Furman, a professor of psychology at Denver University, explains that the amount of conflict between children is not related to the affection they feel for one another. Dr. Furman does not consider name-calling worrisome, for example, but does comment that he would feel more concerned "if the children were very aggressive toward other kids outside the family, as well."

SIBLING FIGHTS HAVE SOME HIDDEN BENEFITS

Psychologists now believe that periods of animosity among siblings (as long as no physical or long-term emotional abuse is going on) can have a beneficial effect on social development later on. *New York Times* columnist Lawrence Kutner explains that a child may take more risks in being aggressive with her siblings because they are not as likely to reject her as friends would. Kutner quotes Dr. Frances Fuchs Schachter of Metropolitan Hospital in Manhattan, who points out that "These fights are a way for children to learn and practice conflict resolution skills they'll need when they grow older."

There are other hidden benefits to sibling fights, as well. Kutner explains that family squabbles help children to differentiate themselves from one another. That's why fighting can be most heated when it occurs between siblings of the same gender who are close in age. Sibling spats also provide an arena in which children can safely vent displaced frustration and anger that they feel toward their parents. Finally, fighting may be a way for children to try to determine who is the favored child in the family. According to Dr. Furman's research, children who feel their parents treat them unfairly are more likely to fight. Unfortunately, understanding the benefits of sibling rivalry doesn't lessen the toll it takes on your kids or on you.

GIFTEDNESS AND SIBLING TENSIONS

In all families, intense competition can exist among siblings not only for the glory of achievement (who won the piano competition, who has the best earned-run average, who finished dinner first) but for the anointing of your recognition.

A child's giftedness may influence how the rivalry is expressed. Whereas a less verbally adept youngster might vent his frustration and anger by shoving his siblings away, a gifted child could train her prodigious verbal sights on her siblings: A razor-sharp mind coupled with a razor-sharp tongue can reduce a sister to a pulp in no time, flat. Of course, a gifted child is not above punctuating her tirade with pinches, kicks, bites, and shoves, too.

Unfortunately, a parental attitude that emphasizes achievement above all else may exacerbate this jockeying for praise and attention and the inevitable tattling when a sibling falls short of the mark (see chapter 8 on perfectionism). As Dr. James Alvino and the editors of *Gifted Children Monthly* explain in their book, *Parents' Guide to Raising a Gifted Toddler,* sibling rivalry occurs in most families where education and success are valued. "Perhaps as parents with well-intentioned, high expectations for our children," they point out, "we tend to reward most lavishly the accomplishments of whoever does 'the best'."

On the other hand, some children deal with the issue of competition by sidestepping it altogether. If Johnny cuts a wide swath as he makes his way through school (as first-born children often do), Janey and Billy—gifted though they may be—can feel hard pressed to follow in their big brother's footsteps. Johnny is a math ace so Janey won't even try to vie in that arena; she makes her mark in composition and reading. And Billy, who finds the range of possible areas of expertise already severely limited by his older siblings' dominance, chooses to excel in basketball, computer games, and skateboarding. I'll talk more about this "second child syndrome" below.

Sometimes parents encourage this "specialization" process as a way of averting undue competition among siblings and bolstering individual egos. Unfortunately, it can backfire. In my family, for instance, my older sister was labeled the "creative one"—she did well in music and art—while our parents saw me as the "smart one" because I excelled in school. It has taken us decades to undo these labels and to risk crossing over into each other's "territory." None-theless, we have managed to cross the lines so well that today she is completing a Ph.D. in psychology while I have become a "creative" writer.

Bear in mind also that even if siblings have identical IQ scores, they are individuals with different personalities, interests, and abilities; IQ tests define only a narrow array of characteristics (see chapter 5). These skills represent only a small part of what's important in life. Yet, teachers can hold rigid—even overwhelming—expectations for gifted younger siblings. Little Billy may feel that he is always the subject of comparisons and that he is not appreciated for his own talents. He may simply stop trying for fear of never living up to his big brother's reputation, or he may rebel out of a sense of injustice. These perceptions are bound to create anger and resentment.

HOW BIRTH ORDER CAN AFFECT IDENTIFICATION

Psychologist Dr. Linda K. Silverman, the director of the Gifted Child Testing Service in Denver, Colorado, has found that many parents are reluctant to have a child identified as gifted for fear of what such a designation might do to the other children in the family. Their fears may be unfounded. In an article on parenting young gifted children, Dr. Silverman explains that of fifty sets of siblings tested at her institute, two thirds scored within ten IQ points of each other. "It would follow that a gifted child who is viewed as 'nongifted' would resent a brother or sister who is recognized and labeled as gifted."

In fact, in the eight sets of siblings that contained one gifted and one nongifted child, one of three circumstances intervened: One of the children was under three (and too immature to understand what was required of him) or over nine (when scores of most gifted children are considerably lower due to the difficulty of the questions) when tested; different IQ tests were used; or one of the children had a history of chronic ear infections that could interfere with language development and rote learning skills.

According to Dr. Silverman, many parents are unaware that giftedness runs in families, and therefore may not look for signs of giftedness in brothers and sisters of the labeled child. Traditionally, psychologists have come to believe that giftedness most often visits the first-born. In fact, of the first forty gifted children who came to Dr. Silverman's testing service, 70 percent were first-born. But then a few of the parents brought in younger siblings for testing. To everyone's surprise, these children's scores were almost identical to their older brother's and sister's.

"The parents were puzzled," Dr. Silverman writes, "because their second children were 'so different' from the first-borns that they didn't seem gifted at all." By the time 500 children were tested, Dr. Silverman realized that this similarity in IQ was the norm. "Most parents would have brought in only the eldest child for identification," she explains, "if we had not informed them of our observations that giftedness tends to run in families."

Dr. Silverman believes that a "second child syndrome" makes giftedness hard to recognize in younger siblings. It is characterized by the younger child wanting to do just the opposite of the eldest, as a way to differentiate himself and establish his own separate identity. "If the first child is a high achiever in school, the second child doesn't seem to care much about school. If the eldest is intense, the second is easy-going. If the first-born has no friends, the second-born is everyone's buddy. If the first child is a clutz, the second child is an athlete." These opposing character traits certainly held true in our family.

Dr. Silverman cautions, however, that teachers and parents are more likely to look for the classic signs of giftedness in the "unencumbered behavior" of eldest children. These signs may be less evident in the second-born who may be "desperately" hiding his giftedness in order to be different from his sibling. These second children "might be coaxed out of hiding to demonstrate their capabilities" if we anticipate that they may also be gifted.

RIVALRY WHEN SIBLINGS ARE NOT EQUALLY GIFTED

Highly gifted children are as different from moderately gifted as the latter are different from more typical children. These variations can further complicate comparisons and competition among the children in your family.

In the rare household (such as mine and my parents') in which only some of the children have been found to be gifted, the labeled child might feel burdened by his parents' expectation that he continually perform at the top of the class. This can create resentment if his unlabeled sibling is given permission to be flaky and flighty. "How come Steven can go out and play when I have to stay home and study?

It's not fair!'' Or, the gifted child may be allowed to be absentminded and creative, while his nongifted sibling must fill in for him and hit the books.

The unlabeled child may also envy his gifted sibling's facility with school work. The gifted child seems to get the answer so quickly whereas his sibling may work twice as hard for a poorer grade. He may hold the accurate perception that his talented sibling receives more parental and societal attention, an exalted position in the family, and an unequal share of the family's resources.

In fact, research has shown that when one child has been labeled gifted in a family, the unlabeled sibling can suffer at least a short-term loss of self-esteem. One study by Dr. D. G. Cornell reported in the *American Journal of Orthopsychiatry* in 1983 found that the label of giftedness itself elevates that child's status in the family. Dr. Cornell discovered that shortly after the gifted child was labeled, his siblings were less well adjusted socially and emotionally. The siblings felt less valued and had lower self-esteem as a result of constant negative comparisons and a relative lack of recognition from parents and the community. It's not surprising that Dr. Cornell found a good deal of sibling rivalry in these families.

At McGill University in Montreal, Canada, Dr. Marcella Evan Grenier followed up Dr. Cornell's research by studying the short-term effects of competition on gifted children and their unlabeled siblings. Her study, published in the *Gifted Child Quarterly* in 1985, showed that competition seemed beneficial for the self-concept of the gifted child but was detrimental to the unlabeled sibling.

In more recent studies, however, Dr. Nicholas Colangelo, professor of counselor education at the University of Iowa, and Penny Brower, a doctoral student at the same institution, found that after five years had elapsed, an unlabeled child "comes to terms" with his sibling's giftedness and doesn't seem to harbor negative feelings or recollections. It seems that the unlabeled sibling experiences negative effects that dissipate with time.

Interestingly, the twenty-eight nongifted siblings in this study scored higher on personal adjustment and "endurance" scales (these indicate a positive attitude toward life and a readiness to adapt) than did their gifted brothers and sisters. Perhaps because of their position in the family, these children needed to develop superior coping skills. One surprising discovery was that the gifted youngsters (now twenty-year-old college students) imagined that their siblings were more ill-at-ease with their placement in gifted classes than the siblings actually were.

In families in which the gifted (or highly gifted) child is the younger of two same-gender siblings who are relatively close in age, tensions can be exacerbated. There's no way out of it—it's hard on an older child when her baby sister outdoes her performance in school.

A case in point: Acquaintances of mine have two children. Paul is a happy-go-lucky youngster of nine who is content to play baseball and skim the surface of his schooling. His eight-year-old sister, Gina, on the other hand, has been identified as gifted. She has won schoolwide spelling bees and has competed on behalf of her school in district-sponsored math contests. Although Gina is in the third grade, she has completed all of the fourth-grade curriculum. In the coming school year, she will be placed in a fifth-grade room with her brother. Unfortunately, this school district offers few other options for gifted education.

Although I am happy for Gina's progress, I can't help thinking that her placement in the same grade with her brother will create tensions between them and potential problems for his self-esteem. I know that when I accelerated to the same grade as my sister, she very naturally felt threatened by my presence. Acceleration of the gifted sibling would be easier for both siblings if the children were more than a year apart in age. In the case of this family, Paul may never get away from the constant reminder that he may not do as well in school as his sister.

Finally, a gifted child may, paradoxically, feel jealous of a handicapped sibling. A severely learning disabled child, for example, could receive more (if negative) attention, more academic help at home, and more nurturing. In this case, parents need to be careful of not trying so hard to make the nongifted child feel okay about herself that they assume the gifted child will be rewarded by his academic and creative awards, alone.

If ignored, the gifted child may engage in negative attention-getting behavior such as fighting or biting. It would be best to equitably look after the needs of all of the children in the family.

PARENTS DO PLAY FAVORITES

Whether you're comfortable admitting it or not, research has shown that most parents do favor one child over another. We often identify with the child that most resembles us in personality—the old "chip off the old block" syndrome. A highly energetic dad who was a college athlete, for instance, may feel a greater kinship to his varsity softball daughter than to his reserved, scientifically inclined, book-toting son. The opposite is also true: A dignified parent may feel closer to a child who is quietly learning how to read than to a rambunctious teenager.

Interestingly, it's not the person that parents favor or dislike, necessarily, but rather it is the child's behavior. In a second article in the *New York Times* on the topic of sibling rivalry, Lawrence Kutner explains that parents who have the most problems admitting to or recognizing their own favoritism (and feel the greatest guilt and shame about it) are those who "have difficulty distinguishing between who their children are and how their children behave." To avoid unconsciously expressing favoritism, it helps to be mindful of your own natural inclination to feel more comfortable with one child's behavior over another's.

In some cases, as within our household, the allegiances seemed to be split. Cherie and I are much more alike in our intellectual approach to problems but Aimee and I are closer in personality—we are both relatively easy-going. On the other hand, Aimee and my husband are both intuitive, divergent thinkers but Cherie and he are closer in their personality style—they are both more emotionally volatile. This symmetry, however, does not always make for harmony. Often, we parents are quick to criticize personality traits in our children that we dislike in ourselves. And if there has been a divorce, we can become enraged when we find our ex-spouse's traits somehow reborn in our kids.

Whether or not you feel drawn to one child over another at any given moment, it is imperative that you not show your favoritism by treating your children unfairly. Such an inequitable approach on your part can have destructive consequences for the whole family. It's better to appreciate each child for his unique gifts. This may not mean that everybody is treated *identically,* but that the *amount* of attention is equal and it's provided differently to each child based on his needs and personality.

Expressed favoritism severely undermines the "unfavored" child's self-esteem. He may feel that he can never live up to your expectations. In addition, the "favored" child will live with the burden of guilt—he has your admiration, but it's at the expense of his brother's happiness. Finally, your response is sure to set off more intense rivalry and resentments as both children vie for your attention and recognition.

To become aware of possible expressed favoritism, examine your family dynamics closely. The following suggestions will help you to do that while you also resolve conflicts among your children.

RELIVING THE PAST

It's important to bear in mind how your own experience growing up in your parents' household can color your reactions to your children today. Over the years, I have come to realize that I relive with my children every step of my own development. When they were infants, they rekindled my own feelings of helplessness; as preschoolers, their struggles brought up specters of my own attempts to master the world around me; during adolescence, I rocked and rolled with their hormonal swings coupled with my own recollections of hurts endured and loves lost.

Our emotional responses to these memories often imprint the way that we parent our children. The influence of your own childhood on your current child-rearing practices is vast and multifaceted. In general, your own experiences can prompt how much and in what way you empathize with your children, your feelings concerning competition and achievement, and the methods you use to break up family squabbles.

To discover your own patterns, you might begin by asking yourself the following questions. These are based, in part, on a family relations checklist my husband and I devised for our book *Disciplining Your Preschooler and Feeling Good About It:*

1. Were you the eldest, middle, or youngest in birth order?
2. Were you the only child of your gender in the family? How close in age were you to your nearest sibling(s)?
3. Did your position in the family empower you relative to your older and/or younger siblings? (Were you more powerful than they toward your parents, or more powerful within the sibling relationship?) Did you take the role of bully or victim, achiever or underachiever, caretaker or risk-taker? Did any of your siblings take these roles?
4. Is there a similarity in power structure between your children or between them and *you* as parents? If so, how? (For example, if you were too often a caretaker as a child, do you now resent the helplessness of your kids?)
5. Were you or any of your siblings identified as gifted?
6. How did your parents react to that news?
7. How did the other siblings treat the gifted child(ren)?
8. If no such identification occurred, was it clear to the family that one of the children was "the smart one?"

9. Was there intense competition and jealousy among the children in the family? Did you spend a lot of time fighting with one another?
10. Do you feel that one child was favored?
11. How did your parents respond to sibling fights?
12. Did they take sides and did you experience favoritism?
13. Do you feel that your parents treated you fairly or unfairly?
14. Did your parents demand high achievement? Did they reward the ''best'' accomplishments while ignoring the effort that went into a less-than-perfect performance? Did they criticize or deride the idea of being ''second place?''
15. Have you been able to resolve conflicts with your adult siblings today? Have you been able to talk with your siblings about these childhood battles?
16. How do your experiences as a sister or brother affect the way you treat your own children? (Have you vowed never to repeat your parents' mistakes yet find similar reactions creeping in? Or, conversely, do you go too far in the opposite direction, feeling unsure of how to find a middle ground?)
17. How would these sixteen questions apply to your spouse and affect his/her behavior with your children? Do your parenting styles conflict in this regard?

The personal information that you unearth in answering these questions may help you to understand and resolve recurrent family conflicts. If you can become aware of the way you were treated, then you have the opportunity to do things differently from your parents in your own family.

FAMILY MEETINGS

Holding regular family meetings is a great way to resolve conflicts and create a feeling of cooperation and equality in your family. We have held regular family meetings since our kids were toddlers to air our grievances and settle arguments. In addition, sometimes my husband or I (or even the kids!) call a special meeting when one of us feels that a family member (adults included) is unusually angry or acting out of character.

The best way to start a habit of family meetings is to set aside time routinely, like every Saturday afternoon at 2 P.M., as well as on those occasions when you feel that something in the family is amiss. You can allow ten or twenty minutes or more, depending on your children's ages and attention spans, to deal with a *single* subject such as jealousy or competition. Make sure you don't confuse the discussion by bringing in extraneous complaints like inadequate room cleanup or shirked piano practice. See to it that you are not interrupted by phone calls or other distractions.

During these meetings, each person must get equal time to have his or her say. Each must feel listened to. This equality helps your child feel his own importance in the family and engenders a sense of responsibility for his own acts.

You may ask Seth, for example, to help you understand why he has been acting so angry lately. It's not like him to withhold his toys from his little brother and call him "stooopid." This gentle confrontation will give Seth the leeway to express his needs. He may respond, for example, that you have been pressuring him lately or that he hates his violin teacher or that it's not fair how Mikey always gets attention. You can use the communication techniques outlined below to show Seth that you're really listening to him.

If what your son says during the meeting causes you to reassess your own behavior, Seth will come to appreciate his power in the family. He will feel that you take his words and feelings seriously. This can abate anger leakage at his helpless sibling. (Seth has a chance to *act,* not *act out,* with the person he's really in conflict with—you.)

COMMUNICATION SKILLS DURING MEETINGS

Certain communication skills help to assure the success of your meeting. For example, if you're critical and yell at Lauren for not completing his assignments like his sister does, the meeting will probably escalate the tension and unhappiness rather than resolve it. Such an attitude on your part might even cause Lauren to increase the level of hostility between his sister and himself. The following are some guidelines that you may find helpful:

1. **Sit down.** You've probably forgotten how vulnerable a child feels in relation to adults. You are big and powerful and most likely have a loud voice when you become angry. Imagine how intimidating it can be for a child to try to confront you about his own anger or pain. You need to be on your child's level both

physically and emotionally if she is to believe that you will listen to her.

2. *Really listen.* You may have a lot on your mind, especially if you're irritated by your youngsters' constant bickering and name-calling. I know that Cherie's endless put-downs of Aimee used to drive me wild. Yet, before you follow your instinct to let your erring youngster have it with both barrels, you need to pay attention to what he has to say, too.

Listening is an active form of communication. A child who is listened to feels cared about and valued. Listening implies mutual respect. Both you and your child will need to feel listened to in order for your family meeting to be successful. If your child cuts you off in mid-thought, you can remind her that you heard her out when it was her turn to speak; now it's only fair that she listen to you, too.

3. *Make eye contact.* Poets have called the eyes the windows to the soul. Emotions, especially love, are expressed through the eyes. From earliest infancy onward, children understand these nonverbal cues. When you look into your child's eyes, you are letting him know that your attention is focused on him and him alone.

If Matt has a tendency to cast his eyes downward, you can gently remind him that you find it hard to know what he's feeling inside if he's staring at the floor. You can say, "I'm afraid I may miss what you're trying to tell me." You might also reinforce Matt's eye contact with praise.

4. *Ask questions in nonthreatening ways.* If you say "What's wrong with you, Melissa? I'm sick of telling you to stop poking Allison! Why can't you keep your hands to yourself?" you're apt to get defensive defiance such as "She started it," "I didn't touch her," or "You're always picking on me," in response. Expressions such as "You always . . . " or "You never . . . " are the stuff that power struggles are made of, and nobody wins a power struggle.

It's best to approach difficult situations with an element of curiosity in your voice. You can say, "Help me understand what's going on with you, Melissa. I want to know why you are fighting with your sister." In this case, Melissa may reply, "Allison never wants to play with me." From this, you would glean that your younger daughter is seeking attention from her more aloof older sister. It opens the way for your discussion with both daughters about their relationship.

5. *Use mirroring.* The technique of mirroring validates your child's emotional experience by communicating *your* understanding of what *he* is feeling. You say, for example, "Jonathan, I can see that you're angry and upset at Eric because he's making fun of you, but it's not okay to hit him. Use your words to tell him to stop. Or, if he won't listen to you, come to me or Daddy to help you settle your argument." By mirroring your child's emotions, show him that you understand him, while providing ideas to help him work out the problem.

6. *Separate the child from her actions.* In order to keep your child's self-esteem intact, it's important to distinguish between *the child* and her *behavior*. Focus on the act, rather than on the person. If you say, "Heather, I love you, but I don't like it when you say mean things to Nicky. It makes me angry because you really hurt his feelings. He looks up to you and values your opinion of him," you communicate that you continue to value your daughter, even though you find her behavior unacceptable.

   On the other hand, if you were to say, "Heather, you're a bad girl. I left you alone with Nicky and the next thing I know, he's crying. Can't I depend on you?" you are criticizing your child's value as a person, labeling her as being untrustworthy and mean. She is now more likely to act out aggressively to fulfill the role implied by her new label. Even when your child's actions are unacceptable, her inherent worthiness should never be called into question.

7. *Express your love.* Despite the angry feelings often aired during our family meetings, we always found some way to express our underlying feelings of love for one another. Inevitably, our meetings ended with a "huggie sandwich"—a family love-in.

   Although you may not always resolve all of your problems during your family meetings—and it's quite all right to leave issues unsettled and open to further discussion—they help create feelings of closeness and understanding that have a lot to do with cementing family ties and resolving sibling difficulties while keeping open the lines of communication.

WHEN YOUR KIDS ARE IN THE HEAT OF BATTLE

Family meetings can be very fruitful if you have some distance from the conflict. But if you walk in on your kids while the fur is flying it is more difficult to help them resolve their differences before they resort to mayhem. Authors Adele Faber and Elaine Mazlish offer some great suggestions that I've adapted from their book *Siblings Without Rivalry*.

If your kids are engaged in bickering (such as "It's mine!" "No, I had it first!") you can simply ignore it. More likely than not, they will settle the dispute without your intervention. If you perceive that the situation is getting more volatile, however, Faber and Mazlish suggest that you:

1. *Acknowledge your children's emotions.* This is much like the mirroring that I discussed above. You can say, "Kevin and Eric, you guys sound angry!"
2. *Reflect each child's point of view.* Again, as in mirroring, you would say, "Kevin you want to play with the superheroes. Eric feels left out and would like to play with them, too."
3. *Describe the problem with respect.* You could say, "I see that you have a tough situation, here: two boys and only one set of superheroes."
4. *Express confidence in your children's ability to find their own solution.* "You guys are smart. I'm sure you can figure out a way to solve your problem that will be fair to both of you."
5. *Leave the room.*

If, on the other hand, you see that your children are actually hurting one another, or if the fighting continues in the same vein, step in with a loud and definite *"Stop!"* to get their attention. Then add, "It's okay to be mad but it's not okay to hurt each other." *Don't take sides*. Rather, acknowledge that you see two very angry children, and send them each to separate neutral territory so that they can cool off alone and think about what has just occurred. While they're doing this, you can speak to each child about what he thinks went wrong and what his recommendations might be for the future. It might also make sense to call for a family meeting shortly thereafter to seek a more permanent resolution to the fighting.

OTHER WAYS TO MINIMIZE SIBLING CONFLICTS

Several experts provide excellent suggestions for diminishing sibling rivalry over the long haul:

1. ***Don't try to treat your children identically.*** Aside from being impossible, strict adherence to "identical" treatment will encourage your children to "keep score." *New York Times* columnist Lawrence Kutner quotes Dr. Lillian H. Robinson, emeritus professor of psychiatry and pediatrics at Tulane University, who explains, "If you had ten children and you made them ten identical sandwiches, each one of them would think that another got the best sandwich." Also, with identical treatment, neither child feels special or recognized for their unique talents. Such an approach mutes the blossoming of each child—it's like tending two different plants exactly alike.

   Besides, children are not like so many cookies cut by the same cutter. James loves piano lessons but Francine may be more interested in taking up tap dancing. Certainly you can offer both children the opportunity for enrichment, but why force both into activities for which one has little interest, just for the sake of "equality"? The same can be said for academic achievement.

2. ***Recognize and show respect for your children's differences.*** This is a corollary to the first point. When you value a child's *stated* preferences and interests (*not* ones *you* choose to validate), he gains a stronger sense of self-esteem and individuality. By respecting individual differences, you avoid the trap of trying to treat your children identically. You can be fair without playing favorites and without trying to fit square pegs into round holes. Certainly Samantha can love horses while Tony dreams of becoming an astrophysicist.

3. ***Pay attention to your children's accusations of favoritism.*** Even if you believe that you have been scrupulously even-handed, your child may complain of favoritism. According to Dr. Kutner, it may be the result of misplaced frustration. He suggests that instead of arguing the point, stick to the task at hand, such as room cleanup. If your child is still upset later, you could ask what the problem is. Perhaps you will discover an underlying sibling conflict or perhaps you will see, from your child's point of view, how he could perceive your favoring one sibling over another. This would make an excellent topic for a family meeting.

4. ***Don't dismiss or repress resentment.*** Nothing makes a child (or adult, for that matter) angrier than to be told "You really shouldn't feel that way." There are no rights or wrongs about

feelings; they simply exist. In truth, inequities do occur in the world and your child may be justified in feeling envious or resentful. The trick, here, is to give your child permission to discuss and work out his feelings in an appropriate way during a family meeting or in a conversation with you. Ask him if he wants to talk about what's bothering him. If he is forced to keep his true emotions inside, he is apt to give vent to them in more destructive and veiled ways.

5. *Be honest and accepting.* Make it clear to your children that all people, including their sisters and brothers, have talents and weaknesses in different areas. This will help them to develop appropriate expectations of themselves, their siblings, and others in their world. Dr. James R. Delisle of Kent State University, author of *Gifted Children Speak Out* and *Gifted Kids Speak Out,* suggests that you talk about your own strengths and weaknesses as well as those of your spouse, your own siblings, other family members, and friends. Make sure to mention areas in which you wish you could do better and model an attitude of self-acceptance. For example, you could say ''I wish I were better at playing tennis, but I guess I do the best I can.''

In the course of this conversation, you can convey that neither the gifted child nor his siblings should be expected to be great in all areas and that one ought to recognize and nourish those talents that one does have.

6. *Encourage individual areas of interest.* It may be great fun—and flattering to your ego—if you see that your gifted child follows in your footsteps. Parental pride is perfectly natural. During Cherie's sophomore year at college, for example, she found herself choosing between psychology and literature as potential majors. (She decided on my husband's profession rather than mine!) Aimee, on the other hand, is pondering possible careers in wood sculpture and furniture design, areas in which neither my husband nor myself are well versed.

Both children, however, should receive our enthusiastic support regardless of their choice and despite our natural unconscious desire that they be mirrors of ourselves. Parents often do bring children into the world with the unspoken wish to correct what went wrong in their own lives. It's okay to acknowledge these hidden motives but it's also necessary (because we love *them* more than we love our own needs) to let our kids evolve as *they* choose. Besides, in the long run, it's more healing for us to see them resolve conflicts in their own way than to watch them struggle with our agendas.

7. **Be careful how you portray "special" programs.** In an article on the heterogeneously gifted family, Diane Peterson of the Mt. Diablo School District reminds us that parents would be wise to not look upon or portray gifted programs as "privileges." Rather, they are a part of the gifted child's regular school work and as much a part of daily life as any other lesson.

8. **Don't compare your children with one another.** Comparing siblings is one of the cardinal ways of worsening sibling rivalry and of eroding your child's self-esteem. Dr. Rita P. Underberg, a child psychologist at the University of Rochester Medical Center, was quoted in Lawrence Kutner's article as saying that this type of comparison "just makes the unfavorable one feel angry and inadequate. It also puts a terrible burden on the favored child." I'm certain you wouldn't enjoy being told you should be more like someone else, either, or worse yet, being warned that your rival is gaining ground on you.

The best way to avoid these comparisons is to help your child compare his current performance with his own past record and his own individualized goals. For instance, when Aimee received her first SAT scores (these days, kids take college entrance exams three and four times), her immediate reaction was, "Cherie scored 200 points higher the first time she took the test."

I reminded Aimee that she was being unfair to herself by comparing her scores with Cherie's. Aimee's undiagnosed learning disability had interfered with her enjoying reading the way her sister had, so, of necessity, her vocabulary would not be as large or her reading comprehension as thorough. In addition, for years, Cherie had been enrolled in honors and advanced courses that had given her prolonged practice in dealing with difficult material.

"You and Cherie are very different people and you do things in your own ways," I explained. "Besides, this SAT score is vastly improved over your PSAT score from earlier in the year. In a very short time, you've come a long way in knowing how to take this kind of test. I think you've done really well, so far. Instead of comparing yourself to Cherie, why not just compare yourself to *you?*''

You can guide your child in creating these reasonable and realistic goals without undue pressure from himself, from his siblings, or from you.

AM I MY SISTER'S KEEPER?

In the sixth grade, I was faced with the difficult decision of eclipsing my older sister at school. I chose my own agenda over hers, for which I felt elated as well as guilty. While I was happy to be included in a gifted program, I also knew that my skipping into my sister's grade was a self-interested act that threatened her self-esteem and caused her pain. It also seemed patently unfair to her, since she, too, was quite capable: She began reading at the age of three, and by the sixth grade, she read at the twelfth-grade level. Her difficulties in math had kept her from skipping a year; she had barely missed the entrance requirements for the gifted program herself.

But life has a funny way of mitigating some of our decisions. The ninth grade was difficult for my sister but in the tenth grade we rarely saw one another. I was part of an honors program that met on the top floor of an old elementary school, several blocks from the overcrowded main building of our high school where my sister was a student. Although we were both enrolled in the same institution, essentially we attended different schools with entirely separate student bodies.

Two months into our junior year, our parents decided to move from New York to Los Angeles, much to our mutual chagrin. In fact, during that tumultuous year, we attended three high schools. Making and leaving friends so frequently, we both felt that at least we had the stability of our sibling relationship. Flung together by decisions we could not control, we began to cling to one another. Eventually, we took solace in the fact that we were in the same grade—at least we each had a built-in friend. We took some of the same classes and attended college together, at times competing with one another but also helping each other through, as best as we could.

While I can't say that our experience lessened my sister's feelings of inadequacy in relation to me, I do know that she learned to compensate. She became a hard worker and in college often received A's, especially in English, psychology, history, and education courses. As I mentioned earlier, she is completing a doctorate, a distinction that I have not achieved despite my many honors classes and academic awards. I feel proud of her perseverance, strength of character, and intellect. She is my friend.

As parents, sometimes it's difficult to see beyond the immediacy of our children's squabbles. I know that I often felt like tearing my hair out when my kids got into it with each other. But it's also helpful to keep in mind that circumstances can unfold that teach our children to rely on one another and to settle their own differences peacefully. For many siblings, learning to get along means learning how to balance healthy self-interest with a spirit of generosity. This comes with time, experience, and your patient guidance. You fulfill your role by keeping communications open among all family members and by valuing and treating each child as the complex microcosm that he is.

PART IV

The Hidden Challenges for Parents

CHAPTER 12

Parental Responsibility: Your Secret Challenge

*I will become engulfed with all I did or did not do,
with what should have been and
what cannot be helped.*

—TILLIE OLSEN, "I STAND HERE IRONING"

I REMEMBER THE FIRST MOMENT I SET EYES ON MY OLDEST CHILD. THE doctor was holding her aloft for me to see. Wrapped in a receiving blanket, she sported a shock of black hair, a red face, and the beautifully rounded head of a C-section baby. I was thrilled that she had my eyes and my husband's lips. She was as I had envisioned. I could let go now and give in to the healing sleep, the nepenthe of the anesthetic as the surgical team sewed me up.

It wasn't until many hours later, when I was permitted to hold my baby in the quiet of the hospital room, that I actually fell in love with her. And *falling* in love is, in truth, an inadequate term to describe the feeling. As I held her close and looked into those eyes that so much resembled my own, I was awe-struck. Who is this person, I asked. Where did she come from? Certainly I understood the biology of it, but that did not prepare me for the sense that I was holding a new soul in my arms—nothing could explain that—or the intensity of love and awe that I experienced.

She was not passive, either. She gazed with similar concentration and curiosity into my own eyes. She could look into my very being and I into hers. She was completely open to me.

As I studied and learned her every little feature, I came to realize the unfathomable responsibility that lay nestled at my bosom. This new person, I thought, has an enormous potential. Will I help that potential to come to fruition or will I stifle it or allow it to be stifled by the vagaries and vicissitudes of life?

I began to cry. I feared I was too young, unworthy, and ill-equipped for such an obligation—I was twenty-one years old. "How can I be a

mother to this baby if I am still a child myself?'' So began my
relationship with Cherie.

OUR INFLUENCE ON OUR CHILDREN

You may feel overwhelmed, as I did, by the magnitude of your
influence on your gifted child's growth and development. You exert
that influence both actively and passively—by what you do and simply
by who you are.

I was struck by the power of parental influence when a friend
described to me how her seventeen-year-old son came to be an
achiever. Sally explained that in her and her husband Frank's eyes, son
Jason had always been a rather lackluster student. "He was so shy,"
she told me one day over a cup of coffee, that "he seemed to hang back
and observe but he never really performed. He was late to read. We
always had to push him: 'C'mon Jason, don't you want to learn to
read?' we used to say."

This couple's younger daughter Hilary was as sharp as a tack.
Hilary seemed to run rings around Jason and had been identified as
highly gifted in the third grade.

When Jason entered the seventh grade, the school counselor
approached Sally and suggested that the boy be tested for the gifted
program. "Frank and I were in shock," Sally explained. "We were
sure that Jason would not make it into the program but we decided to
give it a try anyway. And you know what?" she asked, lowering her
voice to a whisper, "We were wrong. Jason did quite well on the test.
We could hardly believe it.'

The test results rattled this couple's beliefs about their son, and it
reoriented their behavior toward him. "We realized that we had not
encouraged Jason the way that we should have done. My husband
began working with Jason every night on his homework. Jason had no
study skills, so Frank was like a private tutor. Frank saw that Jason
could memorize anything."

Frank's influence made a difference in Jason's performance and his
perception of his own abilities. "From the seventh grade on, Jason
ended up getting almost straight A's," Sally explained. "Now, he
thinks of himself as a good student. He's at the top of his physics class
[in a highly competitive math-science magnet high school]. I think a

lot of Jason's success was due to Frank's working with him saying, 'You can do it, you can do it.' "

Jason did not actively display his potential and his family had done little to bring it out. Once the test results gave Jason and his family permission to believe that he could excel in academic areas, his family used their new perceptions and their actions to help him actualize that potential.

As I'll outline below, many researchers stress the importance of family influences on gifted children. In a chapter on the influence of family values on the development of talent published in the book *Patterns of Influence on Gifted Learners,* educational psychologists Marilynn J. Kulieke and Paula Olszewski-Kubilius at the Center for Talent Development at Northwestern University explain that the family is "the *critical component* in the translation of talent, ability, and promise into achievement for gifted individuals."

A 1961 study by Drs. W. Morrow and P. Wilson published in the journal *Child Development* that examined the relationship between achievement and the home environment reported, for example, that parents of high-achieving elementary, high school, and college students tend to:

- Use more praise and approval
- Take a more active interest in their kids' lives
- Feel more affectionate toward their youngsters
- Express a stronger sense of family and belongingness
- Feel closer to their own parents than do parents of underachievers

How you live your own life and your verbal messages to your children can make a great difference. For example, if you model diligence and mastery by your own actions, achievements, and successes, or tell your children how much you value hard work by praising their efforts, your youngsters will absorb these ideas from you.

According to Drs. Kulieke and Olszewski-Kubilius, you also may act *directly* on your children's talent development process by straightforward intervention such as:

- Selecting certain activities for your children
- Monitoring, organizing, and prioritizing your children's time
- Setting, communicating, and reinforcing high standards of performance

GOING OVERBOARD

While it's true that as parents we have great influence on our children's achievements, it is equally true that a balance must be struck between constantly striving for excellence and the comfortable ordinariness of childhood. It's difficult for some parents to control the impulse to inappropriately push their children (see chapter 13), or to remember that even though their youngster has the vocabulary of a twenty-five-year-old, she is still only five and needs to be treated accordingly.

Researchers often point out that *gifted children are children first*. "Gifted" is merely a descriptive label that we attach to them: It is no different than "athletic" or "musical." Their needs as children must be respected before all else.

I, unfortunately, occasionally fell into the habit of going overboard with my daughter. At birth, I certainly had no way of predicting how Cherie would score on an IQ test, but having been identified as gifted myself, I was convinced that no child of mine would be "just average." For me, it became a question of ego.

Knowing full well that my husband and I would have an enormous impact on our daughter as she grew, we set about shaping her development. We cheered her first smile, first word, first step. We held her hand and dried her tears when the going got rough. We played with her, talked to her, and loved her as only parents can do. Indeed, sometimes it felt to us that we poured the best of ourselves into her. We owed that to her for she was our child. So far so good.

In those first years, we created a home filled with toys, books, and affection—not that it lacked conflict or stress, for we certainly had our share. But underlying it all was a deep love that we held for one another—a love that sustained us through illnesses and death in the family, car accidents, financial struggles, the demands of graduate school, and several moves to different apartments. We were in our early twenties, naive, and inexperienced, and so we dreamed of our own successes as well as those of our child. We knew that we could make it, if only we persisted and tried hard enough.

In 1970, the Women's Movement had not yet come to the fore, and so I felt content in my role as full-time mommy. I had many hours to spend with my baby, hours that I used to stimulate her and talk to her. As I explained in chapter 1, Cherie was my companion. During her first six months, I took her wherever I went. (Besides, on my husband's beginning teacher's salary, hiring a nanny or live-in help was simply unthinkable.) I talked to Cherie all day as I performed my chores. Much as my mother had done with me, we counted "eggies" at the supermarket, looked at animals in picture books, and played with puzzles and blocks.

When Cherie was about six months old, I returned to my graduate studies in French literature and took a job at the university as a graduate teaching assistant. I worked half-days and took my classes several evenings a week, reserving the afternoons and weekends for family time and studying (during Cherie's naps).

In order for me to teach, I prevailed on my grandmother (who lived close by) to watch our child. That worked out fine until Cherie was about a year old and my grandmother moved away. I then placed Cherie in a daycare situation with a licensed daycare mother. My daughter was happy there, as she was surrounded by other children and the woman caring for her was warm and loving. At Tammy's house Cherie began watching the new (at that time) show "Sesame Street." She also started talking.

This began to trouble me. As a literature student, I understood that language helps to shape the way that one thinks. It was ironic to me that a woman other than myself was teaching my child how to speak English so that I could go to my job—where I taught strangers to speak French! So, when Cherie was about eighteen months old, I decided to limit my outside involvements to my own graduate studies, devoting the rest of my time to my child. I would have to say that at this stage I inappropriately projected my own very strong need for achievement onto my daughter, especially because she was already exhibiting the extraordinary behavior I described in chapter 1.

Our connection was so intense that at one point my mother chided me to "Stop pushing! Leave the baby alone" when I persisted in having Cherie complete a puzzle. But I would not relent. I acted as if I were a woman possessed. I knew that she could do it. Inside, I fervently believed that no child of mine could be anything but super bright.

I encouraged Cherie to attempt more and more difficult puzzles, to recite the alphabet, and to recognize letters and numbers by making games out of these activities. Once when Cherie was about four years old and I was being particularly controlling, she turned to me and said, "Mommy, stop pushing me around. I'm not a meatball, you know!"

Fortunately, my husband was a mitigating factor in my behavior. He had neither the legacy of being labeled gifted nor the need to see his child as brilliant. His play with Cherie was wide-ranging, physical, and fun. While I was more of a taskmaster, he became the "silly

Daddy,'' playing hide-and-seek, gently roughhousing, scribbling, making up great stories, and creating a general environment of hilarity. Our parenting styles were complementary; neither of us felt threatened by the other's approach. This can be a problem in some families, however, where conflicts over differing parenting styles may heighten the potential for stress in a sensitive gifted child.

Nonetheless, despite my husband's valuable contributions, I still had taken my sense of responsibility a bit too seriously. In my need to ''create'' a perfect child, I became invasive and intrusive. I was overly involved in shaping Cherie's reality. I hadn't allowed her enough space to simply have her own thoughts and ideas. I needed to be in control. No wonder she had told me to back off. It's true, she was not a meatball! The amazing thing is that at four she was aware enough of the negative aspects of our interactions (more so than I was, I'm ashamed to say) to try to alter them.

If I had it to do over, would I do it differently? You bet. In fact, when Aimee joined our family some three and a half years after Cherie's birth, I was much more relaxed and far less intrusive as a parent, as are most parents of two or more children.

The truth is that I needed a break. I couldn't deal with two children as verbal as Cherie was. It took a lot of energy to respond appropriately to her curiosity and to listen to her long-winded hyper-detailed explanations—the ones that made us shout ''Cherie, get to the point'' in utter exasperation. Unfortunately, first-born and only children are destined to become their parents' laboratories, and so I'm afraid that Cherie got the worst of me as well as the best. At times I felt that I had created a monster.

This is not to say that we did not attempt a sort of correction. When Cherie was ready for nursery school, I sought out a program at some distance from our house that was oriented toward socialization, not academics. To begin with, I could see that the academics were already coming by themselves. More importantly, I felt in my gut that Cherie needed an unstructured environment in which she was free to explore ideas and people on her own. Other, more convenient and conventional schools felt all wrong to me. I realized that I had been too controlling and overbearing. I didn't want preschool to mean more of the same.

OVERSCHEDULING

It's easy to see how once bitten by the ''gifted'' bug, it's tempting for parents to enroll their children in all kinds of enrichment classes from violins for tots to gymnastics, conversational French, and gourmet Chinese cookery. This impulse is a manifestation of the sense of responsibility that we feel to make sure that our children become the "brightest" and the "best."

While a certain amount of enrichment is fine—I have nothing against classes once or twice a week, especially if the program enhances an area in which your child has already demonstrated an interest, curiosity, or ability—too much leaves children with little time to explore the workings of their own minds or to discover the world on their own. The overscheduled child is a stressed child (see chapter 13). Time and time again, experts in this field emphasize that gifted children need time off, just to think. If we deprive our youngsters of opportunities to find their center, to listen to their inner promptings, to ignore external stimuli, then we rob them of their *selves*.

In an article published in the *Gifted Child Quarterly*, Lita Linzer Schwartz at Pennsylvania State University explains the developmentalists' point of view that overscheduling a gifted child in after-school lessons and activities can make those fun activities seem like work. "Many gifted children will resent both the emphasis on achievement and the too-demanding schedule," Dr. Schwartz writes, "and will ultimately rebel, dropping out of school or special studies in body as well as mind."

Unfortunately, parents are not heeding this advice. In fact, these days moms and dads of younger and younger children seem to be pushing their tykes into classes on Mozart and painting, long before they are appropriate. In a recent article in the *New York Times*, for example, Carol Lawson reports that the proliferation of enrichment classes seems to be invading even the playpen. She tells of one little boy living in Manhattan whose mother scheduled him in "courses" much as she had scheduled herself during her own freshman year at college. "Simon goes to gym class on Monday and Wednesday, art class on Tuesday, and music class on Friday. Simon is a year old."

Child developmentalists are sharply critical of most such programs, pointing out that classes for the very young are appropriate only if they are simply unstructured fun. Exploration and socialization—not academics—are important for toddlers and preschoolers. According to Lawson, experts warn that "pressuring toddlers to learn creates stress that backfires academically and emotionally later in life."

Dr. Benjamin Bloom, professor of education at the University of Chicago and originator of the famed Bloom's taxonomy described in chapter 6, has researched with several colleagues the childhood factors that produce superior musicians, artists, athletes, and math/science scholars. Dr. Bloom's study of superior achievers, as reported in his book *Developing Talent in Young People,* reveals that while most of these children did eventually become involved with lessons, typically early experiences were merely playful.

The future pianists "plunked" on the keys as toddlers and picked out tunes with one finger as five-year-olds. The future neurologists performed their own little "science" experiments with play microscopes in the basement. First lessons were also considered fun and not serious "work" and the children were amply rewarded by their kindly teachers' "smiles, positive reinforcements, and rewards." There was little or no pressure. Serious instruction did not begin until quite a bit later.

I believe that one of the hidden burdens of parenting gifted children is feeling guilty when others are given the responsibility to do what should come so naturally and enjoyably to you as a mother or father. It is especially painful if you're busy or overwhelmed with your own job or career. It's hard to provide enrichment when you don't even have a moment to yourself. Classes may seem like a viable solution, and they can be, if they are not your child's sole source of stimulation and if they're not overdone. One of the challenges of parenting any child is knowing how to strike a balance between your own needs and those of your kids.

THE CURSE OF MEDIOCRITY

As adults we have learned about our own limitations. We realize that if we're excellent artists, we may not be top-notch mathematicians. Or, if we do excel in these two areas, we usually admit that we can't write for beans. We understand that we have strong points as well as weak ones. Why is it, then, that many of us expect our gifted children to be exceptional in all areas at all times?

While your gifted child may have many diverse interests and areas of expertise, it is also true that other fields may hold little appeal. It is no crime if your children have little ability in those areas. They can't be expected to be geniuses in everything.

Take math. (Take it, please!) When I was in the ninth grade, all students at our school were required to take a standardized achievement exam called the "Iowa tests." While I scored in the ninety-ninth percentile (meaning that I outperformed 99 percent of all other ninth graders in the nation taking the test) in such areas as reading comprehension, vocabulary, social studies, and science, I was dead average—at the fiftieth percentile—in math.

This was all the more puzzling to me because I was getting A's in algebra. In truth, I never really understood math. I just had an excellent memory. In fact, I was able to memorize my way through algebra 1, geometry, and algebra 2. When I got to trigonometry, however, the truth became apparent. The logarithm tables presented an enigma. I had no idea where they came from, what they meant, or how to use them. I certainly couldn't memorize them all. I was doomed to a C, and rightly so. I was not gifted in math and neither, as it turns out, are my daughters.

All children are entitled to fall in with the crowd in some areas of their lives. Certainly we're entitled to strive toward functional mastery, but there is no harm in allowing a child to be a child—to make mistakes, to fall down and get up again, to struggle and persist through failure. How else can he learn? When your expectations for excellence become overwhelming, your child may freeze in his tracks, a victim of his own perfectionism (see chapter 8).

Your unrealistic expectations of achievement also can skew your child's perception of what it means to be a successful person. In an article published in the *Roeper Review,* Dr. Leslie Kaplan, a counselor of gifted children, explains that "Overvaluing the cognitive leads gifted youths to see their worth only as performers. They see their value as individuals dependent upon their heads, nothing more."

This theory is not as farfetched as it sounds. When I was about twenty-four years old, I painted a self-portrait that consisted of simply my eyes, forehead, and curly hair. What about my womanly body, my sexuality, my feet? What about my heart? In truth, at that time I considered the rest of me rather insignificant and worthy of attention only because it supported and carried around my intellect.

Our gifted children are children, first and foremost. It's necessary and normal that from time to time they become bogged down with the normal baggage of childhood. Broken arms, petty fights with friends, sudden growth spurts, the flu, and the other normal aches and pains of growing up can get in the way of consistent high achievement. Larger issues such as the birth of a sibling, moving, parental unemployment, divorce, illness, and death in the family (even the death of a beloved pet) are highly stressful for you and your children alike and should be taken into account. As I explained in chapter 7, gifted children are exceptionally sensitive, and this sensitivity can cause their work to take a nose dive if they're upset. Your support—not criticism or demands— is what's called for in such cases.

DISCOMFORT WITH THE ROLE OF PARENTING A GIFTED CHILD

Recently I had a talk with my sister about her role as a teacher of gifted children. She explained to me that in her experience, some parents become intimidated when their youngsters are identified as gifted. Apparently, these parents fear that they will have little to offer their talented children. In some instances, she said, these parents attempt to deny or suppress their children's giftedness and may go as far as pulling them out of school.

You may also feel ambivalent about your gifted child's accomplishments. In an article published in the *Roeper Review,* Dr. Phillip M. Powell and Tony Haden of the University of Texas at Austin explain that parents may vacillate between feeling pleased and frightened by the achievements of their highly gifted child. "Parental pride in achievement," they explain, "can quickly turn to a fear of social stigma which can cause parents to give their gifted child inconsistent feedback." As a result, the child may be unsure whether it's good or bad to be gifted.

In *Bringing Out the Best* author Jacqulyn Saunders describes that many parents felt comfortable in their roles *until* their child was identified as gifted:

> The mother of five-year-old Larry says, "I've never been very self-confident, but I've really enjoyed being a parent. Larry was an easy baby, and we had a lot of fun together before he started school. Now he's in the gifted program and suddenly my in-laws don't think I can handle a gifted child 'right.' "

Saunders cautions that "When it comes to a child with special abilities, there is more at risk from overreacting than from underreacting. Do what *you* feel right about. And politely, but firmly, let others know that *you're* the parent, thank-you very much."

Saunders also points out that some parents have a tough time when they perceive that their child knows more about certain subjects than they do. "None of us wants our child to look at us with disappointment when we have to answer 'I don't know' to questions about electricity, bathroom plumbing, and the nature of God—for the thirty-seventh time in one day."

Again, I believe that these issues revolve around our underlying sense of responsibility. As parents we like to feel that we are in charge, and we fear that we cannot be in charge if Jesse knows more than we do or somehow causes us to feel limited, vulnerable, or inadequate. The truth is, however, that even though you can't explain why a television works, you are not diminished as parents. You still love Jesse and want the best for him. More importantly, Jesse loves you and needs your love far more than he needs your electronic expertise. It takes more strength of character to admit that you are at a loss than to cover up your ignorance.

Indeed, you can use your own lapses to show Jesse how to get at information that you don't have at your fingertips. Take him to the library. Look up *television* in the encyclopedia and read the entry together. See how much sense you both can make of it. In this way, you will be modeling for your son appropriate behavior that he can use as he gets older. He learns that if he doesn't know, there's no harm in admitting it and then seeking a way to find the solution. He doesn't have to be perfect.

Remember also that even if you don't have all the answers, you still have lots more life experience than your child. According to Jacqulyn Saunders, "It's not always necessary for you to know more than your child, or even to be smarter than he or she is. It *is* important to show more in the way of wisdom. . . . [That] takes years to accumulate, and years are what you'll always have more of than your child."

OH, THOSE INCESSANT QUESTIONS!

Questioning is one of the hallmarks of giftedness that is by turns thrilling and exasperating. It is wonderful to watch your child's mind at work seeking out answers to life's mysteries. Yet, you may have also felt barraged by your youngster's innumerable queries about the workings of the world and all those that inhabit it.

Experts advise that parents of gifted children ought to take their children's questions seriously and answer them as fully as they can. But what if you feel exasperated? Overwhelmed? Rushed? That feeling of responsibility rears its ugly head again. For your child's good you *must* reply to every query, no matter how tired you are.

I take issue with that. Not being a saint, I sometimes lacked the patience for all those questions, especially the ones that sounded as if Cherie were trying to be silly. After all, by the tenth explanation in a row, I needed a bit of quiet for my own thoughts. Besides, sometimes I believed that Cherie continued with her questioning as a way to maintain her emotional connection to me: As long as I was still talking to her, my attention was focused on her and not on her baby sister or on some other activity.

And so, there were times when I asserted a limit. I wouldn't do it angrily—I didn't want her to feel bad about her curiosity—but I would turn the question back onto my daughter. When I had reached my own internal breaking point and she continued to ask me, ''Why?'' I would simply ask her what *she* thought.

This approach proved to be quite fruitful. Sometimes Cherie's explanations were perfectly reasonable and I complimented her on her astuteness. At other times, she missed the mark completely and I helped her to set about finding the correct answer, as I explained above. There also were occasions when her responses were quite fanciful. I enjoyed watching where her mind would go and I praised her for her ability to have new and interesting ideas.

At other times, I used a different tactic. Rather than asking Cherie what she thought, I asked her *why she wanted to know*. If the question was serious, then my daughter would verbalize the thought processes that led her to query me. If the question was asked for attention or merely because she wanted to be silly, Cherie would giggle, blurt out, ''I don't know,'' and then get involved in something else.

In turning back the question in these ways, you can help your child take some responsibility for his thirst for knowledge. Otherwise, you may become a slave to the questions—and that's no fun for either of you since sooner or later your resentment and irritation will be evident. You also may struggle with guilt feelings. You feel that you *should* respond to the questions fully and with patience. But you are also human and are entitled to your own limitations. Indeed, it's important that your child be aware that you do have limits.

This is not to say that your gifted child's questions are inherently bad or that you should ignore or criticize them. On the contrary, you should make yourself available to your child, but just be aware of your own limitations.

CURIOSITY CAN BURN THE HOUSE DOWN

As a child, I remember asking appropriately ''gifted'' questions such as ''Where does the sky end?'' ''What's at the edge of the universe?'' ''How can I know everything in the world there is to know?'' Curiosity was always a part of my nature as it is of most gifted children.

At seven or eight, I fancied myself in such varied careers as archeology, paleontology, microbiology, and astronomy. I wanted to discover an "answer" to where we come from and where we're going, to what makes the universe work as it does. On warm summer evenings, I would lie on the grass and stare at the stars, trying to fathom my tininess in the great scheme of things and then, remembering about atoms and molecules, try to conceptualize my enormity. I was fascinated by the idea of relativity—not Einstein's theory, but my own.

As a writer, I am constantly exploring new areas, seeking to learn new information. That curiosity and an excitement about learning have stayed with me for a lifetime.

Most gifted children are consumed with curiosity. In addition to engaging in active discovery by asking you 100,000 questions, they also engage in a certain measure of mischievousness when they ask themselves, "What if . . . " in such statements as:

- "What if I poke a stick in the bicycle wheel spokes while the wheel is still turning?"
- "What if I climb up on daddy's desk to see what's in those cabinets?"
- "What if I bring my goldfish in the bathtub with me?"
- "What if I take apart the stereo to see how it works?"

In his marvelous book, *"Surely You're Joking, Mr. Feynman!" Adventures of a Curious Character,* the late Nobel Prize–winning physicist Dr. Richard Feynman delineates some of the ways that this sort of curiosity made itself evident quite early in his life: At the age of eleven or twelve, Dr. Feynman built an electronics lab in his room in which he constructed among other things, a bank of lamps, a fuse system, crystal radios, an electric burglar alarm, an amplifier for a photoelectric cell, a rudimentary telephone, and a microphone.

He also got himself into a heap of trouble:

I had a Ford coil—a spark coil from an automobile—and I had spark terminals at the top of my switchboard. I would put a Raytheon RH tube, which had argon gas in it, across the terminals, and the spark would make a purple glow inside the vacuum—it was just great!

One day I was playing with the Ford coil, punching holes in the paper with the sparks, and the paper caught fire. Soon I couldn't hold it anymore because it was burning near my fingers so I dropped it in a metal wastebasket which had a lot of newspaper in it. Newspapers burn fast, you know, and the flame looked pretty big inside the room. I shut the door so my mother—who was playing bridge with some friends in the living room—wouldn't find out there was a fire in my room.

Fortunately for his whole family, Dr. Feynman was eventually able to put out the fire and get rid of the traces of smoke in the room. You may (or may not) be relieved to learn that this curious and fertile mind went on to become one of the developers of the atomic bomb!

Should you limit your child's curious explorations? Obviously safety factors must be taken into account. Indeed, if Jennifer is just crazy about her chemistry set—and you're loath to take it away from her—make sure that you have a fire extinguisher handy and that she knows not only how to use it but also how to call you and the fire department for help. Alternatively, you should set up clearly defined limits on her use of the chemistry set, such as only when you're nearby. Limit a child's curiosity only if her activities create a danger for herself or others. Of course, it's entirely up to you to decide what constitutes a danger.

Overall, you can see that the sense of burden that sometimes comes from parenting a gifted child derives largely from your feelings of responsibility. Sometimes, by letting go of the expectations that you hold for yourself and your youngster, both of you can enjoy a much more relaxed experience. Sure, your child is gifted, but it doesn't mean that you have to *work* with him or stimulate him every minute, night and day. Parenting gifted children—as with any other children—can be fun if you allow it to be so.

CHAPTER 13

Whose Life Is This Anyway?
Ego and Letting Go

I love my daughter. She and I have shared the same body.
There is a part of her mind that is a part of mine. But, when
she was born, she sprang from me like a slippery fish, and has
been swimming away ever since.

—AMY TAN, *THE JOY LUCK CLUB*

AN OLD NEIGHBOR RECENTLY REMINDED ME OF AN INCIDENT THAT occurred at our daughters' elementary school: After her son's rousing performance during a school play, one mother ran up and down the narrow aisle of the stuffy, jam-packed auditorium crowing, ''That's my son! That's my son!''

My friend and I chuckled at this obvious display of parental pride, but it got me to thinking about just how deeply my ego is attached to my children's achievements. At the very least, we parents bask in the reflected glow of our youngsters' glory. At the most, we take their glory to be our own.

GIFTEDNESS AND YOUR EGO

If your child is gifted and does well at most tasks that are set before her, you may feel as if you are also blessed. This feeling is natural: What parent doesn't derive joy from observing a child's flourishing growth? Indeed, in Yiddish there is a term, *nachas,* which literally means the pride and pleasure that one feels from the achievements of one's children. In the course of my kids' lives, I have had many *nachas* attacks and I suspect you have, too.

I saved a letter of recommendation, for example, from one of Cherie's high school English teachers in which he had declared that in his eighteen years of teaching gifted adolescents, he had never encountered a student quite as articulate or mature in thinking and analytic abilities as Cherie. The day Cherie brought the letter home, I immediately phoned my husband and our parents and read it to them. All of us felt as if we had been similarly praised.

These feelings of pride come from our deep attachments to our children: We feel that they are part of us, an extension of our bodies, and, in fact, they *are* at a DNA level! This feeling of unity is biologically natural as well as psychologically true. Our perception of oneness may also be, in part, a vestige of our early *symbiotic* attachment to our children and our own attachment, as children, to *our* parents.

SYMBIOSIS: WE ARE ONE

The dictionary tells us that *symbiosis* means the mutually beneficial living together of two dissimilar organisms. Psychologically, it means the fusion and enmeshment of parent and child.

Symbiosis is a normal part of a young infant's relationship to his parents. According to developmental psychoanalyst Margaret Mahler, author of *The Psychological Birth of the Human Infant,* when a baby is first born, he has no sense of the distinction between himself and mother: Psychologically he is completely fused with her, as if still in the womb. Slowly, over the first five months of life, the infant learns to differentiate what is "me" from what is "not me." Such an awareness is marked by his sucking on his toes (thereby defining the boundaries of his body), his purposefully grabbing for a toy, and his recognition of your presence and absence in games such as peek-a-boo. These are his very first strides toward the development of a separate self.

The early months of symbiosis are essential to a child's feelings of safety, security, and bonding to his parents. But what is appropriate during one period of a child's development may be inappropriate at another. A toddler needs a less intense attachment in order to successfully undertake the two-decades-long journey toward adulthood. As he goes forward in the world under his own steam, he gains feelings of competency and self-esteem.

At about nine months, the child actually puts physical distance between himself and his parents: He has learned to crawl. But he doesn't go far. He returns frequently for cuddling, praise, and reassurance that his parents are still there, watching out for his welfare.

Even if he plays quietly on the floor, he looks toward mom or dad every few minutes, renewing his connection to them.

As the child becomes more physically adept, he takes his first tentative steps away from his parents. It is a moment of great exhilaration for parent and child alike. Yet the eighteen-month-old's joy in being able to walk, climb, and explore is tempered by an equal and opposite need to cling to a parent's leg: He reassures himself of his secure base before venturing further into the world. Finally, by the end of his second year, the child has created a more stable inner sense of himself and the others in his world. He need not return to you as often. Yet, the push and pull process of connection versus *separation* and *individuation* continues in ever-widening circles as a child grows into the independence of childhood, adolescence, and beyond.

I can see this process still occurring in my teenage daughters today. (Indeed, in his book *The Adolescent Passage* psychoanalyst Peter Blos calls adolescence "the second separation-individuation.") When Aimee finally procured her driver's license, for example, she was eager to be in Los Angeles traffic. Some three weeks later, however, when she got her first traffic ticket, she tearfully stormed into the house, threw her car keys at my feet, and demanded that I take the old blue Volvo away from her! Driving suddenly seemed too great a responsibility. I couldn't comply with her demand, since she needed her car to get to and from school. So, Aimee promptly misbehaved in another way, which then caused us to ground her for the weekend— with nary a complaint from her. One way or another, she got her unconscious wish: to be reined into a place where she felt safe.

Cherie has taken the next step. After her freshman year at college, she spent the summer back in Los Angeles with us. Following her sophomore year, however, she felt ready to try living on her own in an apartment some 300 miles from home with only our Sunday afternoon phone calls and perhaps a weekend visit or two still tethering her to our nuclear family. This is as it should be—she is twenty years old.

THE ROLE OF EMPATHY

Ideally, the intense bond that is created between parent and child from earliest infancy onward is founded on mother's and father's empathy toward their baby's emotions. Mother is at one with her infant's needs. If he is crying, her face reflects his feelings of distress. If he is happy, she is all smiles, too. As psychoanalyst Alice Miller explains in *The*

Drama of the Gifted Child, when a mother is appropriately empathic, baby will gaze into her face and see himself there. When a parent acts as a mirror to the baby's emotions, he feels "noticed, understood, taken seriously, and respected." This mirroring, which is so essential to the early symbiotic connection, helps to build a child's feelings of self-esteem and security.

Ideally, an empathic parent will allow a child his emotions. He can express anger or sadness or hurt without the parent's feeling insecure about his or her own performance. He need not always be the best or the fastest or the smartest; he need not always try to please his parents by being a "good little boy" or by "making nice." The empathic parent will say (like our old friend, Mister Rogers) "It's you I like" or "I like you just the way you are."

This is the ideal. In truth, however, we cannot always mirror our children's emotions. We may experience moments of exasperation, exhaustion, or boredom with the endless routines and constant demands of parenting; we may feel temporarily distracted by problems at work, with our spouse, our parents, or our other children; we may worry on occasion over illness, financial crises, or family conflicts. These problems are part of the normal wear and tear of life. In the words of pediatrician-turned-psychoanalyst Dr. D. W. Winnicott, we need not be perfect—only "good enough." If we expect perfection of ourselves, we may expect the same of our children, and that's unfair to them.

However, Dr. Alice Miller also points out that rather than reflect our child's emotions, we may also project our own "expectations, fears, and plans for the child" when we gaze at him. In that case, mother's face would not mirror her gifted child's experience but rather her own unconscious "predicaments"—her anxiety, insecurities, and even hostility. Her face would belie the hurts and failings experienced during her own infancy and childhood—it would reflect her own inner needs and not his.

When this occurs, the child's own emotions become lost. He feels that he isn't good enough or acceptable to his parents. To survive, he has no choice but to conform to their expectations. He develops what Dr. Winnicott calls a "false self," behaving in accordance with his parents' expectations rather than his own inner promptings.

REWORKING THE PAST

It is inevitable that we attempt to rework our own childhoods in raising our children. If we feel that our parents made mistakes with us, we vow to do better now that it's our turn to take the reins. Sometimes those vows are made consciously. We buy the fancy new baseball glove our parents couldn't afford to give us; we send our children to "the best" private school because we were disappointed in our own education.

I recall a friend who had complained that her intellectual life was stunted by a lack of the arts and esthetics in her home. In response, she saw to it that her children received music and painting lessons at astonishingly young ages. She took them to concerts and the ballet. She would not allow them to lose out on these gifts, in much the same way that I couldn't tolerate the thought of my children languishing in boring classrooms.

Such an approach is acceptable, provided that the child enjoys the activity. But, if a child is forced to take piano or ballet at the expense of basketball or time for silly games with playmates, resentment and power struggles can ensue. We need to establish a happy medium between our own desires and those of our children.

At other times, we decide what is good for our children out of our own *unconscious* need to fix what had been wrong in our families of origin. Our identification can be so strong that we may see our child as our own injured self. In our actions with that child, we try to effect some form of healing *for our own lives*.

We may rationalize that we are acting on our kids' behalf, not our own. As a first-born, for instance, we may have felt abandoned at the birth of our younger sister, so now we shower attention on our first child, at the expense of child number two or three. "But she feels left out," we exclaim, "She needs the extra time with me." It is possible that we are filling the unmet needs of our own inner little girl who felt so hurt rather than the actual needs of our offspring. In truth, these may be our attempts to reparent ourselves.

In this case, try to see what your child *really* needs in relation to what you are offering. Maybe she would benefit from extra attention, but maybe she wouldn't. Perhaps her bids for independence explain the friction between the two of you. As parents, we can gain insight into our own projected needs by examining areas of conflict with our children.

HOW OUR KIDS MIRROR US

Mirroring is really a two-way street: Our children reflect our emotions while we reflect theirs. In his book, *A Good Enough Parent*, eminent child psychologist Dr. Bruno Bettelheim explains that our innermost feelings may remain hidden from us because they are too painful for us to face. But we do express these in our interactions and expectations for our children. In fact, Dr. Bettelheim makes the point that children are more impressed by the emotions that they feel *emanating* from us than from the conscious intentions that we convey. This is why a child may take on traits that we particularly disapprove of or reject in ourselves.

For example, a parent may feel very insecure but may decide that his anxiety is irrational or weak. Not wanting to project a negative image, he suppresses the feeling and belittles its cause. In fact, to cover his fears, he may become boastful and act macho. (''There's nothing to worry about here! Just get out and do it!'') But a child identifies with the emotion, not one's efforts to conceal it. And so, he incorporates the insecurity into his personality, much to the parent's chagrin and disappointment.

You could see how this theory of interaction between parent and child relates to your role with your gifted youngster. If, for example, you have the unconscious need to see yourself as special, successful, on the leading edge, or in charge, or if you have repressed these feelings for fear of seeming antisocial, grandiose, or insecure, your child may still read your underlying emotions and act them out in the world. He might become smug or arrogant, for instance.

As Dr. Bettelheim explains, ''To many parents' dismay, the child builds into his personality those aspects of their personalities which make the deepest impression on him, not those which they would most wish him to internalize.''

THE DANGERS OF TOO MUCH ATTACHMENT

I was brought up in a household in which I was symbiotically attached to my parents; a home in which my mother said to me, ''I know you better than you know yourself''—and I believed her; a family in which I only risked adolescent separation at the ripe age of twenty-three, after my mother suffered a serious illness, and I realized that if I was to survive, I would have to define my own self.

Once, when Cherie was a preschooler, my mother asked me to taste a veal stew she had been cooking to determine if *my daughter* would like it. At that moment, I understood that I had been raised as if we were all one person. ''How would I know?'' I replied rather sharply.

"I'm not in Cherie's mouth!" It was hard for my mother to gauge where one of us started and the other one left off (and sometimes it's hard for me, too).

My mother's deep attachment was, at least in part, a result of her experiences in the Holocaust. She had suffered unutterable losses and could not bear the thought of another separation. Today, I can only feel compassion for her pain and sorrow. Yet, as vigilant as I had been not to repeat the childrearing practices that I felt were inappropriate, at times I easily fell into the same unconscious patterns in parenting my own children. Such is the fate that most of us suffer.

I know that I have overinvested in my children's lives: Their successes were my successes, and by the same token, their failures were my failures, too. When things go well, I somehow feel validated. When they go badly, it's not enough that my kids have to reckon with the disappointment, but they also have to put up with my inappropriate (spoken or tacit) laments: "Why are you doing this to *me?*" "Where have *I* gone wrong?" I see that I haven't been fair to them.

Such intense attachment can have negative effects. When we see our children as extensions of ourselves, we place heavy expectations on them. If we were unable to attend Harvard or Yale, then, by golly, Justin will go in our stead. If our children are unwilling or simply unable to live up to these expectations we feel triply hurt: We are disappointed that our youngsters have lost an opportunity that we deemed important, our wish for validation and accolades as a parent is unfulfilled, and our unconscious need to have our children make up for our own personal deficiencies has been thwarted.

Our overidentification with our children can also spark our intruding into their lives. We may find ourselves constantly interceding on their behalf at school or among their playmates. (This is easy enough to fall into, since our gifted youngsters may need our advocacy at school in some areas.) We may feel torn by their hurts and engaged in their battles.

I remember during Cherie's painful sixth grade, she had been excluded from an end-of-the-year class party. My husband and I seethed about the slight for weeks. It was all that I could do to hold myself back from calling the household where the party was held and excoriating the parents, whom I knew well, for their child's thoughtlessness in snubbing my daughter. (The incident brought back painful memories of my sixth grade, when I was "disinvited" to a party!) Cherie, on the other hand, cried that Friday evening, but then took the hurt in stride. Monday, she returned to school, head held high. The affront bothered us more than it did her.

When we get caught up in our own ego needs, we miss who our kids really are, seeing them, instead, as reflections of our own personalities. We fail to have empathy for their struggles and life issues and can become authoritarian and demanding. (An extreme example of this was portrayed in the movie, *The Dead Poets Society,* in which a father was so insistent that his son become a doctor at the expense of drama, his chosen avocation, that the boy felt he had no choice but to commit suicide.)

Under normal circumstances, our demandingness may have damaging effects on a youngster's self-esteem: He may feel that he is never good enough to please us or that he is important to us only in proportion to how well he fulfills our needs. In this situation, the parent-child roles become reversed. Such a youngster may even feel that he has never been truly heard or understood, causing resentment, underachievement, and rebelliousness.

Through overattachment, we may blind ourselves to the unique and individual struggles that our children must go through in order to mature. And their first order of business is to find out who *they* are—to separate and make lives for themselves. Without this separation, they cannot flourish. As Judith Viorst so aptly put it in her book *Necessary Losses,* "Inextricably our losses are linked to growth."

How can parents deal with this tendency to become overly attached? Dr. Bettelheim suggests deep reflection about your own motivations and feelings. Try to dig beneath the layers of your own needs and look at your children with fresh eyes. Ask yourself the following questions about your gifted child:

- Who is this person?
- What does he really need?
- If I didn't know that he was gifted, would I expect as much from him?
- Aside from my own wishes, hopes, and dreams, how does he want to live his life?

Psychologist and learning specialist Dr. Thomas Armstrong reminds us in his book, *In Their Own Way: Discovering and Encouraging Your Child's Personal Learning Style,* that parents need to believe in their children on their own terms. "In many cases, [your child's] hopes, dreams, ambitions, loves, and abilities won't coincide with yours. In fact, it may be difficult for you to even recognize his talents because of this very fact." In other words, not only do our children need to separate from us in their growing up but we also need to separate from them.

THE DANGERS OF OVERSCHEDULING AND PUSHING

Over and above our gifted youngsters' natural inclination to jump eagerly into activities with both feet, I suspect that our ego needs (as well as an overdeveloped sense of responsibility) may fuel our tendencies to push our gifted children too hard and to involve them in far too many structured activities such as Japanese classes, violin lessons, and computer literacy programs for toddlers (see chapter 12). We may secretly derive pleasure from thoughts of our youngsters' future successes, imagining them as world financiers, concert musicians, or the inventors of new software systems. This may well be true in the future, yet our overinvestment today may be more gratifying to our own unfulfilled needs than to our children's.

We may push our children into gifted programs, despite the fact that they may not actually belong there. Having a child identified as "gifted" (even if the designation is marginal) can be a way of keeping up with the Joneses. Even if a youngster is intellectually able, but socially unready or simply unwilling to do the work, he may fare poorly in a program that stresses pure academics at the expense of social learning or nurturance. Each child's needs and temperament must be considered individually.

I know from my experiences with Aimee that bright and verbal as she is, it did her little good to be placed in a highly structured academic environment. Her learning problem coupled with her learning style interfered with her picking up the material with the same ease as her classmates, and that only served to frustrate her and lower her feelings of self-esteem. It's probably more damaging for a child to be placed in a gifted program and be removed shortly thereafter than for him never to have been placed at all.

According to Dr. David Elkind of Tufts University, author of *The Hurried Child*, children who are pushed and overscheduled are in danger of becoming a "surrogate self" or "status symbol" for their parents. I'm the sort of person who wants to see herself successful in everything she does, including parenting. If my children are successful, I like to think that I have done a good job. Yet, I must also remember that parenting a child is nothing at all like succeeding on an exam or in business. Children are human beings, not objects or responsibilities or data that can be manipulated to our own ends.

In addition, it's one thing to help a child along who is eager to begin reading on his own, memorizing his picture book stories and joyfully calling out words he recognizes on the cereal boxes at the supermarket. It's quite another thing to push and drill a youngster, forcing him into formalized school work before he is raring to go. Dr. Bettelheim points out that in the latter case the child will perform only to please his parents (or he may refuse to perform, altogether).

Your pressure can have damaging effects. First, there is an inherent danger that your youngster's involvement in learning is not intrinsic but comes from observing your enthusiasm over his achievements. This could lead to his valuing performance and grades over his enjoyment of the process of learning—all of which may reinforce perfectionism (see chapter 8). As a result, the gifted child may develop only a limited sense of his own self-worth. He may become outer-directed, constantly needing the approval of others in order to feel good about himself.

We all know adults who are the product of such upbringing. They may either come across as highly insecure in their personal relationships and work, always seeking acceptance from those around them, or, conversely, they may feel driven to remain center stage, endlessly drawing attention to themselves to validate their shaky self-confidence.

Dr. Bettelheim also explains that this early push for academics may backfire later. Suppose your child is caught in a conflict with you during adolescence, as a natural part of his individuation. Knowing how much you value his performance, he may use academic under-achievement or failure as weapons as well as a means to separate from you. His rebellion may make sense in this larger, deeper context, but as a parent, you may see the underachievement as defiance. In effect, however, the child is trying to rebalance the relationship in the only way he knows how.

NOT ENOUGH STRUCTURE

Although the perils of overscheduling your gifted child are legion, if you suffered from the demands of your own overbearing parents, you may feel driven to let go of the reins entirely, allowing your gifted child to seek her own level. While this may give her the freedom to explore many possible activities, insufficient guidance and supervision on your part may lead to her feeling anxious, lost, and stressed.

A child who has too many choices and possibilities (from what she's going to do this afternoon to what she wants to be when she "grows up") may feel paralyzed by indecision: Being told she can do everything, she may feel incapable of narrowing her options to anything. She may need your guidance to create constructive boundaries that make her feel safe. You might lend a hand by showing her how to list and prioritize her options (or by doing it for her, if she's not yet able to write). Once she sees her choices set down concretely, she may find it easier to focus her energies and decide how to proceed.

THE TELLTALE SIGNS OF STRESS

How can you tell if you're expecting too much or too little from your child? Understimulated kids may become bored, petulant, unruly, and angry. Overscheduled, pushed youngsters often act stressed, anxious, and overwhelmed. With too many activities on the agenda, a youngster won't have enough time to play or explore his surroundings as he wants to. He'll be deprived, not only of the opportunity to learn how to manage his own activities but also of his sense of self. He loses touch with what *he* wants and just goes along with your demands. In effect, you are separating him from his identity and replacing it with *your* agenda.

This can cause your youngster to rely on you more and more heavily to make his arrangements, a burden for you and an unhealthy situation for him. He should be learning autonomy during his childhood. Alternatively, your overinvolvement can become the source of power struggles between the two of you. You may knock yourself out planning what you think is a terrific outing at the museum only to have him stubbornly refuse to participate because he had no hand in establishing the itinerary.

In addition, if your youngster is inappropriately placed in an academic program that's over his head, the effects will manifest themselves as negative feelings about himself and as symptoms of stress, not simply as poor performance.

Although children may not be adept at expressing their level of discomfort in words, they do let you know that they are experiencing stress by their behavior. *A word of caution: Persistent headaches, stomachaches, or any other continuing physiological symptoms should be investigated by the appropriate physician.*

If she experiences *any one* of the following, your child is telling you in subtle and not-so-subtle ways that she is feeling stressed:

- Sleep disturbances
  Waking up in the middle of the night
  Nightmares and night terrors
  Sudden difficulty falling asleep
  Somnambulism (sleepwalking) in severe cases
- Eating disturbances
  Sudden loss of appetite
  Overeating
  Frequent stomachaches, nausea, or diarrhea (when physical causes have been ruled out)
- Frequent physical complaints such as headaches
- School phobia
- Hyperactivity or unusual tiredness
- Persistent boredom (psychologists often view boredom in children as a precursor of depression)
- Aggressiveness toward other children or with toys and pets
- Drawings in which family members are represented as disproportionately large or small
- Repetitive, ritualized behavior such as chewing the corner of a blanket, stroking a toy, or twirling a strand of hair
- Clinginess
- Whininess
- Regressive behavior such as bedwetting and thumb sucking
- Withdrawal from normal family interactions
- Frequent, unwarranted temper tantrums
- Accident-prone behavior and personal injury

Many of these behaviors in children are a cry for help. The rule of thumb: Any behavior that is unusual or that you can characterize as an extreme change should be investigated by your pediatrician and/or a child psychologist as a sign of stress.

STRIKING A BALANCE

In defining your gifted child's activities, it is difficult to know how much involvement is too much and how much is not enough. Striking a balance between a laissez-faire and a more structured approach depends on your child's temperament and his own expressions of self-reliance, as well as how relaxed you feel about his preferences.

How can you find that happy medium? Let your child be your guide. Attend to her naturally abundant curiosity, abilities, and interests. If you want, you can expose her to lots of fields of endeavor, but don't force her into the one that *you* feel is important. Offer guidance and choices, but then let her take the lead. As Dr. Raphael Diaz, a Stanford University developmental psychologist, explained in a *New York Times* article by Lawrence Kutner, ''Provide support when and where it's needed, not everywhere and not all the time.''

What's the point of insisting that Bonnie take Saturday morning computer classes if her heart is set on being shortstop on the Little League baseball team this summer? Try to put yourself into your child's shoes and remember what it was like to be eight years old. What would your agenda be like? Then, call on your inner source of empathy and give your kids an opportunity to be themselves, not a replica of what you might need them to be.

GROWING UP; GOING ON

I only began to understand how attached I was to my children when they pulled away from me and vigorously asserted their independence as teenagers. I will spare you the gory details of their escapades, both out of respect to their privacy and because of my aversion to dragging myself through those moments again. But I will tell you that I experienced my daughters' *very typical* teenaged acts of rebelliousness, as innocuous as *they* judged them to be in comparison with their classmates' seditions, with such intensity that I felt as if one of my limbs were literally being torn off without benefit of anesthetic. One cannot go through such an experience without at least a modicum of hollering. It hurts!

My rage was mixed with a certain measure of indignation. I hadn't fully separated from my mother yet! (Who has?) What were these pipsqueaks doing, pulling away from me? How dare they grow up! To make matters worse, having been a rather compliant adolescent, I had no personal role model other than my husband's tempering voice of reason.

Indeed, my sense of loss was so great that at one point I considered approaching my own parents to apologize to them for any hurt I had caused them during *my* delayed adolescence. I fancied that maybe they would lift the traditional curse: "I hope one day you have children just like *you!*" Enough, already. I give.

I tell you this not to frighten you about what's to come but rather because my reaction, as extreme as it may sound, seems to typify how many parents feel about their offspring. When, during adolescence, our children declare their independence, we are forced to confront our enmeshment. We may understand the drama of adolescence intellectually but it can be awfully hard to let go emotionally. Yet release our children, we must, if they are to become whole, well-functioning adults. The tighter we hang on, the more authoritarian our approach, the more rebellious or withdrawn they become. And in truth, despite our feelings to the contrary, our children are not extra limbs that we have sprouted. They are people emotionally attached, yet still separate from us. They must soar toward their own future.

ON GUILT AND HOPE

It is easy to become guilt-ridden about how we use our gifted children to meet our own needs. Certainly the psychological literature is full of theories about the many ways that overinvolved parents can create pathology in their offspring. But we also have to take into consideration how the child effects his own evolution. No tabula rasa, an infant is born with a temperament already intact. It would be wise to acknowledge the impact of this temperament, along with a rare intelligence, and the unique set of experiences that will shape your gifted child's eventual emergence as an adult.

When I was a child, I fantasized about becoming a pathologist. I imagined that I would somehow rid the world of a deadly disease such as cancer—just as Dr. Jonas Salk had recently done with polio. I wanted to make the world a safer place in which to live. Today, I believe that this rather grandiose fantasy of saving the world had its roots in the psychological reality that my parents conveyed to me. For them, the world was a threatening and perilous place filled with people and events that could not be trusted. Their aim was to protect me at all costs from anything that could spell harm—even though we were living in the relative safety of the middle-class suburbs of New York City. Indeed, I believe that my birth, while a source of great joy, also kept alive in them the memory of the tremendous physical and emotional losses that they had sustained and would always fear sustaining again. The more they loved me, the more anxious they were about losing me, and the tighter they hung on. Despite their new lives, they could not separate themselves from the horrors of war.

My parents' underlying attitudes and fears had a profound impact on me. At a very young age, I came to see the world as flawed, and therefore, in need of correction. As a child, I sought to find a way to effectuate that healing: I took on the impossible task of making the world perfect for my much-loved parents. Curing illnesses became a metaphor for my desire to relieve hatred and suffering. My parents never actually said, "This is what you should do!" They probably would have been appalled at the idea of encouraging anyone to "save" such a flawed world. But their pain and longings were in the air, available for me to take into myself. I became the sponge that soaked up their fears and wishes and made them my own. My parents couldn't help themselves in this commerce and neither could I.

While it's easy to see how this legacy can be a burden to a young child, it's also important to recognize that in the course of my absorbing my parents' disturbing experiences, I also found a way to use them constructively in making a life for myself. They are what drive me to write books that help others. They fuel my interest in exploring altruism. They have forced me to come to terms with life and death, good and evil, faith and despair, compassion and apathy. These are not bad things.

And so, there is an irony here. We may feel guilty for unconsciously imposing ourselves on our gifted children, but we must also bear in mind that we are not omnipotent in shaping their successes or influencing their failures. Our youngsters will take our issues and come up with original solutions that are theirs alone. In that transformation lies the mystery and the wonder of parenting. In that mystery and wonder lies hope.

CHAPTER 14

Nerds, Geeks, Eggheads, and Know-It-Alls: The Changing Image of Gifted Children in Our Society

Much madness is divine sense
To a discerning eye;
Much sense the starkest madness.
'Tis the majority
In this, as all, prevails.
Assent, and you are sane;
Demur—you're straightway dangerous,
And handled with a chain.

—EMILY DICKINSON

"You're gifted. You figure out how to get home."
BOBBETTE COLLIER, Illinois bus driver, after getting lost while driving home a load of gifted students

—*NEWSWEEK*, DECEMBER 25, 1989

DURING ANCIENT TIMES, THOSE WHO POSSESSED EXTRAORDINARY abilities were thought to be divinely inspired. Primitive peoples believed that the superior intellectual powers of the seers among them emanated from supernatural forces. (Even today, we refer to the brightest members of our society as being *gifted,* which implies that they have received special *gifts* at birth, perhaps gifts from God, that they had little to do with.) These people became the leaders of the clans, the shamans, and healers.

Over the centuries, however, our society has taken a less admiring view of the gifted in its midst. For instance, in 1891, J. Nisbet wrote in his book *The Insanity of Genius,* "Originality of thought and quickness or preponderance of the intellectual faculties were organically much the same thing as madness and idiocy." In the same year,

Cesare Lombroso, an Italian criminologist and professor of forensic medicine and psychiatry expounded, "Genius is a true degenerative psychosis . . . a symptom of hereditary degeneration of the epileptoid variety and is allied with moral insanity."

These negative attitudes toward giftedness—ridiculous as they may seem to us today—frightened parents into protecting their children from possible madness and mental degeneration even into the 1920s. The expression "early ripe, early rot" came into vogue. Parents of the gifted purposely shielded their kids from too much intellectual activity, fearing that their bright children would become adult simpletons, or worse yet, would betray their precocity to their teachers. In her book *Growing Up Gifted* Dr. Barbara Clark explains that parents actually resorted to punishment to curtail any such tendencies in their children.

It wasn't until 1922 when Stanford University professor Dr. Lewis M. Terman began his famous long-term studies on 1,470 children with IQ's over 135 that some of these more pernicious notions about giftedness were dispelled—among scientific researchers, at least. At the outset, the children in these studies were in grades three through eight and averaged eleven years old. The research team followed up on them every five to ten years until 1972, when they reached their sixties.

Dr. Terman found that when compared to control groups of average-intelligence kids, the gifted were remarkably well adjusted: They were more socially poised, suffered from fewer nervous tics, headaches, or other signs of anxiety, and excelled at schoolwork. These children were also far from the bespectacled, enfeebled caricatures thus far proposed. They were heavier, taller, and more active in play than their average IQ counterparts. They became leaders of their communities, enjoyed greater popularity, and demonstrated superior moral attitudes when compared with the control population.

Despite Dr. Terman's findings, the debates rage on regarding genius and madness even today. Indeed, as recently as 1989, the *Los Angeles Times* published a front-page article entitled "Madness and Creativity: Scientists Hunt for Links" in which the reporter, Anne C. Roark, cited Winston Churchill, Edgar Allan Poe, F. Scott Fitzgerald, Michelangelo, and Vincent van Gogh as creative individuals who are "known to have suffered from some form of mental illness."

While it's true that madness might have struck certain brilliant individuals during the course of history (and others might have experienced their more creative moments during a fit of manic activity), to my knowledge, most gifted people are not mentally ill. They may simply perceive and act upon the world more intensely than do other members of the human race, which may set them slightly apart.

DOUBLE MESSAGES

Today, our culture experiences a sort of schism when it comes to being "brainy." On the one hand, society deifies Albert Einstein, and more recently, Cambridge physicist and best-selling author of *A Brief History of Time,* Stephen Hawking, but on the other it derides gifted people to the point that gifted children have now taken to making fun of themselves. (The *Los Angeles Times* recently reported on a winning junior high academic decathlon team, for example, that dubbed itself the "Nerd Herd.")

In 1954, the famed anthropologist Dr. Margaret Mead decried what she saw as the double bind that our educational system imposes on the gifted. "If they learn easily," she wrote in an article entitled, "The Gifted Child in the American Culture of Today," "they are penalized for being bored when they have nothing to do; if they excel in some outstanding way, they are penalized as being conspicuously better than the peer group." Dr. Mead complained that parents were terrorized by stories of "infant prodigies who go mad at twenty." She went on to explain that our culture attempts to squeeze gifted children into a stereotype (that of the frail, overly studious bookworm) and to cause them trouble in making friends. "Neither teacher, the parents of other children, nor the child's peers will tolerate the *Wunderkind.*"

HAVE ATTITUDES CHANGED?

I believe that remnants of the old prejudices against gifted children persist still today, albeit in a less overt and laughable form. The media are often accurate reflections of our cultural norms. The following news items, gleaned from recent magazine and newspaper accounts, betray our culture's anti-intellectual bent:

> **ITEM:** A banner headline emblazoned across the top of a recent *Newsweek* cover: "Not Just for Nerds: How to Teach Science to Our Kids." Within the article, the team of journalists makes the following startling statement: "Brains are beautiful! The nation needs its nerds; maybe we all [sic] better become nerds" and quotes Lewis Lapham, editor of *Harper's* as lamenting, "The society bestows its rewards

on the talent for figuring a market, not on the proofs of learning or the subtlety of mind.''

ITEM: In a companion article, Harvard biology professor Stephen J. Gould recalls what it was like to be a boy interested in dinosaurs in the 1940s: "Any kid with a passionate interest in science was a wonk, a square, a dweeb, a doofus, or a geek. . . . I was called 'fossil face' on the playground. It hurt.''

ITEM: The *Los Angeles Times* recently ran a story on a new club on the campus of Harvard University: SONG, an acronym for Society of Nerds and Geeks. Most members are math majors but other esoteric departments, such as Sanskrit, are represented as well. The club has a "Nerd Manifesto" about the dangers of anti-intellectualism. According to Jeremy Kahn, the club's founder, there's a saying going around campus, "Blessed are the nerds and geeks for they will become trend-setters.''

Often, these negative attitudes are unacknowledged, much like the elephant in the middle of the room that everyone pretends isn't there and politely steps around. Whether or not we admit to them, however, the prejudices do make their presence felt. You may find yourself wrestling with them, as I did during my own childhood and as a parent of gifted children. You may wonder, for instance, why your child feels alienated and rejected by his peers; why your child abandons her beloved chemistry lab for the lure of the cheerleading squad just for the sake of belonging; why the teacher and school administration seem so mean or unhelpful.

Our kids may encounter hostility from the general public that ranges from classmates' spiteful teasing and name-calling to well-intentioned but misguided efforts on the part of educators to eliminate programs for the gifted under the guise of fighting "elitism.'' Research shows that parents and teachers of the gifted as well as the gifted children themselves understand the crying need for these classes while regular classroom teachers, school administrators, and parents of nongifted kids feel they cheat the rest of the population of money for regular programs.

PREJUDICE IN THE CLASSROOM

Teachers, of course, are responsible for creating an accepting environment in their classrooms. If they fail to do this, they also fail our children. Yet teachers often greet the gifted with irritation, if not hostility. In 1976, in a book about the socioeducational environment of gifted children, T. E. Newland showed that in general, educators express disconcertingly low sensitivity to their gifted population. Other researchers, including former Secretary of Education Sidney P. Marland, Jr., in his Report to Congress, have described counselors and other pupil personnel as apathetic and even hostile toward the gifted.

As California State University Education professor Dr. Barbara Clark points out in her book *Growing Up Gifted,* teachers' statements such as " 'If you are so gifted, figure it out,' 'Of course you don't need any help; you know everything,' 'You're capable of better work than that' are unlikely to support a positive view of self.'' They also belie the teacher's hostility.

The plain truth is that gifted kids make a teacher's life more difficult. Unfortunately, many teachers are not educated about the specific needs of the gifted. Few take courses on gifted education as a part of their teacher preparation.

When a child is many years ahead of his grade level within an average group of kids, the teacher, if she is at all sensitive to his needs, will create separate lessons for him, thereby doubling her own work. Cherie's second-grade teacher resourcefully solved this problem for herself by sending my daughter to a fifth-grade room during reading time. But how many other teachers do this? The highly gifted daughter of a friend of mine recently complained to me that she had completed the curriculum for sixth-grade math at least five months before the school year was over, yet her teacher made no effort to provide additional materials. "I've come to the end of the book, so I just sit there bored during math,'' she said with resignation.

Gifted kids present other problems to teachers, as well. What if, in her lesson plans, the teacher anticipates a project to take a week while her gifted students finish the assignments in only two hours and come back begging for more and different work to do? What if the gifted student, in his desire to know and understand, pushes the teacher with questions that she is unprepared to answer? What if those questions take up too much class time from the other students or scheduled activities? What if the gifted child learns the material on the first go-round and refuses to do drill work? (In his book, *In Their Own Way,* Dr. Thomas Armstrong gives the example of the little girl who says, in effect, if three plus two always equals five, why do we have to keep doing it?)

Let us also not forget that gifted children can be highly sensitive, intense, perfectionistic, demanding, extremely verbal, challenging, single-minded, and rambunctious. They may approach education with a sense of entitlement. In her book *Growing Up Gifted* Dr. Barbara Clark explains that while these traits are not problems in and of themselves, they can present difficulties to teachers who have not been properly trained. "Some teachers," she writes, "do not know what to do with these youngsters and feel incompetent and threatened by them." And, some teachers may simply feel annoyed.

Those feelings of incompetence, threat, and irritation may translate into a hostile attitude. In an article on the intellectual and psychosocial nature of extreme giftedness, Dr. Phillip M. Powell and Tony Haden of the University of Texas, Austin explain that threatened teachers and administrators may give these children and their parents inaccurate information about their abilities by "highlighting mistakes, and by insisting that learning occur in a particular fashion, usually lockstep." This can diminish a child's understanding of his true potential, which can result in poor self-esteem.

How difficult would it be for a child's classmates to suppress their own anxiety and hostility if they sense their teacher expressing hers toward a gifted child?

IT'S HUMAN NATURE

Most likely, the prejudices against gifted children spring from human nature. From early childhood onward, we teach our children not to point and stare at individuals who are "different" or have been afflicted with obvious disabilities. This is part of our accepted socialization practice. Yet, frequent letters to "Dear Abby" and Ann Landers attest to the fact that many adults would think nothing of approaching a stranger whom they deem too fat, tall, thin, or short (among other anomalies) to comment on the weather "up there" or "down there" or on that person's eating habits. Giftedness, of course, is not a disability but an increased ability that is not immediately apparent from one's outward demeanor. Nonetheless, experts tell us that people feel anxiety about others who seem different from themselves.

And being gifted *does* mean being different. In an article on parenting young gifted children, University of Denver professor of gifted education Dr. Linda Kreger Silverman explains that part of our children's difficulties may arise from our lack of understanding that adjustment in childhood differs from how we adjust as adults. Adults spend time with others who share their "interests, abilities, sensitivities, and appreciations. Their friends are those who genuinely enjoy their company, who laugh with them, not at them. . . . We fit in with others who are most like ourselves."

Children, on the other hand, have a more difficult time finding true peers. "Those who play chess and love Mahler," Dr. Silverman writes, "may be very lonely in elementary school and may only find each other in an advanced mathematics class in high school." As I explained earlier, opportunities for gifted children to locate others like themselves may be severely limited.

HOW OUR CHILDREN RESPOND

What's the safest way for children to deal with all of this negativity? In elementary school, I took the tack of becoming the class superstar. If I didn't have many friends, at least I got the teacher's admiration. It was better than nothing. For many other gifted children, however, the answer is simply to hide. They do this in ingenious and original ways.

Some children withdraw from social interaction. They have no one to talk to, and believe they will never be accepted for who they are, so they retreat into their world of ideas and the "nerd" stereotype. According to Walter B. Barbe, who studied gifted children's reactions to social stigmatization, this retreat occurs most often when the learning situation offers no challenge.

Others take on the role of class clown. They show off to get attention and, they hope, peer approval. Often, however, teachers and classmates find the clown's behavior irritating and silly. They shut him out and put him down. The tragedy here is that such a child not only isolates himself socially but he is also unlikely to be thought of as gifted. Since he doesn't fit the stereotype of a cooperative, studious "teacher's pet," he may not be sent for testing and therefore won't benefit from special programming, should any be available.

Another group simply tries to blend in by feigning ignorance. These kids hide their talents in an attempt to relieve the pressure of being different. They avoid gifted and advanced placement classes and cover up their knowledge and abilities by faking wrong answers on tests, explaining to friends that they made "lucky guesses," or simply refusing to study.

This approach is unproductive, too. As Linda Silverman explains in her insightful article, "Children cannot be gifted and average simultaneously.'' Besides, this attempt to blend in leads to a sense of deep alienation from the self. The child denies a core aspect of his personality in order to fit in. Since he's not okay or good enough just as he is, he feels intrinsically unacceptable and unlikeable. Unfortunately, this approach can also lead to underachievement and permanent loss. With intellect, if you don't use it, you lose it. As Dr. Silverman explains, ''There is even some question as to whether adults who have not developed their potential can be considered gifted or whether their giftedness is permanently lost.''

I suspect that there's at least a fourth group, those who make fun of themselves, as did those young people in Harvard's Society of Nerds and Geeks and the junior high ''Nerd Herd'' that I mentioned early in this chapter. This behavior is something like identification with the aggressor: Better to put myself down than to wait for someone else to do it. If you can't beat 'em, you might as well join 'em. Such self-deprecation has to hurt a child's self-esteem, for he will find, in the long run, that the others will laugh *at* him and not *with* him. (I don't believe that banding together in mutual self-deprecation helps either. These children are simply reinforcing negative stereotypes among themselves.)

WHAT ARE WE PARENTS TO DO?

What's missing in these negative attitudes and our gifted children's responses is a basic respect for the marvelous uniqueness and potential of each human being. It's our task as parents to help our children *own* and *integrate* their giftedness, not in a boastful or overbearing way but as a part of who they are, like their brown hair, blue eyes, and cute button nose. Just as there's nothing wrong with being talented in athletics or mechanics, so should there be nothing wrong with being ''smart.''

In her article on parenting young gifted children, Dr. Linda Silverman writes that most often parents long for their children to be ''normal.'' Understandably, they want to protect their youngsters from the pain of feeling different. Yet, when parents equate giftedness with abnormality, a label they dread most, they may deny their children's unique talents:

The hardest part of my job is trying to convince parents not to ''normalize'' their children—that is, not to try to make their children be like everybody else. In order for human beings to develop their fullest potential, their gifts or differences must be recognized and nurtured. I have parents imagine what would have happened if Isaac Stern's mother had just wanted him to be a normal little boy and took away his violin.

Silverman urges parents to support and nurture their children's giftedness, to help them find other playmates with similar abilities, to provide a rich and loving home life that can offset some of the loneliness that a gifted child may experience. She asserts that not all gifted children are lonely. Indeed, she writes:

> They may have delightful, happy, well-adjusted childhoods, complete with many meaningful friendships, *particularly when they are helped to find gifted peers*. Gifted children are more apt to laugh at the same jokes, share similar dreams and interests. They experience their lives as "normal" when they are with others who are like themselves.

You can also help the process along by talking with your youngsters. Encourage your children to value and understand the differences among people. Show them that while they may be different in some areas, commonalities exist among all children. According to Wendy C. Roedell, director of the Northwest Gifted Education Center in Seattle, Washington, these discussions can "enhance peer relationships and individual self-concepts."

Finally, you may want to become politically involved. You can join statewide associations for gifted children and speak out on behalf of the gifted at your school board meetings, especially if the administration has rejected gifted education as "elitist." Again, to quote Dr. Silverman:

> There is absolutely no support for the claims that placing gifted children together creates elitism or snobbery, or inability to appreciate the "common man." . . . These fears seemed to be based on a pervasive anti-intellectualism in our society. Talented football players are not prevented from associating with each other for fear of creating an elitist group; why, then, this irrational fear of congregations of talented artists and mathematicians?

THE CHALLENGE AND THE JOY

By our own actions and attitudes, we give our gifted children a solid base from which they take their first steps into life. By our own actions and attitudes, we can also help our youngsters understand that intelligence is something they can feel comfortable with and even good about. As we express pleasure in watching those young minds at work, formulating ideas and carrying them out, so do we teach our children to enjoy their own intellectual processes. As we stand in awe of our youngsters' abilities and capacities to understand and learn difficult concepts, so do we help them to commit themselves to finding new avenues to explore and new ways to stimulate their minds.

It should be our wish for our gifted children that they take risks to become fully who they want to be; that they make their lives wonderful surprises, even to themselves; that they allow themselves the freedom to create the content of their own beings; that they use their many talents to dedicate themselves not purely for personal gain but also in the service of the greater good of humanity.

It should be our wish for our gifted children that they find joy in their giftedness. In the words of George Bernard Shaw:

> This is the true joy in life: the being used for a purpose recognized by yourself as a mighty one; the being thoroughly worn out before you are thrown on the scrap heap; the being a force of nature instead of being a feverish little clod of grievances, complaining that the world did not make you happy.

I believe that the fulfillment of these goals is the ultimate challenge we face in raising our gifted children.

APPENDIX

RESOURCES, MAGAZINES, AND GAMES

Marcy Cook Math
312 Diamond Avenue
Balboa Island, CA 92662

The Good Apple, Inc.
Box 299
Carthage, IL 62321
Ask for their catalogue of
activities for the gifted.

Midwest Publications
P. O. Box 448
Pacific Grove, CA 93950
Ask for the Mindbenders
catalogue.

Scholastic Publications
730 Broadway
New York, NY 10003

Dell Puzzle Magazine
Games Magazine
World Magazine (by National
Geographics)

BOOKS

Burns, Marilyn. *The Book of Think: Or How to Solve a Problem Twice Your Size*. Boston: Little, Brown & Co., 1976.

Burns, Marilyn. *The I Hate Math Book*. Boston: Little, Brown & Co., 1975.

Dell Big Book of Crosswords & Pencil Puzzles compiled by the editors of *Dell Puzzle Magazine*.

Dell Book of Cryptograms compiled by the editors of *Dell Puzzle Magazine*.

Dell Book of Logic Problems compiled by the editors of *Dell Puzzle Magazine*.

DeMille, Richard. *Put Your Mother on the Ceiling: Children's Imagination Games*. Santa Barbara, CA: Santa Barbara Press, 1981.

Doty, Roy. *Puns, Gags, Quips, and Riddles*. New York: Doubleday, 1974.

Hall, Rich. *Sniglets*. New York: Collier Books, 1984.

Hughes, Patrick, and George Brecht. *Vicious Circles and Infinity: An Anthology of Paradoxes*. New York: Penguin Books, 1975.

Koch, Kenneth. *Wishes, Lies and Dreams: Teaching Children to Write Poetry*. New York: Harper & Row, 1980.

McGuire, Jack. *Creative Storytelling: Choosing, Inventing and Sharing Tales for Children*. New York: McGraw-Hill, 1985.

Moscovitch, Rosalie. *What's in a Word*. Boston: Houghton Mifflin, 1985.

Pentagram. *Puzzlegrams*. New York: Simon and Schuster, 1989.

Perry, Susan K. *Playing Smart: A Parent's Guide to Enriching, Offbeat Learning*. Minneapolis, MN: Free Spirit Publishing, 1990.

Price, Roger. *Droodles*. Los Angeles: Price, Stern, Sloan, 1966.

Simon, Sarina. *101 Amusing Ways to Develop Your Child's Thinking Skills and Creativity*. Los Angeles: Lowell House, 1989.

Stenmark, Jean Kerr, Virginia Thompson, and Ruth Cossey. *Family Math*. Berkeley, CA: University of California Press, 1988.

Striker, Susan. *Anti-Coloring Book of Masterpieces*. New York: H. Holt & Co., 1982.

BIBLIOGRAPHY

Adderholdt-Elliott, Miriam. "Perfectionism and Underachievement." *Gifted Children Today*, 12:19–21, 1989.

Adderholdt-Elliott, Miriam. *Perfectionism: What's Bad About Being Too Good*. Minneapolis, MN: Free Spirit, 1987.

Alvino, James. "Guidance for the Gifted." *Instructor*, November/December: 64–66, 1981.

Alvino, James, and the Editors of *Gifted Children Monthly*. *Parents' Guide to Raising a Gifted Toddler: Recognizing and Developing the Potential of Your Child from Birth to Five Years*. Boston: Little, Brown, & Co., 1989.

Anastasi, Anne. "Coaching, Test Sophistication, and Developed Abilities." *American Psychologist*, 36:1086–1093, 1981.

Anastasi, Anne. "Heredity, Environment, and the Question of 'How?' " *Psychological Review*, 65:197–208, 1958.

Anastasi, Anne. *Psychological Testing*, 3rd ed. New York: Macmillan Co., 1968.

Armstrong, Thomas. *In Their Own Way: Discovering and Encouraging Your Child's Personal Learning Style*. Los Angeles: Jeremy P. Tarcher, 1987.

Austin, Ann Berghout, and Dianne C. Draper. "Peer Relationships of the Academically Gifted: A Review." *Gifted Child Quarterly*, 25:129–133, 1981.

Barbe, Walter B. "Differential Guidance for the Gifted." *Education*, 74: 306–311, 1954.

Bayley, Nancy. "On the Growth of Intelligence." *American Psychologist*, 10:805–818, 1955.

Bettelheim, Bruno. *A Good Enough Parent*. New York: Vintage Books, 1988.

Bigg, Morris, L. *Learning Theories for Teachers*, 2nd ed. New York: Harper and Row, 1971.

Bloom, Benjamin. *Developing Talent in Young People*. New York: Ballantine Books, 1985.

Bloom, Benjamin, M. D. Engelhart, E. J. Furst, et al. *Taxonomy of Educational Objectives: The Cognitive Domain*, Handbook I. New York: Longmans, 1956.

Blos, Peter. *The Adolescent Passage, Developmental Issues*. New York: International Universities Press, 1979.

Bothmer, Richard. "A State of Mind: On Defining Giftedness." *Gifted Children Today*, 12:36, Jan/Feb, 1989.

Bowen, Ezra. "Launchpad for Superachievers: A Remarkable Junior-High Plan Turns Out College-Level Pupils." *Time*, March 18, 1985, p. 66.

Brody, Linda E., and Camilla P. Benbow. "Accelerative Strategies: How Effective Are They for the Gifted?" *Gifted Child Quarterly* 3:105–109, 1987.

Buescher, Thomas M., and Sharon J. Higham. "A Developmental Study of Adjustment Among Gifted Adolescents." In *Patterns of Influence on Gifted Learners: The Home, the Self, and the School*, Joyce L. Van Tassel-Baska and Paula Olszewski-Kubilius, eds. New York: Teachers College Press, Columbia University, 1989.

Carroll, John B., and John L. Horn. "On the Scientific Basis of Ability Testing." *American Psychologist*, 36:1012–1020, 1981.

Chamrad, Diana L., and Nancy M. Robinson. "Parenting the Intellectually Gifted Preschool Child." *Topics in Early Childhood Special Education*, 6: 74–87, 1986.

Clark, Barbara. *Growing Up Gifted*, 3rd ed. Columbus, OH: Merrill Publishing Company, 1988.

Colangelo, Nicholas, and Penny Brower. "Gifted Youngsters and Their Siblings: Long-Term Impact of Labeling on Their Academic and Personal Self-Concepts." *Roeper Review*, 10:101–103, 1987.

Colangelo, Nicholas, and Penny Brower. "Labeling Gifted Youngsters: Long-Term Impact on Families." *Gifted Child Quarterly*, 31:75–78, 1987.

Coleman, J. L. *The Adolescent Society*. New York: Free Press, 1961.

Cornell, D.G. "Gifted Children: The Impact of Positive Labeling on the Family System." *American Journal of Orthopsychiatry*. 53:322–335, 1983.

Cowley, Geoffrey, with Karen Springen, Todd Barrett, Mary Hager. "Not Just for Nerds: How to Teach Science to Our Students." *Newsweek,* April 9, 1990.

Cramer, Roxanne. "Gifted Traits Can Cause Classroom Problems." *Gifted Children's Monthly,* Feb, 1988; p. 18. Based in part on work by May V. Seagoe, cited in *The Identification of the Gifted and Talented,* by R. A. Martinson (Ventura County Superintendent of Schools, California, 1974).

Delisle, James, R. *Gifted Children Speak Out.* New York: Walker, 1984.

Delisle, James, R. *Gifted Kids Speak Out.* Minneapolis, MN: Free Spirit, 1987.

Dowling, Colette. *The Cinderella Complex.* New York: Summit Books, Simon & Schuster, 1981.

Duncan, Scott. "The Social Dilemmas of Real-Life 'Doogie Howsers.' " *Los Angeles Times,* September 28, 1989.

Eccles, Jacquelynne, S. "Why Doesn't Jane Run? Sex Differences in Educational and Occupational Patterns." In *The Gifted and Talented: Developmental Perspectives,* Frances Degen Horowitz and Marion O'Brien, eds. Washington, DC: The American Psychological Association, 1985.

Elkind, David. *The Hurried Child: Growing Up Too Fast Too Soon,* rev. ed. Reading, MA: Addison-Wesley Publishing Company, Inc., 1988.

Elkind, David. *Miseducation: Preschoolers at Risk.* New York: A. Knopf, Inc., 1987.

Endler, N. S., L. R. Boulter, and H. Osser, eds. *Contemporary Issues in Developmental Psychology.* New York: Holt, Rinehart and Winston, Inc., 1968.

Engel, Joel. *It's O.K. to Be Gifted or Talented!* New York: TOR Books, 1987.

Enriquez, Sam. " 'Nerd Herd' of Sepulveda Wins Battle of the Brain." *Los Angeles Times,* March 22, 1990.

Faber, Adele, and Elaine Mazlish. *Siblings Without Rivalry.* New York: Avon Books, 1987.

Feldhusen, John F., and Steven M. Hoover. "A Conception of Giftedness: Intelligence, Self Concept and Motivation." *Roeper Review,* 8:140–143, 1986.

Feynman, Richard P. *"Surely You're Joking, Mr. Feynman! Adventures of a Curious Character."* New York: Bantam Books, 1986.

Fiske, Edward B. "Lessons: Even at a Former Women's College, Male Students Are Taken More Seriously, a Researcher Finds." *New York Times,* April 11, 1990.

Fox, Lynn H. "Identification of the Academically Gifted." *American Psychologist,* 36:1103–1111, 1981.

Fox, Lynn H., and Jerrilene Washington. "Programs for the Gifted and Talented: Past, Present, and Future." In *The Gifted and Talented: Developmental Perspectives,* Frances Degen Horowitz and Marion O'Brien, eds. Washington, DC: The American Psychological Association, 1985.

Freeman, J. *Gifted Children.* Baltimore: University Park Press, 1979.

Galton, Francis. *Hereditary Genius.* London: Julian Friedman, 1892. (Original work published in 1869.) Quoted in Grinder, Robert E. "The Gifted in Our Midst: By Their Divine Deeds, Neuroses, and Mental Test Scores We Have Known Them." In *The Gifted and Talented: Developmental Perspectives,* Frances Degen Horowitz and Marion O'Brien, eds. Washington, DC: The American Psychological Association, 1985.

Gardner, Howard. *Frames of Mind.* New York: Basic Books, 1983.

Ginsberg-Riggs, Gina, "Questions to Ask About G/T Programs." *Gifted Children Monthly,* December, 1986.

Golant, Mitch, and Susan K. Golant. *Disciplining Your Preschooler and Feeling Good About It.* Los Angeles: Lowell House, 1989.

Golant, Mitch, and Susan K. Golant. *Finding Time for Fathering.* In press. New York: Ballantine Books, 1991.

Golant, Susan K. "Research Shows Fetuses Can Learn from Conditioning." *Los Angeles Times,* VIEW Section, December 28, 1982.

Golant, Susan K. and Mitch Golant. *Kindergarten: It Isn't What It Used to Be.* Los Angeles: Lowell House, 1990.

Goleman, Daniel. "Envy Emerges as a Measure of What Matters Most in Life." *New York Times,* February 27, 1990.

Green, Bert F. "A Primer of Testing." *American Psychologist,* 36:1001–10011, 1981.

Grenier, Marcella Evan. "Gifted Children and Other Siblings." *Gifted Child Quarterly,* 29:164:167, 1985.

Grinder, Robert E. "The Gifted in Our Midst: By Their Divine Deeds, Neuroses, and Mental Test Scores We Have Known Them." In *The Gifted and Talented: Developmental Perspectives,* Frances Degen Horowitz and Marion O'Brien, eds. Washington, DC: The American Psychological Association, 1985.

Guilford, J. P. *The Nature of Human Intelligence*. New York: McGraw-Hill, 1967.

Hall, Eleanor G. "Longitudinal Measures of Creativity and Achievement for Gifted IQ Groups." *The Creative Child and Adult Quarterly*, 10:7–16, 1985.

Haney, Walt. "Validity, Vaudeville, and Values: A Short History of Social Concerns over Standardized Testing." *American Psychologist*, 36:1021–1034, 1981.

Hatch, Thomas C. and Howard Gardner. "From Testing Intelligence to Assessing Competences: A Pluralistic View of Intellect." *Roeper Review*, 8: 147–150, 1986.

Herrmann, N. "The Creative Brain." *Training and Development Journal*, 35:10–16, 1981.

Hess, Robert D., and Virginia C. Shipman. "Early Experience and the Socialization of Cognitive Modes in Children." *Child Development*, 36: 869–886, 1965.

Hoffman, Susan G. "What the Books Don't Tell You About Grade Skipping." *Gifted Children Today*, 12:37–39, 1989.

Horowitz, Frances Degen, and Marion O'Brien. *The Gifted and Talented: Developmental Perspectives*. Washington, DC: The American Psychological Association, 1985.

Howley, Craig B., and Aimee A. Howley. "A Personal Record: Is Acceleration Worth the Effort?" *Roeper Review*, 8:43–45, 1985.

Jackson, Nancy Ewald. "Precocious Reading Ability: What Does It Mean?" *Gifted Child Quarterly*, 32:200–204, 1988.

Janos, Paul M., Hellen C. Fung, and Nancy M. Robinson. "Self-Concept, Self-Esteem, and Peer Relations Among Gifted Children Who Feel 'Different.' " *Gifted Child Quarterly*, 29:78–82, 1985.

Janos, Paul M., Kristi A. Marwood, and Nancy M. Robinson. "Friendship Patterns in Highly Intelligent Children." *Roeper Review*, 8:46–49, 1985.

Janos, Paul M., and Nancy M. Robinson. "Psychosocial Development in Intellectually Gifted Children." In *The Gifted and Talented: Developmental Perspectives*, Frances Degen Horowitz and Marion O'Brien, eds. Washington, DC: The American Psychological Association, 1985.

Kantrowitz, Barbara, and Pat Wingert. "How Kids Learn." *Newsweek*, April 17, 1989, pp. 50–57.

Kaplan, Leslie. "Mistakes Gifted Young People Too Often Make." *Roeper Review*, 6:73–77, 1983.

Karnes, M. B., A. M. Shwedel, and D. Steinberg. "Styles of Parenting

Among Parents of Young Gifted Children." *Roeper Review,* 6:232–235, 1984.

Katz, Lilian, G. "Early Education: What Should Young Children Be Doing?" In *Early Schooling: The National Debate,* Sharon L. Kagan and Edward F. Zigler, eds. New Haven, CT: Yale University Press, 1987.

Keislar, E. R. "Peer Group Ratings of High School Pupils with High and Low School Marks." *Journal of Experimental Education,* 23:375–378, 1955.

Kerr, Barbara, Nicholas Colangelo, and Julie Gaeth. "Gifted Adolescents' Attitudes Toward Their Giftedness." *Gifted Child Quarterly,* 32:245–247, 1988.

Kitano, Margie K. "The K-3 Teacher's Role in Recognizing and Supporting Young Gifted Children." *Young Children,* 44:57–63, 1989.

Kulieke, Marilynn J., and Paula Olszewski- Kubilius. "The Influence of Family Values and Climate on the Development of Talent." In *Patterns of Influence on Gifted Learners: The Home, the Self, and the School,* Joyce L. Van Tassel-Baska and Paula Olszewski-Kubilius, eds. New York: Teachers College Press, Columbia University, 1989.

Kutner, Lawrence. "How to Help Children Become More Self-Reliant." *New York Times,* May 31, 1990.

Kutner, Lawrence. "Parent and Child: Keeping a Gifted Child Challenged in School: Special Classes May Not Be the Answer." *New York Times,* October 5, 1989.

Kutner, Lawrence. "Parent and Child: Most Parents Play Favorites, Even If They Don't Feel Good Admitting It." *New York Times,* April 5, 1990.

Kutner, Lawrence. "Parent and Child: Periods of Animosity Between Siblings Actually Appear to Be Helpful to the Children Later On." *New York Times,* February 1, 1990.

Lacy, Grace. "Developing Defensible, Differentiated Programs for the Gifted and Talented." New York State Department of Education.

Lawson, Carol. "Studying Vivaldi and Art, in Diapers." *New York Times,* November 2, 1989.

Loeb, Roger C., and Gina Jay. "Self-Concept in Gifted Children: Differential Impact in Boys and Girls." *Gifted Child Quarterly,* 31:9–13, 1987.

Lombroso, Cesare. *Man of Genius.* London: Walter Scott, 1891. Quoted in Grinder, Robert E. "The Gifted in Our Midst: By Their Divine Deeds, Neuroses, and Mental Test Scores We Have Known Them." In *The Gifted and Talented: Developmental Perspectives,* Frances Degen Horowitz and Marion O'Brien, eds. Washington, DC: The American Psychological Association, 1985.

Ludington-Hoe, Susan, and Susan K. Golant. *How to Have a Smarter Baby.* New York: Bantam Books, 1987.

Mahler, Margaret, F. Pine, and A. Bergman. *The Psychological Birth of the Human Infant.* New York: Basic Books, 1975.

Marland, Sidney P., Jr. *Education of the Gifted and Talented.* Report to the Congress of the United States by the U.S. Commissioner of Education. Washington, DC: U.S. Government Printing Office, 1972.

Maslow, Abraham H. *The Farther Reaches of Human Nature.* New York: Viking, 1971.

Maslow, Abraham H. *Toward a Psychology of Being,* 2nd ed. New York: Van Nostrand Reinhold Co., 1968.

May, Rollo. *The Courage to Create.* New York: Bantam Books, 1975.

Mayr, E. *The Growth of Biological Thought.* Cambridge, MA: Belknap Press, 1982.

Mead, Margaret. "The Gifted Child in the American Culture of Today." *Journal of Teacher Education,* 5:211–214, 1954.

Miller, Alice. *The Drama of the Gifted Child: The Search for the True Self,* Ruth Ward, trans. New York: Basic Books, 1981.

Miller, Henry. "Reflections on Writing." In *The Creative Process,* Brewster Ghiselin, ed. Berkeley, CA: University of California Press, 1952.

Miller, R. "Social Status and Socioeconomic Differences Among Mentally Superior, Mentally Typical, and Mentally Retarded Children." *Exceptional Children,* 23:114–119, 1956.

Mills, B. "Attitudes of Decision-Making Groups Toward Gifted Children and Public School Programs for the Gifted." Unpublished doctoral dissertation, UCLA, 1973. *Dissertation Abstracts International,* 34:1739–1740.

Morrow, W., and P. Wilson. "Family Relations of Bright High-Achieving and Under-Achieving High School Boys." *Child Development,* 32:507–510, 1961.

Mozart, Wolfgang Amadeus. "A Letter." In *The Creative Process,* Brewster Ghiselin, ed. Berkeley, CA: University of California Press, 1952.

Newland, T. E. *The Gifted in Socioeducational Perspective.* Englewood Cliffs, NJ: Prentice Hall, Inc., 1976.

Newton, Edmund. "Sisters Collect Their, Er, Lambskins." *Los Angeles Times,* Part 2, June 9, 1990.

Nisbet, J. *The Insanity of Genius.* London: Ward & Downey, 1891. Quoted in Grinder, Robert, E. "The Gifted in Our Midst: By Their Divine Deeds,

Neuroses, and Mental Test Scores We Have Known Them." In *The Gifted and Talented: Developmental Perspectives,* Frances Degen Horowitz and Marion O'Brien, eds. Washington, DC: The American Psychological Association, 1985.

Olshen, Sylvia R., and Dona J. Matthews. "The Disappearance of Giftedness in Girls: An Intervention Strategy." *Roeper Review,* 9:251–254, 1987.

Olszewski-Kubilius, Paula, and Marilynn J. Kulieke. "Personality Dimensions of Gifted Adolescents." In *Patterns of Influence on Gifted Learners: The Home, the Self, and the School,* Joyce L. Van Tassel-Baska and Paula Olszewski-Kubilius, eds. New York: Teachers College Press, Columbia University, 1989.

Perry, Susan, K. *Playing Smart: A Parent's Guide to Enriching, Offbeat Learning Activities for Ages Four to Fourteen.* Minneapolis, MN: Free Spirit Publishing, 1990.

Peterson, Diane Cyzmoure. "The Heterogeneously Gifted Family." *Gifted Child Quarterly,* 21:396–398, 1977.

Piechowski, Michael M. "The Concept of Developmental Potential." *Roeper Review,* 8:190–197, 1986.

Piechowski, Michael M. "Developmental Potential and the Growth of the Self." In *Patterns of Influence on Gifted Learners: The Home, the Self, and the School,* Joyce L. Van Tassel-Baska and Paula Olszewski-Kubilius, eds. New York: Teachers College Press, Columbia University, 1989.

Plomin, Robert. "Environment and Genes: Determinants of Behavior." *American Psychologist,* 44:105–111, 1989.

Powell, Phillip M., and Tony Haden. "The Intellectual and Psychosocial Nature of Extreme Giftedness." *Roeper Review,* 6:131–136, 1984.

Purkey, William W. *Self Concept and School Achievement.* Englewood Cliffs, NJ: Prentice-Hall, Inc., 1970.

"Questions to Ask About G/T Programs." *Gifted Child Monthly,* December, 1986.

Radford, John. *Child Prodigies and Exceptional Early Achievers.* New York: The Free Press, 1990.

Reis, Sally M. "Reflections on Policy Affecting the Education of Gifted and Talented Students: Past and Future Perspectives." *American Psychologist,* 44:399–408, 1989.

Reis, Sally M. "We Can't Change What We Don't Recognize: Understanding the Special Needs of Gifted Females." *Gifted Child Quarterly,* 31:83–89, 1987.

Renzulli, Joseph S. "The Three-Ring Conception of Giftedness: A Developmental Model for Creative Productivity." In *Conceptions of Giftedness,* Robert J. Sternberg and Janet E. Davidson, eds. London: Cambridge University Press, 1986.

Roark, Anne C. "Creativity: It May Be More Than Biology." *Los Angeles Times,* Part I, September 29, 1989.

Roark, Anne C. "Madness and Creativity: Scientists Hunt for Links." *Los Angeles Times,* Part I, September 30, 1989.

Robinson, Ann. "Gifted: The Two-Faced Label." *Gifted Children Today,* 12:34–36, 1989.

Robinson, Jacqueline. *The Baby Boards: A Parents' Guide to Preschool and Primary School Entrance Tests.* New York: Arco, 1988.

Roedell, Wendy C. "Early Development of Gifted Children." In *Patterns of Influence on Gifted Learners: The Home, the Self, and the School,* Joyce L. Van Tassel-Baska and Paula Olszewski-Kubilius, eds. New York: Teachers College Press, Columbia University, 1989.

Roedell, Wendy C. "Social Development in Intellectually Advanced Children." Paper presented at the Annual Convention of the American Psychological Association, Toronto, August 30, 1978.

Roedell, Wendy C. "Socioemotional Vulnerabilities of Young Gifted Children." *Journal of Children in Contemporary Society,* 18:17–29, 1986.

Roedell, Wendy C. "Vulnerabilities of Highly Gifted Children." *Roeper Review,* 6:127–130, 1984.

Roeper, Anne-Marie. "The Young Gifted Child." *Gifted Child Quarterly,* 21:388–396, 1977.

Sadker, Myra, and David Sadker. "Sexism in the Schoolrooms of the '80s." *Psychology Today,* 19:54–57, 1985.

Samples, Bob. *The Metaphoric Mind: A Celebration of Creative Consciousness.* Reading, MA: Addison-Wesley Publishing Co., 1976.

Saunders, Jacqulyn, with Pamela Espeland. *Bringing Out the Best: A Resource Guide for Parents of Young Gifted Children.* Minneapolis, MN: Free Spirit Publishing, 1986.

Schorow, Stephanie. "Campus Nerds Aim for Last Laugh." *Los Angeles Times,* 1990.

Schwartz, Lita Linzer. "Are You a Gifted Parent of a Gifted Child?" *Gifted Child Quarterly,* 25:31–35, 1981.

Seagoe, May V. "Some Learning Characteristics of Gifted Children." In *A Handbook for Parents of Gifted and Talented,* Second Edition. Jeanne L.

Delp and Ruth A. Martinson, eds. Ventura, CA: Ventura County Superintendent of Schools Office, 1977.

Seagoe, May V. *Terman and the Gifted.* Los Altos, CA: William Kaufman, 1975.

Silverman, Linda Kreger. "The IQ Controversy: Conceptions and Misconceptions." *Roeper Review,* 8:136–140, 1986.

Silverman, Linda Kreger. "Parenting Young Gifted Children." *Journal of Children in Contemporary Society,* 18:73–87, 1986.

Singer, Jerome. "Fantasy: The Foundation of Serenity." *Psychology Today,* 10:32–37, 1976.

Sloane, Kathryn D. "Home Influences on Talent Development." In *Developing Talent in Young People,* Benjamin Bloom, ed. New York: Ballantine Books, 1985.

Smutny, Joan F., Kathleen Veenker, and Stephen Veenker. *Your Gifted Child: How to Recognize and Develop the Special Talents in Your Child from Birth to Age Seven.* New York: Facts on File, 1989.

Snyderman, Mark, and Stanley Rothman. "Survey of Expert Opinion on Intelligence and Aptitude Testing." *American Psychologist,* 42:137–144, 1987.

Sosniak, Lauren A. "A Long-Term Commitment to Learning." In *Developing Talent in Young People,* Benjamin Bloom, ed. New York: Ballantine Books, 1985.

Sosniak, Lauren A. "Phases of Learning." In *Developing Talent in Young People,* Benjamin Bloom, ed. New York: Ballantine Books, 1985.

Sternberg, Robert J. "Identifying the Gifted Through IQ: Why a Little Bit of Knowledge Is a Dangerous Thing." *Roeper Review,* 8:143–147, 1986.

Sternberg, Robert J., and Janet E. Davidson. "Cognitive Development in the Gifted and Talented." In *The Gifted and Talented: Developmental Perspectives,* Frances Degen Horowitz and Marion O'Brien, eds. Washington, DC: The American Psychological Association, 1985.

Sternberg, Robert J., and Janet E. Davidson, eds. *Conceptions of Giftedness.* London: Cambridge University Press, 1986.

Stone, Elizabeth. "A Matter of Class: Do Special Curriculums Really Turn Out Special Students?" *New York Times Magazine,* May 6, 1990, p. 48.

Tan, Amy. *The Joy Luck Club.* New York: Putnam, 1989.

Tannenbaum, Abraham. "Giftedness: A Psychosocial Approach." In *Conceptions of Giftedness,* Robert J. Sternberg and Janet E. Davidson, eds. London: Cambridge University Press, 1986.

Terman, Lewis M. *Genetic Studies of Genius: Vol. 1. Mental and Physical Traits of a Thousand Gifted Children.* Stanford, CA: Stanford University Press, 1925.

Terman, Lewis M., and M. H. Oden. *Genetic Studies of Genius: Vol. 4. The Gifted Child Grows Up.* Stanford, CA: Stanford University Press, 1947.

Terman, Lewis M., and M. H. Oden. *Genetic Studies of Genius: Vol. 5. The Gifted Group at Mid-Life.* Stanford, CA: Stanford University Press, 1959.

Teyler, T. "An Introduction to the Neurosciences." In *The Human Brain,* M. Wittrock, ed. Englewood Cliffs, NJ: Prentice-Hall, Inc., 1977.

Torrance, E. Paul. *Education and the Creative Potential.* Minneapolis, MN: University of Minnesota Press, 1962.

Treffinger, Donald J., and Joseph Renzulli. "Giftedness as Potential for Creative Productivity: Transcending IQ Scores." *Roeper Review,* 8:150–154, 1986.

Tsapogas, John. Personal Communication, November 20, 1990. National Science Foundation, Washington, D.C.

van Gogh, Vincent. "Letter to Anton Ridder van Rappard." In *The Creative Process,* Brewster Ghiselin, ed. Berkeley: University of California Press, 1952.

Viorst, Judith. *Necessary Losses.* New York: Fawcett, 1986.

Wallach, Michael A. "Creativity Testing and Giftedness." In *The Gifted and Talented: Developmental Perspectives,* Frances Degen Horowitz and Marion O'Brien, eds. Washington, DC: The American Psychological Association, 1985.

Weinberg, R. A. "Intelligence and IQ: Landmark Issues and Great Debates." *American Psychologist* 44:98–104, 1989.

Wernick, Sarah. "Hard Times for Educating the Highly Gifted." *New York Times,* May 30, 1990.

Whitmore, J. R. *Giftedness, Conflict, and Underachievement.* Boston: Allyn & Bacon, 1980.

Wilson, John A. R., Mildred C. Robeck, and William B. Michael. *Psychological Foundations of Learning and Teaching.* New York: McGraw-Hill Book Co., 1969.

Winn, Marie. *Children Without Childhood.* New York: Penguin, 1983.

Winn, Marie. "New Views of Human Intelligence." *New York Times Magazine,* Part II: *The Good Health Magazine,* April 29, 1990, p. 16.

Winnicott, D. W. *The Child, the Family, and the Outside World.* New York: Penguin, 1984.

Wolfle, Jane. "The Gifted Preschooler: Developmentally Different But Still 3 or 4 Years Old." *Young Children,* 44:41–48, 1989.

Zervos, Christian. "Conversation with Picasso." In *The Creative Process,* Brewster Ghiselin, ed. Berkeley: University of California Press, 1952.

Zigler, Edward, and Ellen A. Farber. "Commonalities Between the Intellectual Extremes: Giftedness and Mental Retardation." In *The Gifted and Talented: Developmental Perspectives,* Frances Degen Horowitz and Marion O'Brien, eds. Washington, DC: The American Psychological Association, 1985.

INDEX

A

Acceleration programs, 83–84
  arguments against, 84
Achievement
  childhood factors of, 191–192
  home environment and, 187
  as measure of worth, 193
  parental involvement in, 208
  as a weapon, 208
Adderholdt-Elliott, Miriam, 113
Adolescence, 105–106
  gender inequities during, 139–140
  hiding giftedness during, 139–142, 145
  separation and, 201, 211–212
  social adjustment, 141–142
Adolescent girls, 141–142, 145
Alienation, 122–123, 134
Alpha state, 42
Alternative gifted programs, 84–86
Alvino, James, on sibling rivalry, 166
Analytic intelligence, 16
Anti-intellectualism, 216–217
Armstrong, Thomas, 218
  on separation, 206–207
Attention span, long, problems of, 96

B

Babies, stimulating, 40–42
Barbe, Walter
  on sensitivity, 100
  on social stigmatization, 220
Benbow, Camilla, on acceleration pro-
    grams, 84
Bettelheim, Bruno
  on parental emotions, 204, 206
  on pushing children, 208
Binet, Alfred, 14, 35, 48

Bloom, Benjamin
  taxonomy, 86–87
  on unstructured time, 191–192
Blos, Peter, on separation, 201
Boredom, 91
  as sign of stress, 210
  virtues of, 157–158
Brain
  development of, 40
  differences of gifted, 42–43
  growth of, 37–38
    intelligence and, 38
  hemisphere functions, 19–21
  hemisphere lateralization, 20
  structure of, 19–21, 39–40
Brain-wave patterns of creative people, 25
Brody, Linda, on acceleration programs,
    84
Buescher, Thomas, on adolescent social
    adjustment, 141–142

C

Career achievements, gender inequities in,
    140
Cerebral cortex, 19
Characteristics of gifted, 95–97
Children, needs as, 188, 193
Clark, Barbara
  on acceleration programs, 84
  on brain development, 40
  on brain differences of gifted, 42
  on characteristics of gifted, 90–91
  on creativity, 25
  on gifted education, 81, 82
  on high expectations, 109
  on historical view of giftedness, 215
  on identifying gifted, 57

Clark, Barbara (*cont.*)
  on IQ tests, 56
  on perfectionism, 117
  on praise, 117
  on teacher hostility, 136
  on teachers and gifted, 219
Class clown, 220
Clay, 152
Cognitive dissonance, 101
Colangelo, Nicholas
  on hiding giftedness, 138
  on siblings and giftedness, 169
Communication skills, 174–176
Competition, among siblings, 166–167, 169
Convergent thinking, 21–22
  school advantages and, 22
Cornell, D. G., 169
Corpus callosum, 19
Crayons, 152–153
Creativity, 25
  definition of, 22–23
  development of, 154–157, 157–161
  IQ and, 23–24
  IQ tests and, 56
  major elements of, 22–23
  phases of, 20
  pleasures of, 24–26
  problems of, 96
  society and, 24
Csikszentmihalyi, Mihaly, on creativity,
  24–25
Curiosity, 195–198

D
Davidson, Janet
  on giftedness, 28
  on intelligence, 16
Delisle, James, 179
Development, uneven, 134
Diaz, Raphael, 210
Differentiated education, 86–88
Differentness, 143–144, 219–220
  feelings of, 130–131, 132–133
  reactions to, 220–222
Divergent thinking, 21–22
  school difficulties and, 21–22
Dropouts, 126–127

E
Eating disturbance, as sign of stress, 210
Eccles, Jacquelynne, on gender inequities,
  139–140

Elitism
  fallacy of, 92–93, 222
  gifted programs and, 69, 217
Empathy, 201–202
Energy, high, problems of, 96
Enrichment
  danger of too much, 191
  programs, 87–88
Envy, 135–136
  dealing with, 136–138
Excellence, successive approximations and,
  118–120
Expectations
  adult, 134
  high, 109–111
  social, 126
Extracurricular acceleration classes, 85–
  86

F
Failure, handling, 116–117
Family influence, 187
Family meetings, 173–176
Family relations checklist, 172–173
Fantasy, importance of, 153–154
Farber, Ellen
  on feelings of differentness, 132
  on hiding giftedness, 138
Favoritism, 170–171, 178
Fox, Lynn, on gifted programs, 80
Friends, 132–133
  gifted
    need for, 126, 127–129
    older, 130–131
    opportunities for, 127–129
  highly gifted and, 133–134
Fung, Hellen, on differentness, 132
Furman, Wyndol, on sibling conflict,
  165

G
Gaeth, Julie, on hiding giftedness, 138
Galton, Francis, on intelligence, 14
Games, 158–159
Gardner, Howard, 15–16
  on identifying gifted, 58
Gender inequities, 139–141
Giftedness
  among siblings, 167–168
  brain differences of, 42–43
  characteristics of, 90–91, 95–97
  concepts of, 17

definition of, 27–28
displaying of, 30–31
Gould on, 217
hiding, 138–142, 145, 220–221
historical view of, 215
identifying, 29–31, 56–58, 167–168
madness and, 215
misconceptions of, 118
nature of, 28
precociousness and, 31
prejudices against, 216–220
sense of humor and, 29
societal view of, 214–217
Gifted program
acceleration programs, 83–84
alternative programs, 84–86
choosing, 88–90
determining appropriateness of, 64–65
as differentiated education, 86–88
as elitism, 69, 217
as enrichment, 87–88
extracurricular acceleration classes, 85–86
feelings of differentness and, 133
individualized instruction, 82
limitations of, 143–144
need for, 90–92
options of, 80
parental activism and, 63–65
personal experiences with, 71–79
portraying, 180
pull-out programs, 81–82
pushing into, 207
questions for administrators, 89–90
regular classroom as, 80–81
revolving door program, 84–85
screening for, 56–58
self-contained classes, 82–83
Glial cells, intelligence and, 40
Gould, Stephen J., 217
Grenier, Marcella Evan, on sibling competition, 169
Guilford, J. P., 15
on model of intellect, 21

H
Hall, Edward, 16–17
Hemisphere lateralization, 20
Hiding giftedness, 138–142, 145, 220–221
Higham, Sharon, on adolescent social adjustment, 141–142
Highly gifted, 219

family complications of, 168–170
friends and, 133–134
need for specialized education, 91
self-contained classes and, 83
social adjustment of, 133–134
vulnerabilities of, 101, 110, 113, 133–134
Hostility
dealing with, 136–138
reactions to, 220–221
in school, 135–136
teacher, 136, 137, 218, 219

I
Identification, parental, 205
Impatience, 114–115
Independence, problems of, 96
Individualized instruction, 82
Inequities, gender, 139–141
Intellect, model of, 21
Intelligence
analytic, 16
brain growth and, 38
definition of, 13–17
fetal development of, 38–39
genetic determination of, 36
glial cells and, 40
influence of nurture on, 40–42
multiple, 14
newborn, 39
nongenetic determination of, 36–37
practical, 16
splitters, 15–17, 54–55
synthetic, 16
temperamental determination of, 37
triarchic theory of, 16
unified, general, 14
Introspection, 103
Introversion, 102–103
IQ test, 35
children and, 58–59
coaching for, 53–54
controversy of, 45–46
creativity and, 23–24, 56
criticisms of, 54–56
evaluating examiner, 51–52
experiences with, 59–63
function of, 46
group testing, 52–53
most common, 47–51
score, definition of, 46–47
as screening tool, 44–46
Stanford-Binet, 48–49
Wechsler, 49–51, 52

J

Janos, Paul, on social adjustment of gifted, 129–130, 132, 133–134
Jealousy, 135–136

K

Kaplan, Leslie
  on achievement, 193
  on perfectionism, 118
Karnes, M. B., on parenting activities, 34
Kerr, Barbara
  on elitism, 92
  on hiding giftedness, 138
Kulieke, Marilynn, on importance of family, 187

L

Learning characteristics of gifted, 31–33
Learning tool(s)
  clay as, 152
  crayons as, 152–153
  nature as, 147–149
  play as, 146
  reading as, 150–151
  story telling as, 151–152
Left-brain dominance, 19–21
  description of, 18
Limbic system, 19
Listening, 175
Logic puzzles, 160
Ludington, Susan, 20–21
  on brain growth, 38
  on stimulating babies, 41–42

M

Madness, giftedness and, 215
Magnet schools, 94
Mahler, Margaret, on symbiosis, 200
Mainstreaming, 69
Marland, Sidney
  on elitism, 93
  on hostility toward gifted, 218
Maslow, Abraham, 106
Mathematics
  games and puzzles, 158–159
  gender inequities in, 140
Matthews, Dona, on hiding giftedness, 141–143
May, Rollo, on creativity, 23, 25
Mead, Margaret, 216
Mediocrity, 192–193
Miller, Alice, on parental empathy, 201–202
Miller, R., on gifted friends, 131

Mirroring, 176, 201–202, 203–204
Morrow, W., on home environment, 187
Multiple intelligences, 14

N

Nature, as learning tool, 147–149
Noncompetitive activities, 116, 149–157
Nongifted siblings, 168–170

O

Observation, keen, problems of, 96
Olshen, Sylvia, on hiding giftedness, 141, 143
Olszewski-Kubilius, Paula, on importance of family, 187
Overscheduling, 190–191
  dangers of, 207–208

P

Paradox of gifted, 131, 216
Parenting
  ambivalence about, 194
  balanced, 211
  Bettelheim on, 204, 206
  child as status symbol, 207–208
  communication skills for, 174–176
  complementary styles, 189–190
  controlling, 190
  coping with giftedness, 221–222
  ego involvement in, 199–200
  emotions, 204
  empathy and, 201–202
  favoritism, 170–171, 178
  of gifted, 34–35
  goals for children, 223
  imposing expectations, 202
  influence on children, 212–213
  influence of past on, 172–173
  learning from past, 202–203
  overinvesting, 205, 207
  overinvolvement, 209
  perfectionism and, 111–112
  power of influence, 186–190
  projecting needs, 203
  role in gifted programs, 63–65
  sense of responsibility, 194–195
  structure, need for, 208–209
Peers, 219–220, 222
Perfectionism, 149, 193, 202, 208
  dealing with, 115–118
  demands on others, 114

high expectations and, 109–111
parental promotion of, 111–112
positive, 113
reinforcement of, 111
Phobia, school, 210
Piechowski, Michael
on differentness, 143–144
on gifted adolescent development, 105–106
Play
different kinds of, 145
importance of, 127, 145–146
noncompetitive, 149–157
parents' role in, 146–147
as teaching tool, 146
unstructured, 157–158
Plomin, Robert, on genetic determination of intelligence, 36
Positive perfectionism, 113
Powell, Phillip
on parental ambivalence, 194
on teacher hostility, 219
Power struggles, 209
Practical intelligence, 16
Praise, 112–113, 117
Precociousness, giftedness and, 31
Prejudices
against giftedness, 216–220
in classroom, 217–219
Pull-out programs, 81–82
Pushing children, 207–208
Puzzles
logic, 160
math, 158–159
word, 160

Q
Quality time, 146
Questions, dealing with, 195–196

R
Radford, John, on temperament and giftedness, 37
Reading, 161–162
as learning tool, 150–151
problems of early, 96
Reis, Sally, on identifying gifted, 57–58
Renzulli, Joseph, 17
on alternative gifted programs, 84–85
on identifying gifted, 58
Reptilian brain, 19
Revolving door gifted program, 84–85
Right-brain dominance, 19–21

description of, 18
school difficulties and, 18–19
Right-brain perception, example of, 17–18
Robinson, Nancy, on social adjustment of gifted, 129–130, 132, 133–134
Roedell, Wendy
on differentness, 222
on perfectionism, 110, 113
on praise, 117
on socialization, 127
on vulnerabilities of highly gifted, 101, 134
Roeper, Anne-Marie
on gifted loss of innocence, 105
on precociousness, 31
Role conflict, of highly gifted, 134
Rothman, Stanley, on IQ tests, 56

S
Saunders, Jacqulyn
on achievement, 118
on handling failure, 116–117
paradox of gifted, 131
on parenting gifted, 194
on perfectionism, 111, 116–117
Schachter, Frances Fuchs, on sibling conflict, 165
Schwarz, Lita Linzer, on overscheduling, 191
Science education, gender inequities in, 140
Seagoe, May V., on learning characteristics of gifted, 31–32
Second child syndrome, 168
Self-actualization, 106–107
Self-contained gifted classes, 82–83
Self-definition, 134
Self-esteem, 144, 178
differentness and, 132–133
favoritism and, 171
of nongifted sibling, 169
parental demands and, 206
socialization and, 124–125
Sense of humor
giftedness and, 29
problems of, 96
Sensitivity, 98–101, 105, 193
problems of, 96
Separation, 204–207
adolescent, 211–212
Sex-role stereotypes, 140–141
counteracting, 142–143
Sibling conflicts
dealing with, 176–177

Sibling conflicts (*cont.*)
  minimizing, 177–181
Sibling rivalry, 164–165, 171, 180
  benefits of, 165
  dealing with, 166–167
  effects of, 169
  giftedness and, 166–167
Siblings
  comparing, 180–181
  giftedness among, 167–168
  nongifted, 168–170
  nonlabeled, 168–170
  reaction to gifted label, 168
Silverman, Linda
  on denying giftedness, 220–221
  on elitism, 222
  on introversion, 102, 103
  on "normalizing" gifted, 221
  on peers, 219–220
  on self-contained gifted classes, 83
  siblings and giftedness, 167–168
Singer, Jerome, on fantasy, 153–154
Sleep disturbance, as sign of stress, 210
Smutny, Joan
  on group testing, 53
  on perfectionism, 115, 116
Snyderman, Mark, on IQ tests, 56
Social adjustment
  of adolescents, 141–142
  differentness and, 132
  highly gifted and, 133–134
  superior, 129–130
  Terman on, 215
Social competence, definition of, 125
Social difficulties, of gifted, 130–132
Social expectations, 126
Social isolation, 91
Socialization
  academic achievement and, 126–127
  definition of, 123–124
  examples of, 124
  preschoolers and, 127
  self-esteem and, 124–125
Society
  anti-intellectualism of, 216–217
  creativity and, 24
Spearman, Charles, on intelligence, 14
Stanford-Binet IQ test, 48–49
Sternberg, Robert
  on giftedness, 28
  on intelligence, 16–17
  on IQ tests, 56, 58
Stimulation, of babies, 40–42
Story telling, 151–152

Stress, signs of, 209–210
Structure, need for, 208–209
Successive approximations, 118–120
Symbiosis, 200–201
Synthetic intelligence, 16

T
Teachers
  gender inequities and, 141
  gifted and, 219
  hostility of, 136, 137, 218, 219
  stress from gifted, 218
Terman, Lewis
  on intelligence, 14–15
  Stanford-Binet and, 48
  study of gifted, 215
Torrance, E. Paul
  on creativity, 22–23, 24
  on developing creative abilities, 154–157
  on divergent thinking, 21–22
  on unstructured play, 158
Triarchic theory of intelligence, 16

U
Underachievement, 91, 113–114, 221
Unstructured play, 157–158, 192
Unstructured time
  Bloom on, 191–192
  need for, 191–192

V
Veenker, Kathleen and Stephen, 53, 115, 116
Verbal ability, problems of, 96, 131

W
Wallach, Michael, on giftedness, 55
Washington, Jerrilene, on gifted programs, 80
Weaknesses, accepting, 179
Wechsler IQ test, 49–51, 52
Wilson, P., on home environment, 187
Winnicott, D. W., on perfectionism, 202
WISC-R, 49, 50–51
Word puzzles, 160
WPPSI, 49–50

Z
Zigler, Edward, 132, 138